THE REVELATION INTEGRATION METHOD

A PRACTICAL GUIDE TO PSYCHEDELIC INTEGRATION

Danielle L.Brooks

The Revelation Integration Method
A Practical Guide to Psychedelic Integration
By Danielle L. Brooks

Hardback ISBN: 979-8-9872920-1-3
Paperback ISBN: 979-8-9872920-2-0
Ebook ISBN: 979-8-9872920-5-1

Published by:
Good Decisions, Inc.
Jackson WY
425445-9065
www.daniellebrooks.com

Printed in the United States of America

TABLE OF CONTENTS

INTRODUCTION

If you've ever thought, I touched infinity... and now I have to do laundry, this book is for you.

Most people don't pick up a book like this because life is smooth, predictable, and spiritually uneventful.

They pick it up because something real happened— something that cracked them open, rearranged their sense of self, or made the old ways of understanding life feel insufficient.

Maybe a psychedelic journey gently (or not-so-gently) dismantled your personality. Maybe breathwork launched you into the cosmos while your body stayed awkwardly snoring on a yoga mat. Maybe meditation revealed that the voice narrating your life is not actually you and now you're wondering who's been running the show.

If "normal" no longer makes sense and pretending nothing changed feels dishonest, welcome.

You're not broken. And you're not required to immediately know what any of it means.

Psychedelic medicines, breathwork, somatic healing, meditation, and other non-ordinary state practices have gone mainstream for a simple reason: they work. They interrupt patterns, unlock emotional release, and offer direct experiences of insight faster than the mind can say, "Wait, what?"

We live in a culture that values peak moments. Breakthroughs. Revelations. High points. In psychedelic and spiritual spaces especially, there can be an unspoken assumption that the more intense or beautiful the experience, the more transformative it must be.

Yet intensity alone does not equal integration. Psychedelic and spiritual spaces are full of:

- Intense experiences
- Beautiful insights
- Symbolic coherence
- Emotional catharsis

But the work of integration is not preserving intensity. It is asking: "What still functions when the intensity is gone?"

I've seen people have stunning, expansive, deeply moving experiences and still feel confused, destabilized, or unchanged months later. I've also seen experiences that were difficult, disorienting, or even frightening contain information that became profoundly healing once it was integrated.

This book was written for that space in between. Not the peak. Not the valley. Not the story we tell right away. But the slower, quieter work of making meaning without rushing, and letting insight actually land in a human life.

It's common after peak experiences for people to return home, go back to work, and try to carry on as if nothing happened, while quietly knowing that something definitely did. Higher states of consciousness often come with clarity, compassion, creativity, and a felt sense of connection.

They're also famous for producing sentences like:

- "I think I met God, but I forgot to ask for instructions."

- "I realized I'm not my ego... yet my ego has a lot of opinions about that."
- Everything is perfect... and I'm still late on rent."

This is where integration comes in.

The Revelation Integration Method was not born out of theory. It emerged from lived experience, pattern recognition, and many conversations with people trying to make sense of what they encountered in non-ordinary states. Over time, clear rhythms began to appear; not universal rules, but recurring patterns in how insight unfolds, stabilizes, and becomes usable.

This work is not about chasing more experiences. It's about learning how to live with what you've already encountered and how to live coherently after profound insight without fragmentation, ego inflation, or getting stuck.

It's also not about dismissing the beauty, mystery, or intelligence that can arise in these spaces. On the contrary, it's about respecting them enough not to rush past their integration.

Integration is the unglamorous—but essential—work of translating insight into something you can actually live. It's what keeps revelation from turning into spiritual bypassing, identity inflation, or floating so far into the cosmic that you forget you still have a body, relationships, responsibilities, and a human life to live.

For centuries, humans have been conditioned to experience themselves as separate from each other, separate from the Earth, and separate from what we call God, Source, Universe, Spirit, Consciousness. Choose which one resonates with you. Many non-ordinary states temporarily disrupt that sense of separation. People often report experiences of wholeness, unity, love, or deep remembering.

Across cultures and modalities, people are asking the same very human question:

"Okay... but how do I live like this on Tuesday?"

Not every insight needs to be interpreted and not every powerful experience is meant to be taken literally. Part of integration is learning how to appreciate what an experience offered without letting it define who you are, what you believe, or how reality must work.

What matters is not whether these experiences are "ultimate truth," but how they are held, translated, and lived afterward.

I've supported thousands of people before and after psychedelic and non-ordinary state experiences. Before that, I spent over a decade helping people unwind limiting beliefs and emotional patterns through nutrition and mindset work. Back then, shifts like self-love often took years. In the medicine space, people sometimes touch it in a single afternoon.

The insight can be immediate. The embodiment takes skill.

I've seen what happens when people integrate well—and what happens when they don't. I've witnessed grounded healing, emotional freedom, and deepened presence. I've also seen people chase peak states, get tangled in spiritual significance, or mistake a powerful experience for a permanent identity upgrade.

What's most challenging is not the revelation itself, it's translating something vast, symbolic, or ineffable into ordinary human life without losing humility, discernment, or one's sense of humor.

This book exists to help you prepare for experiences and to catch you afterward. After the visions fade. After the ceremony ends. After the universe hands you something meaningful without an instruction manual.

By the end of this book, you'll know how to ground, balance, translate, and apply your insights without turning them into dogma, delusion, or a new personality. You'll learn how to stay connected to insight while remaining firmly rooted on planet Earth.

You'll learn how to:
- Integrate insights without over-identifying with them
- Stay grounded while touching the infinite
- Work skillfully with thoughts, emotions, ego, and identity shifts
- Use the "golden window" after an experience for lasting change
- Apply integration tools to any profound experience—medicine or not

This is not a book about chasing peak states. It's a book about integrating them.

If you ever find yourself thinking, "I must be special because I saw something extraordinary," this book will help you gently remember that extraordinary experiences are part of being human—and that integration is what makes them meaningful.

Follow your intuition. Go slowly. Stay curious.

Nothing in this book requires belief. You are encouraged to take what's useful, question what isn't, and laugh when something lands a little too close to home.

It is my greatest honor to share with you the wisdom I have received doing this work. I wish you much joy in your integration process as you find what works for you.

HOW TO USE THIS BOOK: A SIMPLE ROADMAP

This book follows a natural rhythm that many people move through after powerful psychedelic or revelatory experiences. You do not need to move through these phases in order, and you may revisit some phases more than once. This roadmap is here to help you stay oriented, grounded, and kind to yourself.

You may notice that I repeat the same information in different ways throughout this book. This is to help you receive and embody the information presented. When you are reminded of certain concepts at different intervals, in different ways, it makes it easier for the mind to grasp the information and retain it.

Part 1: Preparation

Chapters 1, 2, 3, and 4 focus on the Revelation Integration Method; what supports safety, readiness, and containment before and immediately after non-ordinary experiences. We explore setting intentions, nervous-system readiness, discernment, and how to capture the information from a journey objectively. You will receive tools to navigate the medicine space safely, and strategies that will help you ground, release, receive, reorient yourself, and work with fear and discomfort. This chapter provides information that can help you let go while retaining sovereignty so you are not at the mercy of any medicine experience.

Part 2: Stabilization and Integration

Chapters 5, 6, 7, and 8 focus on how to stabilize you immediately after a journey. We will do a post-medicine check-in, discuss how to organize your revelations and navigate difficult situations. We will normalize what happens during psychedelic experiences so you can stay grounded and expansive. Many people report moments where their usual sense of self fades or disappears entirely. Here we look at what helps experiences like that settle rather than fragment. This includes grounding practices, pacing, and how to recognize when meaning-making needs to wait.

This section explores how insight can be understood without hardening into identity or certainty. We examine pattern recognition, interpretation, translation, and the subtle difference between insight and belief. Meaning is allowed to evolve over time, not be rigid and unmoving. You will answer the question, "Now what do I do with this?"

Part 3: Embodiment and Integration

Chapters 9, 10, 11, and 12 re-orient from insight to living. These chapters restore humility and stability. We will explore the phases of healing many people go through, release expectations, and touch on living the mystery. Integration is what ultimately shows up in behavior, relationships, and daily life. Therefore, this part focuses on translating insight into action, ethics, and lived change.

This phase supports long-term stability and freedom. You may find yourself moving back and forth between these phases. That's expected. Integration is not linear, and completion is not the goal.

Let's start with Part 1.

PART 1

PREPARATION

CHAPTER 1

THE REVELATION INTEGRATION METHOD

In this chapter we will define The Revelation Integration Method. We will discuss the fundamentals of the Revelation Integration Method, and how even bad trips can hold information to integrate. We will talk about the Rhythm of Integration and how some people use it as a road map for healing. We will explore what can happen for some individuals when they go for another high without processing the lows, and how Revelation Integration can become a part of your everyday life, no plant medicine required. This chapter touches on what to look for in an integration guide and will explore a perspective on how humankind as a collective can integrate together.

Before we dive in, let's explore what a psychedelic experience actually does.

Psychedelics in a Nutshell

It is important to emphasize that the medicine doesn't import anything new; it rearranges what's already here, inside of you. It loosens, amplifies, and reconfigures inner architecture such as beliefs, emotions, memory, identity, meaning-making, and depending on how that reorganization is met by you, the results can be stabilizing or destabilizing.

When the experience is understood as internal, several things fall into place:

- There's less fear, because nothing is invading or possessing.
- There's more responsibility, because meaning isn't outsourced.
- There's more agency, because architecture can be worked with.
- And there's less inflation, because insight becomes information, not identity.

In short, the medicine reveals how your internal system builds your personal reality, and that same system can build coherence or confusion depending on many factors.

Your psychedelic experience is internal. The clarity that you don't go anywhere is what allows the medicine to become a tool rather than an authority.

- Psychedelics temporarily loosen predictive filters in the brain and nervous system, allowing new patterns, memories, emotions, and meanings to surface.
- Psychedelics can feel cosmic, absolute, or divine, but the experience is internal, state-dependent, and interpretive.
- Psychedelic experiences reorganize internal architecture (nervous system, perception, identity, meaning-making), not external realities. That's up to you.

- A psychedelic experience reorganizes perception.

However, it is integration that determines whether that reorganization becomes wisdom or confusion.

What is Revelation Integration?

People and professionals approach integration in many ways. Some approach integration from a behavioral, cognitive, or psychological perspective. Others through a shamanic integration ceremony or through a talking circle or bodywork. These are all fine methodologies.

The methodology used in this book focuses primarily on what an individual experiences, or what was revealed in the medicine space, and helps them work with that information. People often find the information in a medicine ceremony to be just what they needed, no matter how uncomfortable it was or how much time had gone by before they were ready to look at the information receptively. Revelation Integration emphasizes individual discernment, curiosity, and investigation. Visions, entities, voices, symbols, and narratives are experiential interfaces, not authorities. Their value lies in what they reveal about your internal system, not what they claim to be. This method increases individual authority, agency, and decreases the risk of confusion, dependency, and harm.

In my work with many people, I've noticed some individuals are in the process of spiritual awakening. Others are healing trauma, learning to self-govern beyond addiction, and leaving the stories of victim and perpetrator behind them. They are doing this by integrating objectively what was revealed to them in their journeys.

Revelation Integration is how you work with what is revealed to you in a journey. It occurs when an individual is willing to see all aspects of themselves, the flattering and not so flattering bits and pieces, and let what was revealed settle within them.

Integration happens when the body is given the opportunity to adapt to a new vibrational set point and come into harmony with the revelation. Integration supports the individual post retreat to continue the process of releasing emotional imprints, negative thought patterns, and false identities. It allows the divine within to be reconciled with physical form in ways that are right for each person. Integration requires time and space to let the mind, body, and spirit align to new information.

The Revelation Integration Method is processing, assimilating, acclimating to, investigating, and embodying the parts of the experience that move you forward and help you live a more grounded, centered, coherent life right here and now. It may include getting used to being empty of what was released and being receptive to new information that is other than what you expected. It is putting the experience on the shelf and pondering it like a Rubik's Cube. It's questioning it, being curious about it, and deciding for yourself what you will keep and what you will discard.

Integration occurs when:
- Insight changes behavior
- Revelation settles into the body
- Understanding no longer needs rehearsal
- What was seen no longer fractures daily life

Integration is translation, not belief adoption. An insight may be real, but how you interpret it and work with it can change over time. You know integration of an insight is complete when nothing needs to be done to remember it. Your system has reorganized around it and you don't even think about it anymore.

Integration is slow, ordinary, unglamorous. It shows up as a steadier nervous system, quieter compulsions, different choices made without effort and fewer internal contradictions. Integration is the rewiring that prevents collapse back to habit.

In the medicine space, you may dip into the belly of creation and know experientially that you are not separate. That's wonderful! Yet, it's one thing to take a dip and another thing entirely to live it here. Integration is the process by which experience becomes lived reality. It is how one lives coherently after profound insight without fragmenting the nervous system, inflating the ego, or getting stuck in delusion.

Integration is how insight becomes usable without becoming identity.

Integration is when the absolute (God, Source, Spirit, Universe, Consciousness), the relative (human), and the mystery in between come together in a dance of Unity. Integration is the end of separation. Integration is the letting go of what you are not and remembering who and what you truly are.

When people integrate their experiences and insights, they take the time to let what has been realized settle; they make course corrections in life, let go of what is not serving them, and call in more of what does. They increase their conscious awareness, get clarity, and expand their idea of who they are. They take action on the self-realizations, directives or information revealed, for example, leaving a relationship that no longer serves them or healing one that does with honesty and vulnerability.

Whether they received a healing, released a limiting belief, or let go of the story of unworthiness, when people integrate, they release what I call low vibrational distortions, such as fear, guilt, shame, judgment, comparison, self-doubt, and acclimate to freedom and love with more ease and clarity. When people integrate, they come home to themselves.

Many individuals don't know what to do with the information gifted to them in the medicine space. I've witnessed people have ineffable experiences and deep knowings of who they are as amazing, incredible, unlimited beings. Those who don't take the time to integrate come home, go to work, and often fall right back into the same habits and patterns. They risk reverting back to their limited humanity.

Psychedelic experiences help us:

- Recognize patterns
- Experience emotional truths
- Gain insight and alignment through symbols and metaphors.

But when experiences are interpreted without discernment or become another false identity we can get into trouble. The Revelation Integration Method is designed to help people translate experiences rather than attaching to them or creating meaning where there is none.

It is common for people who have cultivated awareness or who have meditation practices to have transcendental experiences. Separation can be seen for what it is: an illusion. Transcendent experiences are available to all, so you don't have to do plant medicine to have these types of experiences. But plant medicines can help get you started, speed up the process, and show the way when they are done responsibly with intention and are followed with an integration period to assimilate the experience and information revealed.

The Revelation Integration Method above all else strengthens your ability to know the difference between quality information that supports you and delusion or egoic attachment. One pattern that shows up is identification with the revelation in a way that serves superiority or spiritual significance. It is important to be able to ground yourself and say, "Yes, I just had an extraordinary experience." But I am no better or worse than anyone else. (See my book *The Extraordinary, Ordinary You* for more information on this.)

You must also be able to discern whether you are shying away from important information that needs to be seen. People shy away from the truth of who they are all the time, and a good integration guide can hold up the mirror and encourage them to look again.

Integration is important. I have rarely seen a journal entry, voice memo, or transcript of a medicine experience that doesn't hold valuable information the individual can utilize to move forward. Even a year later I have revisited journals with clients only to find the information they need is often within those pages. I don't do the work. I simply remind people that they have the information; I show them where to look and how to retrieve it, how to discern if it is helpful, and how to apply it so they can move forward in their own authority.

The more willing you are to look at a revelation from many different perspectives the more you may receive from the experience. The integration process is not about analyzing, diagnosing, or prescribing; it's about honoring the revelations, discerning what's helpful and what is not and integrating that information at your own pace.

Revelation Integration Method Fundamentals:

1. **Revelation**: The revelation is often the reason many people take medicine. A revelation is a subjective experience. It could be an experience of healing. It could be a release of pain, suffering, control, or fear. It can be an insight, a realization, a shift in identity that can last

for minutes or permanently affect your long-term idea of selfhood. It can be information that you received. A revelation could even reflect how a person acted in the medicine space; it could mirror to you aspects of yourself you'd rather not see or aspects that you had never considered.

2. **Safety**: Safety is primary. The Revelation Integration Method teaches us how to journey safely. How to integrate safely. How to transition to who and what we are safely. Safety includes stabilization, grounding, nervous system protection and regulation throughout the entire arc of the experience.

3. **Receptivity:** Receptivity involves being open to what the medicine has for us, without giving up sovereignty— no matter how challenging or ineffable the experience may be, no matter what the medicine reveals to us about ourselves. When we are receptive, we are open to transformation and changing perspectives. Receptivity is allowing what is without interpretation.

4. **Discernment**: Discernment takes the time to explore each revelation intuitively. We distinguish between temporary intense psychedelic states and long-term ideas of self. We explore the difference between egoic attachment and authenticity to avoid distortion and delusion. We test reality, we practice humility. We ask, "Is the revelation helpful? Does it align with my principles? Does it help to let go of limitations and deep rooted beliefs? Or is it a distraction?" Not all revelations need to be integrated.

5. **Curiosity**: We put the revelations into quarantine and ask questions; we look at them deeply and stay open to them. Curiosity is the antidote to judgment and helps

us discover when our intentions have been met in ways we did not expect. Curiosity enables us to recognize patterns and helps us make meaning of our experiences with an open mind that is free of judgment. When we are curious, we are more able to understand and translate symbolic experiences intuitively.

6. **Investigation**: This involves returning to the insights in order to broaden the perspectives within them. Insights mature through revisitation. Re-reading, re-speaking, re-sensing the revelations can reveal new aspects you hadn't seen before. We also investigate the quality of the revelation and the source from which it came to ensure it is a quality revelation not an unnecessary diversion from life.

7. **Translation**: Raw revelation often arrives as symbolic, somatic, or imaginal. Often words cannot come close to translating these experiences. This fundamental takes that revelation and does the best it can to put the experience into context and language; so that it becomes a bridge that improves our relationship with ourselves and others. Translation happens when the insight is integrated and aligned with individual principles. It ensures the action or embodiment of the insight is free of distortion.

8. **Adaptivity**: Adaptivity lets the mind, body, nervous system, and spirit adapt, acclimate, and get accustomed to new information and new ways of being and living. We shift perceptions and accept new ideas about ourselves and others. We let go of old constructs and adjust to new ones. Adaptivity involves taking time to be with the revelation so it can settle within us.

9. **Embodiment**: This is the process by which insight

moves out of memory and into the body, shaping how a person feels, responds, and acts in everyday life without effort or rehearsal. This includes True Self integration and what it means to fully embody the mystery of yourself authentically. Silence in this case is what integrates what language cannot.

10. **Continuation**: Continuation involves evaluating a new set point, what's complete and what's not. Then taking what is not complete into the next journey. This is one way an individual can continue to do the work and move forward. This requires immense discernment, intentionality, and awareness to ensure a person is not just tripping or bypassing doing the work. Continuation is only advised when boundaries are created to prevent overuse, dependency, and pacing allows for nervous system regulation, grounding, AND integration time is taken.

The Rhythm of The Revelation Integration Method

Integration has a rhythm, a cadence that moves from an experiential insight, knowing, or realization to a period of adjustment where you get used to and embody that new information. You let go of what did not serve you. You discover a new layer of all-of-you and take the time to ponder it, be curious about it and get used to it, and integrate it into your daily life. You are metaphorically bridging the divine and the physical worlds, so in many ways you receive the information from the non-physical, integrate it, and bring it into the physical world. As above, so below makes perfect sense from an integration perspective.

1. **Intention:** You set the intention and you mean

it. You put some energy and momentum behind your intention and you work with your beliefs to stretch them, opening yourself to the idea that your intentions absolutely can be fulfilled. Intentions are how you create. Core intentions are the most powerful intentions, and as you will soon learn, one core intention can wipe out many other intentions.

2. **Revelation:** You take the journey, and in the medicine, layers of yourself may be revealed to you. The release, the insight, the receiving, the experience, and how you navigated the space completely out of control or courageously faced what needed to be seen are also revelations to consider. Some revelations you keep, some you release.

3. **Settling/Integration:** You let things settle. Your body adjusts. During the settling period of integration your mind accepts and adapts to new information and releases old information. The mind expands. The nervous system adapts. Old patterns fall away; new patterns are created. You continue to journal and play with the revelations. You may continue to let go of what doesn't serve and adapt to new ways of being and navigating the world. This is when you take action on directives even if the directive was to just be. This period can feel like a downward slope as everything you thought you knew falls apart so something new can come through. Insights mature through revisitation. Re-reading, re-speaking, re-sensing the revelations can reveal new aspects you hadn't seen before.

4. **Completion:** You enter this phase when you evaluate what is complete and what is not complete. This is

the time to reflect on what you accomplished and what feels like you still have some threads on it. For instance, is what you released still gone or did you pick it back up? No worries if you did, you can set the intention to go in after it again in your next session. Completion can be immediate or it can take years. Only you know when something is complete.

Note: It is preferable to fully embody one insight mentally, physically, emotionally, and habitually so that the insight means something rather than collecting many insights without embodiment.

5. **New Set Point Evaluation:** If the medicine is calling you back, consider reflecting on your entire intention journal to see what's complete and what is not. Look for common themes, such as fear or unworthiness, that can have threads through all of your patterns. When you know what is complete and what is not complete you have established your new set point. This can help you set your next intention and prepare you for the next experience.

6. **Continuation:** You set your next intention to go after a core pattern, receive clarity or healing. As you move through these phases it is normal to continue to let go of what you are not and adapt to new levels of being and new ways of navigating the world from an evolving and expanding perception. You continually move forward. Again, continuation is only advised when boundaries are created to prevent overuse and dependency. You want to pace your medicine experiences so that the nervous system can settle and regulate. Continuation happens only after integration time is taken from a previous experience.

7. **Healing:** At some point you may realize that you are healed and you are whole and you no longer need medicine unless you choose to utilize it as a tool to help you integrate at deeper levels or just need a tune up to help alignment and coherence. Let's face it, it's dense here and an occasional tune up may sometimes be helpful for some people.

This is the time to celebrate! Many people at this point still look for things to fix. I certainly did. Eventually one can get used to being whole and complete if they choose it. This is when an individual can learn to master their being without medicine.

The Revelation Integration Method emphasizes grounding and continuous evolution. Even after you find yourself healed and whole, the journey continues. This book operates as a guide, as structure so you may use medicine wisely, responsibly, and with intention. It puts you in the driver's seat during both the medicine experience and the integration phase. You are the one who discerns between a peak state and the truth of your being.

For many people this methodology creates structure and a safe container where they can face the crunchy bits with minimal fear and explore peak states while staying grounded. There are many ways to heal. The Revelation Integration Method is but one way of many.

BAD TRIPS: Challenging experiences are what happens when the system is overloaded, an individual feels like they need to respond to the medicine in protection, or when unintegrated material comes to the surface. What some call "bad trips" often hold within them vital lessons to integrate. For instance, how a person acts or responds to the medicine reflects many things. If they lost their shit, it can reflect a need to ground, center, and balance. If they stayed calm and used their breath to ground, release, and harmonize, this may reflect the work they have done. No good, bad, right, or wrong, just insight to be received and integrated.

It is not uncommon for people to blame or project onto someone else for their decision to take the medicine. This is not helpful and reflects where they have given up sovereignty and agency. There is always something revealed to us about us that could use integration. Revelation integration happens when time is taken for the mind to grasp and accept the revelation, regardless of whether it is flattering or not. This is not punishment, failure, or spiritual wrongdoing; it's what healing can look like.

Revelation integration is many things. It is the tears that fall when you realize a new aspect of yourself: whether those tears are from the pain and suffering you have caused yourself because of a key decision to stay safe, or whether the tears are tears of joy at seeing an aspect of yourself that you hadn't taken into account, or even a glimpse of the True Self beyond the stories of who you thought you were. Integration is what happens when an individual is willing to look at oneself with openness and curiosity and is courageous enough to face what arises and move through it into freedom.

In my work I have seen many individuals free themselves from the illusion's humanity has lived with for generations. Freedom from the lies of not enough-ness, freedom from negative thoughts and limiting beliefs and unruly emotions. Freedom from fear, control, and the illusion of separation. People often report who and what they are is something that can never be measured, can never be explained, can never be limited, and can never be taken away.

Revelation Integration Has Highs and Lows

The rhythm of integration can feel like riding a roller coaster. At first, moments of insight and awareness may come only when the conditions are just right. A person may go into the perfect meditation or breathwork session and boom, they find themselves where they never expected to be. Or perhaps they received a glimpse of what lies beyond their ego, and they soared. It is common for people to experience expanded versions of themselves and feel like they left this realm for a while. This is the up part of the roller coaster that is exciting and open to possibilities.

Then, after the meditation is over and the temporary state of bliss wears off, they come back to this physical world and doubt may set in. "Was it real? Did I have that experience or was it my imagination? Am I really all that or am I this limited, fearful human? Am I both? How do I bridge the two so I can navigate this world? Will anyone even believe that I had this experience?" This is the downside of the roller coaster that can be filled with fear, doubt, confusion, and uncertainty.

The downside is the most important part of integration and the point where most people get off the roller coaster, or worse, go for another high without mastering the low. There are gifts in the lows, as this is where the negative thought patterns and limiting beliefs are worked through and released. This can feel like the gunk of the soul is being cleansed like a Roto Rooter on a gunky pipe, when people experience being stripped of false identity and step into the seat as a sovereign being not driven by anything outside of themselves. The downside is when we can let the tears of grief and sorrow fall; when we let the anger rise within us, face it, and feel it move through us and out of us. Most importantly, integration is when you descend from peak states and allow that experience settle within you with humility and grace.

When you are willing and courageous to be present through the downside, to work out the shadow aspects, you allow yourself to experience all aspects of yourself. All of you. Habits and patterns may then slowly drop away, old belief systems can fade, and fear can transform into excitement. Guilt and shame may then be perceived as wisdom gained. If you continue the path, wounds can heal, the past may recede, and your heart is given the chance to open. This is alchemy at its best. This is Revelation Integration.

An upward period of expanding consciousness needs to be balanced by an integration phase. An integration phase is often felt as that downward move, a retraction or stagnation, as opposed to the euphoria of the upward move. This is not bad. It is transformation.

STORYTIME: *I had been asked to create a workshop for some very successful business owners and CEOs. Because of my past experience I took on a teaching style that totally failed me. I talked at them when they wanted to be facilitated. They wanted to engage. They wanted to do the work.*

When I got home all I wanted to do was bury my head into my pillow and never come out of my bedroom. This is the downward move of integration. Where layers of myself were revealed to me about myself, I had to face the truth. I had to own it. It was hard, but it was also one of the most humbling experience I have ever lived. I saw where I went unconscious and pretended to know things I really didn't know. The direct feedback they gave me was brutal. But it was that feedback that enabled me to check myself. The next time I had an opportunity to work with a similar group I did much better because I integrated that feedback.

The downward slope of integration can be difficult. It's

when we face the stuff we would rather not see. However, it is the downhill movement that gives us momentum to travel to greater heights. The good news is that in the long run, you may notice that even the downs are on higher levels than before and things just even out over time. You may also experience a trend towards a greater expansion of consciousness and greater integrity and authenticity.

Revelation Integration Takes Time

Some revelations integrate rapidly. Others may take years or even a lifetime to integrate. I experienced divinity for the first time years ago and am still integrating that revelation today. Integration is most often a gradual process. We acclimate, adapt to, and work with the revelations gifted to us a little at a time. Big realizations take time, years, and lifetimes to integrate. Little revelations can be instantaneous. The most important thing to remember is not to implement big changes right away, to go slowly so you have the time and wherewithal to stay centered and grounded in truth not delusion.

Revelation Integration is a Continuous Process

Revelation Integration is a lifestyle; it's all the time and how you live your life. It is a continuous transformational process and journey where you integrate each step, each experience, each expression, and each revelation. We integrate all the time; there is no stopping and starting life to integrate. For example, if you have an altercation with someone on the street, it is an opportunity to look within and ask, "What is this encounter teaching me about myself? How did I act?"

Integration is your dance with life and you get to choose how you want to approach it. It can be awkward and uncomfortable or exciting and sacred. It's a process of transformation. Integration is how to get the maximum value from any experience. You don't have to force it. It's already happening whether you know it or not.

Revelation Integration is Alchemy

When you are willing to look at the layers of yourself with openness and curiosity, you transform them. When you no longer avoid what many call the shadow aspects of the self, they evolve and often add meaning to life. Just like in dreams when you are being chased, if you just stop, turn, and face what is chasing you, the pursuer or the scene will dissolve. The shadow disappears when the light is turned on. The light is your awareness. The light is the revelation. The light is what is asking to be integrated.

Integrating the Mystery

Integrating the unconditional love of the creator, the oneness of the universe, and your infinite and divine nature is integration at the highest level, integration that has no words. We discuss this in many ways throughout this text.

Integration Guides

A good integration guide can advise you not to be too hasty and to let things settle before making any major decisions. A good integration guide can help future forecast how your life could unfold as you choose, where to take action and where to let things lie, where you may be getting in your own way, and where to ask for help.

Sometimes integration requires courage as you cut ties; write letters; seek a new job, new home, or new partner. Other times it is passive as you learn to stop being a human doing and return to being a human being.

• Integration guidance before any medicine experience can show you how to get the most out of the experience, help you with intention setting and releasing expectations. It can help you navigate the medicine space and prepare you to receive whatever information is revealed to you. But never give up your agency, intuition, or authority to a guide. No one knows like you what is right for you. Use a guide as guardrails but stay in the driver's seat.

• An Integration guide after an experience can be there to catch you if you face a dip in your mood, such as depression or sadness, and reassure you that all is well and normal. When all feels not well and normal, an integration guide can help you navigate that as well.

• An integration guide can create a safe space for you to be uncomfortable and do the work. To face the crunchy bits, to cry, to release, and to be called out when you need to be. A guide can give you the feeling of "I am with you and we will move through this together."

• A good guide will not tiptoe around patterns. They will guide you through them. They will say what is needed kindly and firmly so you can move beyond the constructs of unworthiness, fear, guilt, or shame. The most important thing a guide provides is safety and true guidance.

Just coming out of a journey is the perfect time to strategize with your guide on how to integrate and organize what was revealed. Many people experience a neurological reset or a peak state that questioned identity, so just after a journey is the perfect time to incorporate new habits, new patterns, new ways of thinking and being in the world.

• Strategies on how to maintain and cultivate the peace you accessed in ceremony and preserve the sense of oneness can be invaluable.

• Additional integration guidance every week or two after a journey can help you stay on track and your toes dipped in the proverbial waters of awareness.

• A qualified guide is one who bridges both the physical and non-physical realms with their own experiences, wisdom, and knowing. Use your discernment to find the right one for you. You know you have a good one when they have reached a place where you would like to go.

• An integration guide can help you learn how to work with your emotions, quiet your mind, and let go of what no longer serves you. They can help you get clarity and adapt to identity beyond any stories you've told about yourself.

• The tendency to over-validate the experience, identify with an experience, or create meaning where there is none can be problematic. A guide will ask the questions, "Is this helpful? Is it useful? Does it help you let go of limitations and deep rooted beliefs? Or is this a distraction?"

A good guide can help you navigate the overwhelming experience of True Self and the revelations that come with it. They can help you get used to the intensity of the experience. As you allow these experiences and revelations into your biological form, consciousness can become an embodied experience, not something you jet out of the physical form to experience. The body adapts, and while it still looks like a human form, it may be experienced as an expression of the divine. This is the beauty and sacredness of integration.

Integration means taking the information revealed to you during your experience and allowing it to evolve and expand your life. Integration is when you receive a different perspective and live your life from that new perspective.

The challenges many people face after receiving revelations

is that while you may have a new perspective, your friends, family members, and co-workers may not. The degree to which you allow your own evolution determines the amount of chaos or destruction those around you may experience. A good integration guide can be invaluable at helping you navigate new perspectives slowly, gently, and as comfortably as possible.

Choose an integration guide who is a good fit and will meet you where you are, AND who will still push your limits.

Integration as a Collective

Up until now I've talked about integration on a personal level. But let's take a few brief moments and address integration as a collective. Whenever an expansion of consciousness is reached by a sufficiently large number of individuals, it can create tension amongst mass consciousness. That then may require an integration phase. This happens so the majority can catch up and adjust to the new circumstances. Sometimes though, the tensions are already so heightened that integration at a societal level becomes impossible. Then, instead of integration, an implosion might occur, eradicating many of the advances in consciousness.

Many societies throughout history have experienced great advances in consciousness and technologies of their time but were not able to convert it into wisdom. What can happen when the tensions in consciousness become too huge to be integrated is the downfall of that civilization. Many theorize in the case of Atlantis that the temptations to abuse new technologies proved too strong and they lost control. So whole cultures fell. We have more advanced technologies than ever before, but our level of consciousness has not caught up. If we are wise, we will take the time to integrate these new advances in ways that serve us collectively.

Are we as a collective ready to end the belief that we are separate from the universe and each other? Well, if you were not ready, you would not be reading this book, would you?

Integration is to put all the pieces together, to understand the purpose of everything.

You create and play in the sandbox of life. You experience and express and experiment. Then you have to put together what you learned from it all and organize it in a way that makes sense. That is what humanity is doing now. We've been playing in the sandbox throwing sand at each other, stealing buckets, and hitting each other over the head with shovels. Now is when we put down our shovels, have a good laugh at how unconscious we have been, and clean up the mess.

In the next chapter we will discuss how to set an intention to do just that.

CHAPTER 2

INTENTIONS

This chapter explores what an intention is and why it is important to set intentions before any medicine experience, whether it is breathwork, cannabis, mushrooms, or anything else. We will investigate why some people meet their intentions and others don't. This chapter offers an exercise that many people find grounding in a way that quiets the mind and can assist you in finding one core intention that has the potential to fulfill many intentions at once.

Intentions Create

Your intentions can propel your words into being. Intention focuses attention and organizes energy. For many people, intention acts like a steering wheel rather than an engine. When intention, emotion, and action align, words tend to gain momentum and they become the engine. Intention doesn't create outcomes by itself, but it often sets direction. For example, when you say, "I am going to get myself a cup of tea," you intend it, and when the emotion and action align it propels you to get up and go get that cup of tea.

When words move into action and the intention brings about change, it's usually because of some combination of:

• **Attention:** What is repeatedly noticed, rehearsed, and returned to increases the chances of a fulfilled intention. We could say that intention focuses attention and organizes energy. The more attention you give something the more likely it is to come about.

• **Emotional investment:** The level of desire, passion or fear all play roles in intention completion. If you are afraid of what would happen if your intention were to be fulfilled, it is less likely to happen. If you have a strong desire or passion or excitement at the prospect of an intention fulfilled, it is more likely to happen.

• **Somatic readiness:** Whether your body and nervous system are regulated enough to receive your intention and your ability to act rather than freeze, dissociate, or sabotage also play roles in intention completion.

• **Meaning-making:** The story the mind attaches to the intention also must be considered. Thoughts such as, "This is impossible, what would people think, and who would I be if this intention is fulfilled?" determines how likely I am to align to that intention.

• **Behavioral follow-through:** Small, often unglamorous actions that align with the intention bring it to life. Yes. Action is required. In the medicine space that action can sometimes be your ability to not take action and surrender.

• **Context and conditions:** Is the timing right? Do

you have support and resources? How is your health and environment? These are factors that may not be fully under personal control.

When these align, people experience words as "having power." They are coherent with their intentions because attention, emotion, and choice line up long enough to move the body into action.

When they don't, words feel empty.

The problem is that we often say things we don't mean. We say we are going to eat better, then we have coffee and a donut for breakfast. There is no emotion behind the words. So, when setting intentions, you must put some emotion and action behind your words.

Intention is one of the places we can participate consciously in our lives. When intention, emotion, and action collide it feels like the energy of your intention gathers momentum and off you go.

An intention is not wishy washy.

Intention is Conscious Deliberation

Many of our responses and patterns are shaped by choices, both conscious and unconscious. The distinction between conscious choice and unconscious choice lies in the level of awareness and intentionality behind the decision-making process.

• Conscious choice is when a deliberate and intentional decision is made with full awareness of the desired outcome. The individual knows what they want and takes intentional and inspired action steps toward it. There is clarity, focus, and confidence—no doubt that the outcome will align with their intentions.

• Unconscious choice is when decisions or behaviors

are driven by past underlying thought patterns, beliefs, or external influences without deliberate awareness or intent. The individual might not realize they are "choosing" at all. Choices are often influenced by past experiences, ingrained habits, or societal conditioning. Outcomes may feel random or out of one's control. An individual might say something like, "This always happens to me."

Key Differences: Conscious choice involves mindfulness and deliberate intent. Unconscious choice operates on autopilot, often based on old programming or external factors. Conscious choice empowers the individual to shape their responses, behaviors, and interpretations. Unconscious choice gives us limited access to habits, emotions, or external circumstances.

Responsibility: In conscious choice, the individual takes responsibility for their decisions and consequences. In unconscious choice, responsibility is often projected outward; there is a blaming of others, situations, or past experiences, which leads to feelings of helplessness or victimhood.

These two can operate concurrently so there is often a combination of things going on: Your life as you intend it and your life as you undermine it through your unconscious patterning. The two things create tension all the time. For example, "I want more money; but money is bad" and "I want more love yet feel unworthy of love."

When you have a pattern that sabotages your life, you have an unconscious pattern that needs to be cleared. You can clear it by using your intentions, emotions, and actions effectively. This can be done over time with attention and repetition.

For instance, when you say, "I am done with this thing I don't like, I quit," it is a decree, a choice to be done with whatever it is. When said with energy and you truly mean it, your conscious intentions are how you transform your life. You have the energy and momentum you need to create change in the areas you need it the most.

On the other hand, when you say, "I can't change this thing," it is also a decree, a choice to be a victim or helpless in regard to this thing you do not like.

Whether you intend to change something consciously or are experiencing helplessness unconsciously, you claim that as your truth and that can become your reality.

The more you energize your thoughts with attention and action, the more they come into being. Good or bad.

The degree of self-awareness you have also plays a role. For instance, if you set the intention to eat better and are aware that the old patterning still exists within you, you may use your energy to override that old pattern. You are aware that for a moment you had a craving for that donut, it beckoned to you, and you almost gave in and were out of alignment with your intention. So, through awareness and choice you realign yourself to your intention and say, "No. I have chosen to eat better, and by golly I am going to do it."

You understand you are not helpless, and that donut has no power over you. Truly, who is more powerful? A donut or you? Well, when you are unconscious in autopilot mode, the donut will kick your ass. But if you are aware, it doesn't stand a chance. Even if the craving is physiological, awareness can help.

You are the chooser of your reality, and if you cultivate awareness and stay alert to what is going on in your life, you will know when you are giving up that power and when you are exercising it. It is normal to go back and forth for a while until you master intention setting and how it all works. So be patient and compassionate with yourself as you work towards mastery.

By cultivating self-awareness and giving your intentions some energy and hutzpah—I mean really owning them—you can shift from unconscious reactions to conscious creation.

Here's your first tool to help stand victoriously over that donut:

⚓ Cultivating Awareness Exercise

In this exercise keep your eyes open and loosely focused on something in front of you. Don't close your eyes and disappear inward; expand your awareness. Practice super awareness.

Step 1: Direct your gaze down at a 45-degree angle. Listen to the sounds in the room. Be very aware of your external environment. Don't judge the sounds; see how many sounds you can become aware of.

Step 2: Next, bring your awareness to your body and where it is located in the room. Feel your feet. Feel your legs. Become aware of the weight of your legs. Feel gravity. Release your belly. Become aware of your heartbeat. Can you feel your heart pumping blood to your entire body? (Releasing the belly helps to release stress or tension and the heartbeat brings you to center. This exercise grounds and balances you.)

Step 3: Feel the aware presence that resides within that physical body. Awareness. Consciousness. Experience what some call the 'I am that I am' as a feeling sense. If your mind is active and you sink back into the realm of thoughts, just let them come and go.

Resist nothing. Be curious. Tell your mind to chill out and redirect your focus back to your heartbeat.

Above the Mental Plane of Thought: This exercise can metaphorically rise you above the mental plane of thought; above belief structures, ego, and emotional reactivity. You still see them, but they can't hook you. When witnessed at this level they just disappear. I have found that nothing can withstand the power of pure consciousness. Nothing. No habitual pattern, no belief structure, and no false identity. Cultivating awareness is so much better than the donut. Instead of dropping out with the donut, you rise above the craving.

Above Emotional Reactivity: This exercise also rises you above the plane of emotional reactivity. Emotions may come to the surface to be felt and released, then they just die down and go away. It is the trigger tamer.

The Point Before Creation: Now, cultivate awareness again.

What's the first thought that comes to you?

Become aware that any thought that arises or falls within consciousness is something you can choose to buy into or not, whether it be a thought, an idea, inspiration, or a story. I call this the point before creation because any internal experience, behavior, or meaning-making you choose becomes your creation.

- From this point before creation, choose a negative thought and feel how your body responds.
- Then direct your mind to choose a positive thought and feel that.

You are the chooser, and you can choose consciously!

Cultivating Awareness is Key: You may meld with the universe and experience yourself as whole and complete, but if you aren't aware of the old pattern of unworthiness creeping back in when you land, you can't reprogram it. Awareness is the great dissolver. Again, I have found that nothing can withstand the power of pure consciousness. Nothing. ANY negative thought pattern, belief system, or false identity slowly dissolves in front of me when I expose it to pure consciousness. Try it now. Bring a negative thought pattern to the forefront of your mind. Then become super alert and just watch it. Intensify your awareness to the point where it just disappears. It helps to be fully grounded in your body when you do this.

What better integration tool than this to help you dissolve the patterns of the past and integrate? What better tool to help you stay aware of and aligned with your intentions? We will return to this over and over throughout this text.

Okay, back to intentions.

How to Set and Accomplish an Intention

Setting an intention is an act of creation. It is a powerful practice, especially when made consciously with emotion and energy behind it. Intentions are even more powerful when you work with transformative and catalytic experiences like psychedelics. Many people I work with report that being intentional when they take any medicine, whether it be sound medicine, breathwork medicine, or mushroom medicine, is POWERFUL beyond words and increases the chances of that intention being fulfilled.

♣ **HOMEWORK:** Start an intention journal so you can start tracking the intentions that have been met and the ones you are currently working on. Seriously. Stop reading now and go pull out that old journal tucked away in a drawer or order one online. Use this just for

41

your intentions. You will need it later.

Great!

Here's a step-by-step guide to setting an intention and allowing it to manifest:

1. Set the Intention and Mean It: The first step is claiming the intention. When you do this, you give it emotion and momentum. When I set an intention I often say it out loud with power and energy behind it, "I intend to..." Fill in the blank. And I mean it. For you it could be "I intend to release unworthiness, experience myself as loved, and know myself." Now, look into your heart. What does it really desire? What are your heart's true intentions? Take time now to reflect on what you:

- Want to let go of
- Want clarity on
- Want to receive or invite into your life
- Want to explore

Write them down.

2. Connect Emotionally with Your intention: Once you have set your intention, imagine what it would FEEL like to achieve your intention. Imagine the emotions, sensations, or outcomes associated with it. Emotional alignment strengthens your connection to the intention, making it more resonant and authentic. If you experience resistance, work through that by tweaking the intention or working with your emotions until you can imagine what it would feel like to experience the results of your intentions. Feel it as if it is done, right here and now. Reassure yourself that you are safe to heal, safe to change, safe to make any change you desire. Work through fear by shinning the light of your awareness onto it. Is fear even real? Or is it just a projection of what might happen but never does?

Can you give yourself permission to be empowered?

3. Are You Ready for What You Ask? Too much too quickly can cause nervous system instability, identity inflation, and interfere with your ability to live a fulfilling grounded life here. If you are highly sensitive, have unresolved trauma, are experiencing any identity instability or are seeking meaning or transcendence, go slow. Ponder what it would be like if your intention was fulfilled. Are you really ready for it?

4. Release Expectations and Control: Once you've set your intention, let go of how it will unfold. Trust you've done what is needed and let go. Avoid overthinking or obsessing about how it will happen. The medicine might come in and say, "I see your intentions but in order to get there we have to deal with this first." And it may take you back to sixth grade when Johnny pulled your ponytails or pushed you down. It may not make sense. Go with it. You've done your part by setting the intention. Sometimes the universe delivers outcomes in unexpected ways that serve your highest good—even if they don't match your exact vision.

I can't tell you how many people I've worked with who thought their intentions were not met in a journey. Then, when we scanned their journal discovered indeed their intention had been met in a roundabout way. So, investigate. Be curious. Don't think linearly. Attachment to specific results can block you from receiving your intention. Trust the outcome will unfold in its own way and timing. Letting go doesn't mean abandoning your intention—it means releasing resistance, expectation, fear, and doubt about how it will unfold. By trusting in the process, you allow the energy of your intention to flow freely and naturally to you, without the limitations of your expectations or timeline.

Setting an intention is an act of creation; letting it go

is an act of trust. Together, they form the foundation for meaningful, transformative experiences.

When you state with a strong intention to release something, what can often happen is energy may begin to radiate through your body and begin to dismantle and clear the old patterning from your field. You can feel this if you pay close attention to it. Unless, of course, you are in doubt, constriction, or resistance and not aligned with your intention. To let go means to relax, allow, breathe, and relax even more, so that the outward flow of whatever pattern that is lodged within you can be released. A release can be in the form of an emotional release, a physical purge, a yawn, a deep breath, shaking, or other body sensations. Once you understand how releasing works in any medicine space, it gets more comfortable. A release may be uncomfortable at first but the relief afterwards is worth it.

5. Open and Receive Your Intention: If your intention is to get clarity or receive healing, be in a state of receptivity. Say to yourself, "I am in receivership of what I have called forth" and feel the results of your words. Open yourself and allow yourself to feel the medicine doing its work. It's so fun to set an intention and watch how the medicine goes about bringing it to you! You may actually feel an inflow of energy or the medicine performing cosmic surgery on a part or all of your body. Saying, "thank you" can be very helpful as it is the energy of receivership. You can also just trust and have faith that when you ask it is given.

Note: I've seen many people spend an entire medicine journey begging for what they want. This rarely works. They never even considered creating the space to receive what they desired. Set the intention, let it go, and be open to receiving what you ask for. There is a difference between begging for something and stating your worth and value as the receiver of your intentions.

6. Believe It Is Possible For You: Some people go into the medicine space with the attitude of, "I'm not sure I'll get anything out of it." Others go in with the intention to really destroy old patterns and accomplish their intentions. They know it's possible and approach the medicine with excitement. Beliefs matter. If you believe you can let go of a pattern, you will. If you doubt it's possible for you then it is less likely to occur. Belief is often a missed piece of the puzzle in the medicine communities. For instance, we have a knowing that our beliefs create our reality, but we have never thought to apply that knowledge to our work in the medicine space. Beliefs do matter. But don't take my word for it. Try it yourself.

⚲ **EXPERIMENT:** Write down the top limiting belief or negative thought pattern that your mind thrashes you with. Then take that pattern to the medicine of your choice with the intention to obliterate that pattern.

Once you understand and experience for yourself that you can set an intention, believe it's possible, then watch it happen, you are well on the healing path. You can indeed let go of anything you wish to. You can receive clarity, you can explore consciousness, who you are, and the universe. You can explore anything you wish! All you have to do is intend it and believe it can happen. Starting small can help you build trust and confidence in this methodology.

Be open and curious as to how your intentions are met. This is where investigation, discernment, and curiosity come in. I find that when someone sets an intention with momentum and believes it is already done, roughly 80% of the time it is indeed done. However, it may not have been met HOW they thought it would.

Bottom line: Nurturing positive beliefs increase outcomes greatly.

7. Be Tenacious: In one of my medicine journeys, I entered the revelation or visionary phase and found myself in an experience where I felt like I was kneeling before God. It was intense! God was asking me to be of higher service and I crumbled! I immediately cowered away and said, "I am not worthy! I am so not worthy! Just look at all the reasons why." After the intensity died down and I landed, I wiped the tears away and set the intention to go back and stand before God with a strong, worthy, and serving heart. And I did. And you can, too. All you have to do is set the intention and go for the ride. If you fail, get back up and do it again. It's the best thing in the world to set an intention and fail, then achieve it, especially after you have fallen down a couple of times!

Another example is when I set the intention to stop judging things and people. At first, I failed daily. But then the more I stayed with it and cultivated awareness and let judgment go every time it arose, the less it appeared in my life. This is how intention works. When you mean what you say, magic happens.

A common intention for people is to work through fear. Facing fear and moving beyond fear is a great intention because fear is insidious and at the root of most human problems. Think about it for a moment. What underlies judgment, unworthiness, greed, guilt, shame, and comparison? Fear. Fear is a common core pattern that shows up in a myriad of ways. Setting an intention to face and move beyond fear is a powerful core intention and is worth going after in the medicine space.

Don't let fear prevent you from love, joy, and play. Set the intention to see it for what it really is (a disproportionate reaction or protective illusion) and set yourself free from it. Be courageous knowing when you face it, it dissolves.

Have I effectively emphasized the enormous power of intention when done consciously and with some energy and emotion behind it? I hope so.

8. Take Inspired Action: Once you have set the intention, put some feelings behind it, and let go of expectations that doesn't mean you are done. An intention is nothing if it is not embodied or incorporated into your life. For example, if in a ceremony you intended to have more love in your life and had a self-realization that you need to appreciate your partner and say, "I love you" more, do it. Write a letter to your partner based on your revelations. Tell them how you feel. If you saw the only thing that matters is love, align to love over and over. Practice love. Explore love. Express love, integrate love. Yes, it will be awkward and you may feel vulnerable. The discomfort is worth it.

If you experienced yourself in the medicine asserting your power and setting boundaries, then set them after you land. Allow the new pattern of empowerment into your life by taking action when inspired to do so.

If in the medicine space you saw that the partner of your dreams is on the way, don't cloister yourself in your apartment and do nothing and expect it to manifest. You have to take actions that correspond to your intentions. This doesn't mean you take blind action. No. It means you stay alert, conscious, and present to any inspiration or inner guidance that arises. You take inspired action, not desperate action. You don't run around doubting that the partner of your dream will show. You follow the breadcrumbs spirit lays out before you.

Yes, it takes courage to love more, face fear, and move beyond your limitations, but that's why you decided to take the medicine, isn't it? The worst thing you could do is hop back into your daily routine as if nothing happened. Then you didn't take medicine, you took a trip. See the difference? The medicine will show you what you need to see, but you still have to integrate.

9. Don't Pick Back Up What You Laid Down: Often my clients will release something only to pick it back up again because they "didn't have time to integrate" or it was just easier to stay unconscious. If this happens to you, don't beat yourself up. Set the intention to keep after it. Mastery doesn't happen in one day. It takes time and patience and tenacity to become a conscious creator who chooses intentionally and aligns to those intentions. If you have fallen unconscious, cultivate awareness and set the intention to live without the pattern you released. Say aloud, "I am now choosing consciously to have this cleared once and for all. I now intend to release any unconscious behavior that would have me pick it back up. I am now free." Say this with feeling behind it and mean it.

Intentions are not only used to release things. You can bring forth all kinds of clarity and healing, and they can be used to experience just about anything you wish, including character traits. One of my clients wanted to get over being self-conscious and awkward in social settings. In his journey he experienced himself as witty, sharp, engaging, and wonderful. After he landed, we created a mantra that he repeated with feeling and intention until it was embodied and he no longer needed it. We combined it with creative imagination (that you will experience later) to embody these qualities. Don't play small here. Intentions are how you create, how you choose your experiences from the catalogue of the universe. Isn't it time you chose those experiences consciously?

Exploration: At some point you may experience that there is nothing more to heal. When this happens, exploration may be next on your docket. Setting intentions to delve into this fabulous universe may appeal to you. If your intention is to explore consciousness, meet your guides, or take a joyride into a spiral galaxy or down a black hole, cool! Do it! Know that you can. You're infinite, remember? It may feel clumsy at first and you may feel paralyzed as you stand at the edge of a black hole before you decide to jump, but man, what excitement!

AND always remember that exploration does not replace integration or daily functioning.

Now that you have a firm grip on how to set an intention and accomplish it, the next three chapters will cover how to prepare for a medicine journey, how to navigate the medicine space, how to catch yourself after a journey, and how to receive and integrate the information revealed to you while you were in the medicine space.

You will receive three integration protocols.

Preparation Protocol: In depth information and tools that will help you prepare for a medicine experience.

Post-Journey Protocol: In depth information and tools for after you have landed to stabilize and begin integration.

Integration Protocol: Integration tools on how to discern, translate, embody, and incorporate revelations into your life in a way that leaves you confident that you are receiving all the wisdom from that experience with as little delusion as possible.

These chapters are intended to help anyone choosing to participate in a medicine ceremony do so safely and answer the question, "What does this experience mean and how does that meaning enhance how I now live my life?"

CHAPTER 3

PREPARING FOR A MEDICINE JOURNEY

In this chapter we will cover how to prepare for a medicine experience in great detail. Preparation is an active part of the medicine arc and is integration. You will have the opportunity to set some intentions and discover how to find the one core intention that can fulfill many intentions at once. We will explore how to manage expectations, get the most of an experience, and find your starting baseline. You will discover how to create a safe sanctuary to travel within, how to capture the revelations afterwards, how to mitigate fear and work with the ego, and receive grounding exercises that teach you how to relax and let go. Even if you have difficulty letting go of control.

So, let's get started.

Starting Baseline

The first thing you want to do is capture your starting baseline. This is not who you are, it is where you are starting today. If you don't know where you are now, you won't know what patterns or programming from the past to rocket launch with the help of the medicine.

> 🔖 **EXERCISE:** This exercise will help you establish a starting baseline. It will show you where you spend most of your time and give you a clear picture of what your mind is up to and what patterns are most active. For 15 minutes do the cultivating awareness exercise I gave you earlier (become aware of sounds in the room, your body, release your belly, tune into your heartbeat) and then pay very close attention to your thoughts. When a thought about the past pops in, write that thought down in the column under the past. When you find yourself judging or observing the present moment, put that in the middle column. When you find yourself fantasizing about the future, place that fantasy in the future column. When your mind is quiet and calm, do nothing. Write down any negative thought patterns, limiting beliefs, habitual ways of being, or egoic patterns that arise. Do not try and fix anything. Noticing patterns is the goal. Not fixing them.

Past Memory	Present Judgment or Observation	Future Fantasy

Where do you spend most of your time? What negative thoughts patterns did you observe? What did this exercise show you about your mind and your relationship with yourself? Also write down any other issues you have been dealing with such as unworthiness, fear, or feeling unlovable. This information goes into your intention journal and you get to choose which pattern you will go after first. Think of it this way, your intention journal is the list of patterns you intent to move beyond. It is also a list of things you would like to experience or receive, such as healing and any clarity on life decisions.

You did purchase an intention journal, didn't you?

Your Intention Journal

An intention journal enables you to track your thought patterns, belief structures, ego activity, and emotional imprints or trauma triggers as you go. It also helps you track divine integration, if that is your chosen path. An intention journal will give you the opportunity to reflect on the intentions you have completed and the intentions that are still in process. This will keep you motivated and very clear on how the medicine works from beginning to end. You will see how the intentions you set that are wishy washy may not go anywhere, and the intentions that have some emotion behind them may manifest quickly. Also, some intentions just unfold slowly because they involve deeper nervous-system or identity-level changes. The more you return to your revelations the more layers of your experience will unfold for you. What meant one thing can often unfold to something of greater meaning when revisited later.

An intention journal can be a physical journal or an electronic journal on your laptop.

This is an example of how an intention journal can be structured:

Starting Set Point: A thorough list of negative thought patterns or belief structures, habits of perception, ideologies, storylines, and behaviors that are visible as a repeating pattern that doesn't serve you. This also includes patterns of fear; depression; anxiety; emotional imprints from trauma, grief, guilt, or shame. The exercise you just completed will give you your starting set point. Your starting set point is a picture of your programming right now. Flattering or not, get over it. Be compassionate. You are healing, remember?

Intentions: An exhaustive list of what you want to release or heal, things you want clarity on, what you would like to receive or experience, etc.

Core Intentions: Then look for a core intention, one or two that wipe out many unwanted patterns all at once. We will talk about this more in a bit.

This is an example of how a medicine journey can be documented:

Date:

Medicine:

Dose:

1. Core Intention(s): To go after a core pattern, to get clarity, to release, express, to receive or experience something.

2. Revelations: This is where you journal about everything you experienced in the journey itself. This is what happened. Write down your revelations as objectively as possible as soon as possible so the mind can't grab ahold of the revelation and distort it or put meaning on it that wasn't there. If writing is difficult, record the details using the voice memo app on your phone and journal about it later. Don't judge it, just capture the information no matter how difficult.

Notes: Write down any insights about the experience, the set, setting, or dose to increase or decrease next time. Was your intention met? Free write about your experience.

3. Settling/Integration: Then sit with your experience for a good couple of weeks. At least. Let everything settle. Return to your journal daily to help the mind and body adapt to what happened. Continue to journal. If it doesn't make sense, stay with it, stay open and curious. You just had a neurological reset. Let your nervous system and body adjust; let the mind stretch. Let old patterns fall away; let this new set point settle within you. Be curious about it. Spend the next couple of weeks or longer implementing any directives and practicing new ways of being. During the settling period is when creating new habits or patterns is easier. This takes as long as it takes. Don't rush it. This is when you do the work. The medicine can show you that love is the most important thing in the world, but you still have to implement and practice loving. There is no recipe for how long the integration phase lasts. Only you know. Big revelations tend to take longer; some integrate right away. Take your time. Go slow. The medicine did its part. Now is the time for you to do yours.

4. Completion: When you revisit your journal and ponder the experience after some time has gone by you may intuitively know when the revelation is complete or not. If you spent the ceremony releasing grief from your childhood, is it gone? If so, it is complete. If grief still resides within you, it is still in process. Completion can be immediate or it can take years. Remember that it can be more favorable to complete one insight over accumulating many incomplete insights.

5. New Set Point Evaluation: When the medicine is calling you back, it's time to reflect on your entire intention journal and see what's complete and what is not. Be curious about what you have accomplished and what may be next for you. This inquiry will help you establish your new set point.

6. Continuation: You then set your next intention to go after another core pattern. You continue to let go of what you are not and adapt to new levels of being and new ways of navigating the world from an evolving and expanding perspective. Continuation requires immense discernment, intentionality, and awareness to ensure you are not bypassing doing the work. Continuation is only advised when boundaries are created to prevent overuse, dependency, and pacing allows nervous system regulation, grounding, and integration time.

Eventually, if you walk this path, you may find you no longer need medicine. This doesn't mean things won't arise to challenge you. They will. You just may spend more time integrating and adapting in different ways. You don't need the medicine because you can stand on your own footing.

Now let's dive even deeper into intentions.

Setting Intentions

This book is not about taking a joy ride through the cosmos. Well, actually exploring the cosmos is an awesome intention so I take that back. What I mean is this book does not support the use of psychedelic medicines recreationally, just for the trip of it. It explores how to live coherently after profound insight without fragmenting, inflating, or getting stuck. This is not a moral judgment. It is a distinction. American drug culture is not intentional. Going to a party and taking a hit of acid is not medicine. Getting high on cannabis while you watch TV is not medicine. Taking psilocybin (or MDMA) at a rave is not medicine. No. That's tripping. While you may have many aspects of yourself revealed to you from those experiences, this book is about using medicine intentionally to receive information that helps you evolve, transcend, or explore aspects of yourself and the universe. The more you approach these medicines with humility, reverence, and intention, the more you may get out of them.

Ask yourself, "Why am I coming to the medicine now?"

Some people will know exactly why they're coming to the medicine. They'll say: I want to let go of ancestral trauma or sexual abuse; I want to let go of fear; I want to have a better relationship with my spouse. They may want clarity on what to do next in business or how to be a better parent. People are sometimes very clear on what they want.

Some people who have never had medicine experiences have no idea how to even set an intention.

I find there are five questions that can be helpful in exploring intentions:

1. What do you want to let go of? For instance, if you want to let go of pain and trauma from sexual abuse, what would you experience beyond that pain? Is it

freedom to live your life without unworthiness, guilt, or shame? To let go of victim mentality? Or to be free of the past?

2. On what do you want clarity? People often want clarity on life purpose, relationships, or business.

3. What do you want to receive? Do you want physical, mental, or emotional healing? More abundance? Love? Acceptance? Worthiness? Confidence?

4. What do you want to explore? Do you want to explore yourself? The universe? To understand creation at a deeper level?

5. Is there a spiritual reason you are choosing to have this experience? Do you want to meet God?

How would you word your intention in a way that feels right to you?

📌 **STOP READING:** Take some time now to write down an extensive list of intentions in your journal if you have not done so already. These are the things you would like to go after in the medicine space or dismantle daily with awareness. Don't worry about writing too many. We will organize them in a bit. Just do a huge data dump.

If you still have a hard time setting your intentions, the following section is a list of examples of what's possible for you based on what I've seen or experienced over the years since I have been an integration guide:

Physical Healing: I've seen people with low back pain, neck pain, a frozen shoulder, and knee pain come out of psychedelic medicine experiences completely pain free. I've worked with an eighty-year-old retired football player dealing with whole body aches and pains, who came out pain free and stayed that way three months later. Some people come out partially healed and then slowly over the next few days or weeks heal fully. I had this happen myself with a frozen shoulder.

The physical body is sometimes slow to catch up to the realizations people have of themselves on medicine and if the client has faith that they are healed, then healing is possible for them. It just may not be linear or how we expect it to unfold. Others who come out and doubt the healing experience often pick back up what was laid down. That's OK. People do things when they are ready for it, and many people are attached to identities as a wounded person or a victim. Letting go of that persona may be too much for them. Many people experience receiving surgeries, especially on the brain and heart. Physical healing is possible. There is a reason the medicine is called medicine.

Emotional Healing: I've seen people who have been sexually and emotionally abused as kids go into a MDMA/ketamine session, have an experience, and come out with a new perspective, forgiveness, and understanding. They come out and say, "That wasn't about me." They are ready to move on with life. Same with physical abuse, mental abuse, and traumatic situations. When these are seen from a different perspective they are easier to let go of.

Mental Healing: Many medicines heal the brain and bring the two hemispheres into coherence. Some shut down the thinking mind, enabling people to experience themselves beyond their thoughts and false identities. When people experience the peace, the bliss, the joy that accompanies a quiet mind, they may proclaim that they know who they are beyond the thinking mind and that knowing is something that could never be defined. These individuals have a lovely glow and peace that surrounds them. A quiet mind is common after many medicine experiences.

Ancestral Healing: I've worked with people who have gone into a medicine experience and saw that their habits, addictions, patterns, and ways of being weren't even theirs. They saw clearly how they learned from their parents and their parents learned from their parents and it was handed down through their lineage. I have had more than one client say in the medicine space, "This shit ends here! I will not pass this on to my children!" It is such an honor to witness these humans ending ancestral patterns.

Soul Connections: On some medicines, it is not unusual for people to connect with their higher self, soul, or True Self and receive information and even directives. Others have experienced themselves beyond physical form. I've worked with many, many people who have had conversations with deceased loved ones.

Spiritual Healing: I've worked with people who have connected with what they call God, Source, Spirit, Universe, Pure Consciousness, or Oneness. Many people remember spitting out the religious constructs they grew up with like a bad egg. Not one being with whom I have ever worked reported seeing a gray-haired man with a judgment stick in heaven. Quite the contrary. They report unconditional love and freedom. When I ask if they experienced any judgment in the presence of God, the answer is always a resounding no. Many report that there is no separation between us and God and that God is always with us, in us and permeates all things. They emphasize ALL THINGS.

While many people use different words to describe their experiences, what is experienced is often fundamentally the same. Whether Christian, Catholic, Jewish, or New Age;

whether God, Source, Spirit, Universe, or Consciousness, people who have experienced medicine use the words unconditional love, which is as close as they can come to describe it.

There are as many spiritual orientations as there are people on the planet. They all point to the same thing. Perhaps instead of fighting over language and linguistics we can step out of the constructs and boxes we've put the divine into and experience it for what it is. All religions point to the same thing: love.

Don't take my word for it, discover the truth for yourself, set an intention, and go find out.

STORYTIME: *One of my clients was talking about the will of God and that made me curious. So, I set the intention to go into the medicine space and ask God what his will was all about. In the medicine space I walked right up to God and said, "What is your will?" and the reply was, "To heal the wound of separation." I think my response was something like, "Oh, I'd really like that, too."*

I knew I would fulfill that intention. I knew that I was going to get an answer. I didn't know how it would unfold, but I set the intention, aligned emotionally, and took action. I got busy with it. I feel that is a powerful way to enter the medicine space.

To be clear, my journeys don't always unfold that way. I am never certain what will happen, or if I am aligned with my intention. Alignment varies from experience to experience. In addition, the degree to which I try to control the experience also plays a role. In this case I was not trying to control the experience. No. I set the intention, then let go of any expectation as to how it would unfold or what would happen. In the beginning, my journeys were all over the place. Then as I got to know the medicine, I built a relationship with it. I learned that trust can coexist with doubt. Working with medicine is sacred, and I recommend approaching each ceremony with reverence, personal responsibility, and sovereignty. We will talk more about this in a bit.

IMPORTANT NOTE ON FRAGMENTATION: If you seek ego death or enlightenment, make sure you are ready for it. Receiving this intention can blow you apart and cause an identity crisis that can take years for you to put the pieces back together. Enlightenment may require your whole life to fall apart so that you can align to that which you seek. This can cost you friends, family, and everything in your life that is not in alignment with this intention. Caution is needed to ensure you are really ready for what you ask for.

Even worse, the experience can fracture what needs to stay intact. Identity can temporarily dissolve, nervous system scaffolding can weaken dissolving familiar reference points, emotional imprints can surface, all of which can be very helpful for the individual ready to do that work. But for the individual not ready, too much change, too quickly, without the capacity to integrate can destabilize. Too much change too quickly can dissolve structures, remove filters, and while it can accelerate change, it can also blow out a nervous system not ready or capable of integrating that change. This is why preparation matters.

Risk for fragmentation increases when someone has:
- Unresolved trauma
- Identity instability
- High sensitivity
- A tendency to seek transcendence without integration

It decreases when someone has:
- A strong body awareness
- Ability to ground

- Emotional regulation skills
- Patience
- Comfort with uncertainty

I will reiterate the importance of nervous system stability throughout this book. The nervous system loves change to be gentle and at a softer pace. It loves stability. While many of the experiences can feel expansive, upon landing they can destabilize coordination or tear down old scaffolding before new scaffolding can be built.

It is wise to consider if you are ready for the next expansion before loading your rocket ship up with a hero's dose of fuel! So, look back at your intentions.

Are you ready for that which you seek?

How can you move forward in such a way that honors your system even if it means decreasing the intensity in which you approach medicine work?

These questions offer ways to have a grounded, safe ceremony that increases coherence after profound insight without fragmentation.

Core Patterns and Intentions

By now you may have a whole list of intentions. Good.

Now let's organize them into main themes so we can find a core intention or two.

For instance, you may want to:

- Release anxiety
- Connect deeper with your partner
- Fire someone at the office
- Let go of unworthiness or imposter syndrome

Exploring what's at the root cause of these may take you to the core pattern of fear.

For example,

- Anxiety is the creation of a story about something that might happen in the future but never does. Anxiety and fear are closely related. So, facing fear and seeing it for what it really is—a well-intentioned illusion—can actually heal the pattern you created around feeling anxious.

- If you look at what is getting in the way of connecting deeply with your partner you may find fear of rejection or vulnerability may be in the way. Again, fear is often the creation of a story, not what is real.

- If you need to fire someone at the office and you explore what's in the way, you may uncover a fear of being a bad person, or being afraid of what people think, or fear of confrontation. Again, fear is at the core.

- Exploring unworthiness also brings us to the fear of not being good enough, not mattering, not being worth being seen or known.

Core Patterns: We see from this example there is clearly a core pattern of fear. There may be threads of unworthiness in there, too. This doesn't mean fear is a bad guy that needs obliterating. Fear can be protective as well as illusory, depending on context.

Core Intention: Setting the intention to thank fear for its protection and work through fear can be a powerful intention that takes care of all of these.

Look back at the intentions you wrote down. Is there a main theme that runs through them all? Fear and unworthiness are most common, which is why I use them as examples.

Is there one core intention you could set that would wipe out many core patterns and accelerate your journey?

Lastly, take a moment and ask yourself if you believe it's possible for you to fulfill your intention. For instance, if you set the intention to release fear, do you think you can do it? Can you imagine life without it? Is it too big a leap or is it digestible? You don't have to release it all at once, that may be too intense. You could actually whittle away at it little by little. Set intentions that feel comfortable and doable for you.

Releasing Expectations

Okay, now that you have set your intentions and have chosen one or two core intentions, it is very important to let go of any expectations of what's going to happen or how it's going to unfold in the medicine space. Don't go in thinking that you're going to be facing your darkest shadow, that you will be letting go and struggling the whole time. Don't go in thinking it will be all rainbows and butterflies either. Expectations are a big impediment to people being able to let go and receive what is being revealed to them. Expectations are recipes for disappointment. Always.

Trust that you have done your part by setting the intentions and let the medicine drive the car. You can always exercise sovereignty if the journey takes a dark turn, but in general, let go and trust your decision to take medicine and release any expectations as to what will unfold.

Here's an example of what this can look like: Let's say you set the intention to get clarity on what's next for you in business, and the medicine shows you an aspect of yourself you may not want to see. You may see how you have disrespected the people in your life; taken them for granted; or witness the selfish, petty, needy, or greedy aspect of yourself. This is something that needs to be worked through before you can manifest what's next in business. While it may not be what you expect, it can be exactly what you need. This is a huge gift that many people don't see as a gift. We have to be willing to receive the revelations, even though they may not make sense at the time.

The medicine and Spirit always seem to know what is most urgent for people to work through. So don't be surprised if you set one intention and the medicine takes you down a completely different path. Go with it. The difficult revelations that people want to stuff away and forget are often the most impactful when integrated. People don't often see how their intentions are actually being met in a roundabout way. It may not be clear to someone wanting physical healing why the medicine revealed an onery aspect of themselves or the divine aspect until the experience is looked at from a broader perspective. For example, it could be the orneriness that caused the disease, or it could be the recognition of the divine within that enables healing.

We may not know why the medicine does what it does, but we can trust that it is wise and works with spirit in ways that are beyond our understanding. When we approach the medicine intentionally, with reverence and humility, miracles happen. I am blessed to see them all the time.

So, to recap: Set your intentions. Find a core intention. Then LET GO of any expectations. Period.

Clear Your Schedule

I cannot emphasize enough how important it is to clear your schedule for a few days after you decide to take medicine. Let's talk about why.

Neurological Resets

Many medicines disrupt neural connections within your brain and throughout your entire physical body, interrupting thought patterns, belief structures, habits, and patterns temporarily and sometimes permanently. They can challenge identity and change your whole neural circuitry. So, it's really important to clear your schedule as much as possible after an experience. This gives you the time and space to allow new circuits to form and to implement new habits, new patterns, new ways of thinking, and new ways of being in the world. I recommend clients take at least three days to sit with what was revealed to them, to capture as much information as possible, and to acclimate to their new set point. If you just hop right back into your old routine, the chances are high that you may pick back up the patterns you released and the medicine experience could be for naught.

The neurological reset or the neuroplastic event increases plasticity, which means it boosts the brain's ability to rewire itself, form new neural connections, and adapt to new experiences and learning, or heal from injury. Many medicines increase nervous system flexibility, resilience, and capacity. This makes learning new skills or recovering brain function at any age possible. This can involve strengthening certain pathways, pruning unused ones, and reorganizing neural networks for better function, allowing you to learn languages, recover from strokes, or maintain cognitive sharpness.

Medicine work often makes change happen easier. This is important to emphasize, especially for executives who have a realization that their partner and kids are more important than work. This is an important and common insight. Yet, when no space is taken they often get home and go right back to work as if nothing ever happened. Previous neuro-connections reestablish themselves, old patterns are picked back up and an opportunity to make changes when change is easiest is missed.

A note of warning: There are so many retreat centers that people can visit to have expanded experiences, but an individual's circuitry may not be prepared to withstand these experiences and it can push them past the capacity for the body to integrate these energies and can do damage. Capacity-building is gradual and embodied, not just energetic. Not to mention, some people may not be ready for awakening experiences. Looking for a state change may open you, but if you don't have the circuitry to integrate what you're experiencing it can be challenging. You may have no reference point to process the information you are receiving. This can create more anxiety or dissonance within the system.

So instead of seeking and pushing these high state experiences, consider spending time integrating some of the lower ecstatic experiences until they become a part of you, until it becomes integrated and you have a new set point. Then you can experience the next ecstatic experience and you integrate that.

Neurological Adaptation

The body is the grand alchemizer; it knows the truth. It always tells the truth. The body will ground the mind and help you translate the experience. The body is not delusional. The mind absolutely can be. When we anchor in the body, we can quiet the mind and receive, balance, and harmonize high frequency vibrations. Then the body is given the opportunity to illuminate and vibrate coherently where disease, anger, judgment, and fear can't exist.

When we infuse these frequencies into the systems of the body little by little, it reconstructs who we are. We build the circuitry for the subtle self to be built at a different level where we can embody the wholeness of our being.

When you start experiencing low level joy that sustains itself over time without medicine you know you are on the right track.

The Golden Window

The two weeks after a medicine journey are what some call the golden window, when change is easier because you just had a neurological reset. I will have clients look at their calendar. If there's anything on there that they don't like or don't want to do, I tell them to delegate it, delete it, take a personal day, and do what they can to create the perfect life for them when they return.

Clearing your schedule as much as possible after a journey does many things:

• Some people simply may not feel well or be able to function afterwards, depending on the medicine.

• Some medicines can be extremely depleting and it may take up to two weeks to recover, especially if you have been overdosed. (This can and does happen.)

• It gives you time to acclimate to the information mentally, physically, and emotionally.

• You may still be purging—physically, mentally, and feeling very emotional.

• Spiritually you may have a new set point.

• It gives you time to just be and let all the bits and pieces settle.

Outside Influences

Avoid being exposed to anything beforehand that would distract you or hijack the journey. For example, don't watch a horror movie or take a deep dive into politics or the news. These things could come in from your subconscious mind and hijack the journey. Spend some time in nature in a contemplative, receptive state ideally to prepare for the medicine.

Set and Setting

Set and setting are crucial factors in shaping the experience of any journey.

Set: "Set" refers to your mindset, emotional state, intentions, and expectations before taking the substance. A positive, open, and prepared mindset can lead to meaningful insights, emotional healing, and transformative experiences, while anxiety, fear, or unresolved personal issues may manifest as challenging or difficult.

Having said that, sometimes the unresolved personal issues are exactly why we are taking medicine. For instance, the depression or anxiety we want to release can come into the medicine space with us if our intention is to release it. So having a mindset that is aligned with, "I am going into this experience to get things done. And if that means I am going to be facing and purging anxiety the whole time, so be it." Resolve and dedication to move beyond the things you fear, beyond the patterns of your youth, and beyond your habitual ways of being in the world is a very helpful mindset. Setting clear intentions and ensuring emotional readiness can greatly enhance the likelihood of a beneficial experience.

Setting: Setting encompasses the external environment, including the physical space, social context, and overall atmosphere in which the ceremony takes place. A safe, comfortable, and familiar setting can provide a sense of security, allowing the individual to surrender to the experience without unnecessary fear. Supportive and trusted companions, calming music, and nature can further enrich the sacred ceremony, fostering feelings of peace and connection. Conversely, an unpredictable or chaotic environment can lead to distress and anxiety, reinforcing the importance of carefully curating the surroundings to encourage a positive and insightful experience.

Group Settings: If you are going in for a group ceremony that requires everyone to stay on their mat in silence while everyone works with the medicine in their own way, that is good to know. I was in an ayahuasca ceremony once with a large group and there was a girl who was humming quite loudly. This took everyone out of their own revelations and was a huge distraction. Don't be that person. Of course there are times when being quiet is not an option. Like when you are staring into a puke bucket and it feels like your intestines are being ripped from your body. That's just what is. It can be done with or without drama. The amount of drama is directly proportionate to how loud you are. There is no need to over dramatize anything. Don't stop your own healing experience just to be quiet; simply be respectful and considerate of those around you. This is a time for you to go inward and be with yourself, not emoting or creating drama that could distract the group.

Individual Setting: Many facilitators work one on one, which I love. In this case you can make as much noise as you like. I still recommend leaving the drama out of the experience. For example, if you are crying uncontrollably from sadness or trauma from the past, let it out. Let it all out, but be aware of whether you are wallowing in the sadness, attaching story to it, and holding onto it versus letting go. We will go into this more when we talk about navigating the medicine space. For now, just know there are group retreat offerings and solo offerings, and they differ in how you will work with the medicine, how you express yourself, and what the set and setting look like. Now that some of these medicines are legal, such as ketamine clinics, you may also find yourself in a room sitting upright with an IV in your arm.

Self-Guided Settings: Set and setting are very important. If you will be taking the medicine within the comfort of your own home, be sure that you have a comfortable, warm area with lots of blankets, and a playlist that you know won't take you down a dark hole. I recommend calm, soothing music that makes you feel safe, loved, and held, unless your intention is to traverse the universe, then a playlist a bit more upbeat may be indicated.

If you are journeying alone at home, be sure to cleanse your space with sage, spend some time connecting with the medicine, and call in your guides to create a clean, safe, and sacred ceremonial space. This ensures you are approaching the medicine with reverence, respect, and humility. When you approach the sacred as sacred it can increase your chances of success enormously, because when your space is sacred, it is a high consciousness, high vibrational zone that many low vibrational energies can't or won't enter.

There were a few times when I got lazy and did not cleanse my space or call in my guides, and I got totally tossed. What feels like dark energies or nonphysical low vibe entities that may not have your best interest at heart can come into your space if it is not set up protectively. These can be understood symbolically, psychologically, energetically, or literally depending on your worldview and experience. The times I did not create a safe and sacred space were the times I encountered these energies, demons, or just plain chaos and confusion. I learned fast that my ceremonial space MUST be clean and it MUST be sacred.

I recommend you do the same. Even if you are being served at a retreat center, ensure the space where you will be taking medicine is conducive to a good experience.

Cleansing Your Space

There are many ways to cleanse your space and a quick Google search will give you many to choose from. Here's what I do:

🕯 Step-by-Step Guide for Burning Palo Santo (or Sage)

1. Set an Intention: Before lighting Palo Santo, set a clear intention to cleanse the space and journey safely. Hold your intention for the journey in mind as you do this.

2. Light the Palo Santo: Hold a stick of Palo Santo at a 45-degree angle and light the end. Allow it to burn for about 30 seconds, then blow out the flame.

3. Cleanse the Space: Walk around your space with the Palo Santo, letting the smoke drift into corners and over areas where you want cleansed. Invoke safety, love, peace, and any other qualities that resonate. Speak your intention into the space as you move through the space.

4. Store the Palo Santo: After use, place the stick in a heatproof dish. Palo Santo can be reused several times.

Safety

Once the space has been cleansed, you want to continue to create the container in which you will journey. You want to create a sanctuary so you know you are safe to let go and receive the fulfillment of your intention. This involves calling in your guides, and there is no bigger guide I can think of than the divine, so I recommend calling in the safety of God, Source, Spirit, Universe, Consciousness to watch over you while you are in the medicine.

The Revelation Integration Method recommends strongly that you ensure you have a space in which to journey safely. There are several ways you can do this and no one way is the only way. I will list a few and you can choose the one that works for you or create your own sanctuary.

Sanctuary

There are many ways we can language Sanctuary to invoke it. An invocation is a summoning. It is powerful and it is real. When you invoke God, God is there. When you invoke Source, Source is there. It doesn't matter what name you call it. If you invoke consciousness, consciousness it is right there. It actually never left. You have just increased your ability to be aware of it.

Sanctuary, and the invocation of it, is a method you can use to become aware of your union with the creator and step outside the illusion of separation.

All of creation is one big construct. We live in a world of creation. Any negative thought pattern is a creation. The belief of unworthiness: a creation. The ego: a creation. The government: a creation. Religion: a creation. Fear is a creation. These are the constructs we have created that make up the world we live in. And those constructs were born of a species at a certain level of consciousness. Our species has been asleep. Now we are waking up and have the opportunity to evolve the constructs.

We can clean up our mess and we can do it safely in Sanctuary.

Sanctuary is a vibrational field, a tone that you hold or align to that can be used to heal. Any decision you need to make can be brought to Sanctuary; any issue can be solved in Sanctuary. When you align to Sanctuary you tap into what exists beyond all constructs. You find yourself within the universal field in which all things exist and the answers you receive in this space are always for your highest good and the good of others.

You could say becoming aware of the divine increases and balances your vibrational frequency, your resonance, and things automatically move toward coherence. Dense imprints and patterns can be released; the body can restructure itself and you don't have to do a thing other than cultivate awareness that you set the intention to be in Sanctuary and bam! You are in it.

If you also invoke the presence of your guides, that increases your protection. If things get crazy, you can ask for their help and they will aid and support you.

You are totally safe in Sanctuary. What better setting to create for a medicine journey than this?

Hamilton Souther's Sanctuary

I first learned of Sanctuary from Hamilton Souther at the Blue Morpho Academy when I was being educated on how to sit with others in the psilocybin space. I studied his teachings for two years and continue to follow his work. Sanctuary enables me to connect to a pure field and gives me the tools to hold an impeccable space when sitting for others.

"Sanctuary is a space you create for your consciousness to operate in multiple dimensions. In Sanctuary the room you are in becomes the infinite. No matter where you go or what you find, you are safe." ~ Hamilton Souther

Hamilton's Sanctuary is composed of four tenants:

1. Source/God/Universe/Spirit is in through and around all things.

From the oxygen you breath to the cells in your body, to the subatomic particles and waves that comprise your body and the field you exist within, you can't be separated in any way from it. It is Oneness code, not separation code or delusion. He directs us to use our mind to call on it and invoke it. In Sanctuary there is you, plus Source, plus all your guides that you invoke to help you. It provides absolute protection and absolute safety.

2. Source/God/Universe/Spirit is infinite time and eternal space.

This one can be tricky to understand as in the beginning it feels backwards. You may have to explore it on your own to really grasp it. How I was able to embody this tenant was to ask, "Where am I?" and the answer came, "infinite time." Infinite time is all the time. Eternal space has no borders; it is the stable field of source through which everything manifests. Space is eternal. I discovered that this tenant helps me tap into what exists beyond what is called space time on Earth. This feels like a higher dimensional state. Time may seem like five minutes or five years. Sanctuary gives you all the time and all the space to do what needs to be done anytime, anywhere. Especially in the medicine space.

3. When you invoke Sanctuary it becomes self-balancing, self-grounding, self-harmonizing, self-healing, and self-orienting.

When you combine these two tenants you have God, infinite time, eternal space and you have stability. The field you are in automatically becomes self-balancing, self-harmonizing, self-healing, self-grounding and self-orienting. This is really valuable if you are serving or taking psychedelic medicine. It helps you hold a stable and safe space for your clients. If you are sitting for yourself it helps you journey safely.

4. Sanctuary is safe

After testing Sanctuary for years Hamilton found Sanctuary to be safe. I have also found it to be safe. Anything that comes into Sanctuary or is released in Sanctuary automatically begins healing, harmonizing, and balancing. Sanctuary reorients and grounds. Even the darkest of dark needs healing and all are welcome in Sanctuary. I love this. No more fighting. Just unconditional love.

Sanctuary does all the work for us, so we don't have to. If things get intense, just invoke Sanctuary and call in your guides. They've got you.

In Sanctuary you have the space, infinite time, your allies, the tools, AND a unified field. These principles support your practice and enables you to not only take medicine in a safe space, but they also empower you create a safe and healing space anytime anywhere under any circumstance. Whether you are in the medicine or not.

Think about this as becoming aware of or aligning to the extraordinary, unified field in which we can heal and evolve. Not to mention it is just absolutely delicious to be in Sanctuary. The body just loves it and it has contributed immensely to my own healing.

If you are serving medicine or want the skills to sit with someone in the medicine space in an impeccable way, I highly recommend Hamilton's training. Much of his wisdom has found its way into this book and I am forever grateful to him. I am just skimming the surface here, so for a deeper dive into how to serve medicine and take medicine safely in Sanctuary, his online training can be found at https://bluemorphoacademy.com/

Don't take my word for it; invoke Hamilton's Sanctuary and experience it for yourself. Here's how. Be sure to feel the effects of your words.

✎ Invocation:

1. Source/God/Universe/Spirit is in through and all around all things. Including you.

2. Source/God/Universe/Spirit is infinite time and eternal space.

3. When you invoke Sanctuary feel how it becomes self-balancing, self-harmonizing, self-healing, self-grounding and self-orienting.

Feel how safe you are.

Don't just say the words, feel them, explore them, discover Sanctuary for yourself. Again, there is much more to Hamilton's work than what I am sharing here. So go check it out if you want to learn from a master who knows his craft.

Paul Selig's Sanctuary

Paul Selig and the Guides he channels, who he calls Melchizedek, have also been some of my greatest teachers. Before he channels he does an invocation that he speaks aloud:

"The light of God surrounds us, the love of God enfolds us,

the power of God protects us, the spirit of God watches over us. Wherever we are, God is. So be it. Set the intention that you are open and receptive to those energies and information which are for your highest good in the perfect amounts needed for your healing and evolution at this time."

This is a beautiful invocation and intention that we can use in the medicine space to create Sanctuary. Can you feel the effects of the words? I sure can.

I have explored this invocation and found it to be a very pure way of creating Sanctuary when it is said with meaning and feeling. It is very clear, simple and easy to use.

Deepak Chopra's Sanctuary

Deepak Chopra founded the concept of consciousness as the regulator of biology. He invites us to explore the profound relationship between our awareness and our physical existence. He suggests that time, as we perceive it, is constantly consuming our life force, leading to aging and eventual physical decline. To slow the metabolism of time, he suggests we shift our perspective from a time-bound identity to one rooted in timeless awareness. When we recognize that our true essence is not confined by the passage of time, it opens a sacred space within us, one that naturally moves toward healing and harmony. He is known for the phrase, "Timeless mind ageless body."

In my meditations I have focused on "timeless awareness" and have found it to be self-healing, self-harmonizing, self-grounding, self-balancing, and self-orienting as well.

Ram Dass's Sanctuary

Ram Dass rooted his entire teaching in the practice of loving awareness. Instead of trying to transcend the human experience, he invites us to soften into it, meeting our fears, joys, confusions, and hopes with unconditional friendliness. He often taught that loving-kindness is not something we generate; it is something we remember, a natural presence revealed when we relax the tight grip of the ego. From his perspective, Sanctuary is found not in escaping life but in turning toward it with an open heart. When we rest in loving awareness, we step into Sanctuary where nothing needs to be fixed or controlled, and everything is held within the spaciousness of compassion.

In my meditations, I have focused on Ram Dass's invitation to "be here now," allowing myself to return again and again to the simple warmth of loving-kindness. I've discovered that this gentle presence operates like an inner Sanctuary— self-soothing, self-accepting, and deeply stabilizing. I find a natural healing intelligence that arises on its own: a softening, a grounding, and a remembering of who I truly am beneath all the stories.

My Sanctuary

Years ago I read a book that emphasized the importance of cultivating awareness as a way of accessing True Self. I took this to heart and have practiced it on and off for many years. I had a hard time meditating because I could not quiet my mind. But I found I could cultivate awareness and rise above the plane of thought where thoughts and the constructs of the world could not attach to me.

Here it is again:

ꙮ Cultivating Awareness Exercise

In this exercise keep your eyes open and loosely

focused on something in front of you. Don't close your eyes and disappear inward; expand your awareness. Practice super awareness.

Step 1: Direct your gaze down at a 45-degree angle. Listen to the sounds in the room. Be very aware of your external environment. Don't judge the sounds; see how many sounds you can become aware of.

Step 2: Next, bring your awareness to your body and where it is located in the room. Feel your feet. Feel your legs. Become aware of the weight of your legs. Feel gravity. Release your belly. Become aware of your heartbeat. Can you feel your heart pumping blood to your entire body? Feel your arms. Become aware of how your chest rises on the inhale and falls on the exhale. (Releasing the belly helps to release stress or tension and the heartbeat brings you to center. This exercise grounds and balances you.)

Step 3: Feel the aware presence that resides within that physical body. Awareness. Consciousness. Experience what some call the 'I am that I am' as a feeling sense. If your mind is active and you sink back into the realm of thoughts, just let them come and go. Resist nothing. Be curious. Tell your mind to chill out and redirect your focus back to your heartbeat.

This exercise expands consciousness like the branches of a tree and grounds us in our body like the roots of a tree. This stabilizes our ability to rise above the mental plane of thought where we can experience peace and the interconnectedness of all things, while staying in the body. I have found that when I cultivate awareness I access the infinite and eternal. In the beginning it was to a small degree, but the more I practiced the stronger it got. It takes me to the same self-balancing, self-healing, self-harmonizing, self-grounding, and self-orienting space Hamilton speaks of.

Any of these practices, no matter which we choose, naturally moves us toward healing and harmony. You may even have your own version of Sanctuary. In general, when we become more aware, more loving, and more present, we tap into the profound intelligence of the universe, which inherently knows how to restore balance. In a state of heightened awareness, we may begin to perceive the interconnectedness of all life. We see ourselves not as isolated beings but as integral parts of a larger cosmic dance.

We remember in Sanctuary.

So, when it comes to setting, what setting will you create? How would you choose to create a safe setting, a Sanctuary to journey safely? You only need one practice that resonates.

Let's continue with this chapter on how to prepare for a medicine journey.

Capturing Revelations/Gathering Data

Once you have set your core intentions, released expectations, cleared your schedule afterwards, have your ceremony mindset aligned with a belief that your intentions can absolutely be fulfilled, and Sanctuary has been invoked, you want to plan how you will capture the revelations that are going to be revealed to you.

Talking: Depending on the setting and medicine, you may or you may not be able to talk while you are in the space. Most people are surprised at the idea of talking while in the medicine space, but I find it is a great way to capture the revelations for later integration. I highly recommend talking if you are doing a solo journey as long as it doesn't pull you out of the experience. Many people will use the voice memo function on their cell phone and just let it record through the whole session. This way you can vocalize something knowing it won't be forgotten. I recorded a facilitated mushroom journey, and it was one of the best journeys I've ever had. I talked and laughed the whole time. I still listen to that recording to remind me not to take life too seriously, and I am still integrating that journey today. I am grateful I have the recording.

Ketamine is a medicine that when some people get into the revelation phase, they find themselves to be very talkative. They report having conversations with their higher self, their soul, or God. Talking helps us work through things and helps us see where we are with ourselves. Talking is extremely valuable for the integration process, as long as it's not distracting or pulling you out of the medicine.

The recording of any talking you did while in a session and journal entries are precious. When you make the decision to take medicine, also make the decision to capture as much information from that experience as possible so you can integrate the revelations later.

You may give it a try and find you are not able talk. This is absolutely okay. If you don't talk, it doesn't mean you did anything wrong or the medicine didn't work. Processing pre-verbal trauma, receiving what people call codes, upgrades, activations, healings, restructurings, and working with vibrational frequencies can be silent or verbal. If you don't talk, it just means you will ideally be journaling like a crazy person afterwards. Sometimes people will hum or sing or just go into a quiet mind and deep peace. So, not talking isn't a bad thing.

How you capture the revelations from your experience depends on the setting:

• Are you having a solo experience? Can you speak into a recorder or the voice memo app on your cell phone to capture the revelations? If so, set the voice memo app to record and just let it run. It doesn't matter if you speak or not, just knowing you can speak aloud to capture a revelation anytime can be reassuring. Most apps have a skip silence function that is awesome so you can go straight to the words you spoke.

• If you are not a voice memo person or are with a group and can't talk because it will distract others, wait until you land and find a quiet spot to journal extensively about your experience immediately afterwards while it is still fresh. If you find you can't journal, narrate the experience into your voice memo app for later integration.

Important: Don't wait to capture your revelations. The revelations are the whole reason you decided to take the medicine. The longer you wait to journal about your experience, the more the mind can distort the experience or make things up. The ego can come online and attach meaning or significance to a revelation that wasn't there. Journaling about your experience afterward helps you capture the imprints and remember or embody the revelations at a deeper level. You are exposed to the information twice.

Some people will end up with two pages of journaling from a cannabis session, others may have ten pages from a psilocybin session. Others still can have up to 100 pages of typed transcript recording from a ketamine/MDMA session.

Find a way to capture the revelations in a way that is right for you. If any method of capturing information pulls you out of the experience, capture the information when you land.

The Revelation Integration Method emphasizes heavily the importance of capturing the revelations as soon as possible. This enables you to work with the revelations to see what is complete and integrated and what is not. The more information you capture, the more you can integrate.

Uncertainty and Fear Mitigation

While I talk a lot about releasing expectations, there are some general things you can anticipate from certain medicine experiences, like the onset, the revelation phase, and landing phase general timelines. In general, these are somewhat predictable.

On the preparation calls I have with clients, I talk about common experiences people have on the medicine they will be taking and answer any questions to help them feel safe and mitigate any fear or uncertainty. It's impossible to know exactly what each person will experience, but we do have a general idea of how certain medicines work. For example, if someone is going in for an ayahuasca experience, purging is very typical, and I will give them ideas and tools to work with that medicine, like how to relax, breathe, and let go if they have issues with control.

I often give clients examples of a wide range of common experiences people report if the individual is curious and requires reassurance. This is akin to telling them what to expect in such a way that helps them release expectations. For example, I might say, "Some people report seeing colors, fractals, or sacred geometry; others don't receive any visuals, they receive information through imprinting. They don't see, they know. Some people report receiving restructurings and surgical-like experiences. Others visit a place they call 'the void.' Some say it's the most uncomfortable experience of their life. Others experience pure bliss and what they call 'God.' Some go in and it's like crawling on their hands and knees over broken glass to release past trauma, and others will look at the trauma and say, 'Huh. That wasn't even about me.'"

Preparing for a medicine journey is like opening a Christmas present you haven't peeked at. You never know what will come out of that box. The ultimate reassurance is, of course, that in my years of doing this work, no one I know of has died from medicine work, and there is always something to learn from every medicine experience.

Prep Guides: Before retreats people will often receive a prep guide with information on how to dress, what to bring, how to eat, etc. Going over the prep guide and asking for clarity if you need it can mitigate fear and the unknown. Follow any dietary restrictions to make the most of the experience. They are important. When you eat a clean diet before taking medicine, the medicine doesn't have to deal with the crappy food you have been eating and can take you straight to the revelations. Eating well also indicates you are approaching the medicine with respect and reverence and intention. This is wise and can lead to more impactful experiences.

Other items that help mitigate fear and uncertainty include going over the details of the retreat itself. Did you vet the organization and the facilitator? Does it feel right? What time will you start? How long will it last? Who will be there with you? How is your safety being reassured? How do you ask for support if you need it? This preparation can answer any questions you have about the organization and experience itself.

My favorite way of mitigating fear and uncertainty is by asking one question: is this thing you're afraid or uncertain of true? Can you know without a shadow of a doubt that it will happen? Fear is, most often than not, an illusion. It's a story of what might happen that never does. Changing your relationship with fear by looking at it openly and honestly, seeing it for what it is; a protective biological role that overreacts, can help diffuse any illusions or delusions around fear you may be hanging onto. Truly, what is fear going to do? Hit you over the head?

Acknowledging fear's protective biological role can help when people feel like they are failing and fear persists. Thanking fear, letting it move through you, and shifting your attention to something other than fear (like your breathing pattern) repeatedly can unwind the pattern of fear when done intentionally.

Regardless, it is normal for fear to arise in the medicine space. We are taking a dive into the unknown. There is no way we can be certain of outcome or, in many circumstances, even control the experience.

You and you alone must decide if medicine work is right for you. If you make this decision, there are ways you can mitigate fear and do it safely and responsibility.

Things That May Pull You Out of the Medicine: Having to pee, being cold or too hot, dry mouth, outside noises, and any other distractions can pull you out of the medicine in the middle of an important revelation. Remove all these distractions ahead of time.

Serotonin Depletion: If a medicine, such as MDMA, depletes serotonin in the brain, it is good to know that particular medicine may create a dip in mood after the experience, including sadness or mild depression so you can plan for it. Not always, but this can happen and it's good to be aware of it so you can acknowledge that you just need to rest and restore. A dip in mood can also occur when we experience bliss or divine experiences and then return to what we call our normal 3D life. Prepare yourself for this as a possibility knowing it is normal. Again, it doesn't mean that the medicine didn't work, or that you didn't get anything out of it or that you did it wrong. It just means that your physical form is depleted. Let your body rest.

Pre-Call Tools

Here are some tools I have found helpful when preparing a client for a sacred ceremony.

⚘ Grounding Exercise: 5 Senses Check-In

Sometimes I will have someone who is really anxious or scattered do a grounding exercise or meditation, if they are open to it. These are often people who dissociate: they don't stay in their body or they're not fully present in their body.

If this is you, there are many different grounding exercises that can be found online. Find one that works for you. The following is an exercise I use to help clients ground and center before and after ceremony that you might find helpful.

What do you see? Look around and name five things you can see. Observe colors, shapes, light, or movement. "I see sunlight on the floor... I see the flicker of a candle..."

What do you feel? Tune into your body and notice four things you can feel.

It might be your breath, clothing, warmth, or gravity. "I feel my feet on the ground... I feel the air on my skin..."

What do you hear? Listen quietly and name three sounds you can hear.

They can be near or far, loud or soft. Don't judge it, just listen. "I hear a bird outside... I hear my own breath..."

What do you smell? Take a breath and notice two scents. You might smell the space, nature, incense, or essential oils. "I smell sage... I smell the clean air..."

What do you taste? Notice the taste of your mouth.

Whole Body Awareness: Become aware of the entirety of your body. Feel the weight of it. Feel gravity. Imagine you have roots. Are you safe?

Breathe: Take a deep inhale. Pause. Exhale slowly. Pause. This helps to contain your energy and settle the chaos. You are here. You are grounded. You are safe.

Grounding exercises are great before and after medicine ceremonies because they get us out of our head and into our body. This helps to calm anxiety, fear, or uncertainty and can help us access the revelation at a deeper more heart centered level.

If I notice a client has a hard time relaxing and is clenching or does not know how to let go, I will walk them through this brief exercise:

⚓ Letting Go/Relaxation Exercise

Begin in a comfortable position. Close your eyes if you like. Let your hands rest gently on your body or by your sides. Take a deep breath in...and let out a long, slow breath.

Bring your attention to your shoulders. Notice any tension or tightness. Take another deep breath and on the exhale relax your shoulders. I will usually see their shoulders drop and say, "See. You do know how to relax and let go." Then I will direct them to practice this in the morning and at night while they are lying in bed with their entire body, not just their shoulders.

How to let go exercises condition the body and teach the body-mind that it can let go. As each muscle relaxes, the person gets more and more familiar with what letting go feels like. This can be super valuable for those who don't really know how to let go.

If you can take a deep breath and relax your muscles on the exhale, you know how to let go.

⚓ Receptivity Exercise

Receptivity is one of the Revelation Integration Fundamentals and involves being open to what the medicine has for you, no matter how challenging or ineffable it may seem, no matter what the medicine reveals to you about yourself. When you are receptive, you are open to change. This is an exercise that can enable you to shift into a listening, open state, and it is suitable as a meditation before, during, or after a ceremony, or anytime you want to receive answers.

Begin by finding a comfortable position. You can sit or lie down. Eyes open or closed.

Take a slow breath in, pause. Let out a long, slow breath. Pause. Repeat 3 times. Let your attention rest on your body. Notice where it touches the ground or your seat. Feel the natural rhythm of your breath. No need to change it. Just notice. Now bring awareness to sound. Notice any sounds around you. Allow them to come and go. You're not trying to focus—just noticing. Let sounds arrive and leave without effort. Now bring your attention to sensation. Feel your body as it is. Temperature, pressure, movement, stillness. Nothing to fix. Just awareness. Rest in this space for a few more breaths.

Next ask a question. Then pause again. Stay open and curious. Wait patiently for what wants to come through. You are simply being present and receptive, waiting for what might drop in. Curiosity helps. After you receive something say thank you and feel the results of those words.

Nausea

Some people experience nausea on some medicines. If you are taking a medicine that makes you feel nauseated, use your exhale to send the nausea out of your body; imagine the nauseousness leaving with every exhale. When releasing suppressed emotions or toxicity, the body may respond with physical symptoms like nausea, as the "stored energy or gunk" is processed and released. Using your breath to blow out nauseousness can help the cleansing and purging process along, even two to three hours or more after the experience.

Overall, when preparing for a medicine experience of any kind, the best advice I can give is this:

1. Vet the organization or facilitator so you feel safe.
2. Set your intentions and mean it. Know what you are going in to accomplish.
3. Release expectations. Period.
4. Clear your schedule afterwards to take advantage of the neurological reset.
5. Avoid being exposed to anything beforehand that would distract you or hijack the journey.
6. Mitigate fear and uncertainty as much as possible.
7. Go in with a positive mindset aligned with your intentions.
8. Set yourself up to capture as many revelations as possible.
9. Connect with the medicine with reverence and gratitude.
10. Call in your guides, invoke Sanctuary, know you are safe.
11. Then let go.

While preparation does not guarantee a smooth journey,

it guarantees one that you will be able to work with.

In the next chapter we will discuss how to navigate the medicine space itself.

CHAPTER 4

NAVIGATING THE MEDICINE SPACE

In this chapter you will receive tools to navigate the medicine space safely, and strategies that will help you ground, release, receive, reorient yourself, work with fear and discomfort, and acclimate to your divinity. There are four phases people go through in the medicine experience: Onset, Revelation, Landing, and Integration. In this chapter we will cover them in detail and give you tools to navigate them effectively.

Let's go through these one at a time.

Navigating Onset

The onset is the initial phase when the effects of the medicine of your choice begin to emerge, often marked by physical sensations, changes in perception, and a gradual shift in consciousness. Depending on the medicine, dose, and person (you), onset can be very comfortable and short or long and uncomfortable. Onset is the initial phase when changes in consciousness take place. We could say experientially that it feels like your metabolism and brain chemistry are changing vibration until a dimensional shift in perception can take place.

When people take psychedelics, they are not accessing external dimensions. They are entering altered states of perception and cognition within the brain–body system. The revelations experienced comes from internal sources such as memory, emotion, sensory amplification, pattern-making, imagination, and subconscious material that can be temporarily or permanently reorganized by the medicine. We could say that you are having your quantum and subquantum atoms adjusted. This is a good thing.

RELAX, RELAX, and RELAX some more is the mantra of onset.

The more intense it gets during onset, the more you want to relax and breath through any discomfort until the shift takes place and you enter into the revelation phase. Some people have only experienced onset because they were never able to relax enough to break through to the revelation phase, which is a much more comfortable phase. Here are some tips to navigate the onset phase:

1. PRACTICE RELAXING. Difficulty relaxing is something you can work with. It just takes intention, practice, and working with letting go outside of the medicine space. This conditions the body in such a way that makes it easier to let go in the medicine space. Do a full body scan and anywhere you find tension release it. If your body shakes, vibrates, and moves, allow it and surrender to the experience as much as possible.

Take a deep breath. Pause. Now release the breath. Pause. Did you notice how your shoulders just dropped and relaxed? Did you notice the feeling of energy being released on the exhale? The more you do this in daily life the more you train your body to feel safe letting go.

2. RECEIVE: Imagine letting the medicine into every cell of your body. You took the medicine intentionally so do your best not to fight it. Finding and practicing a breathing/relaxation technique that works for you can be helpful leading up to the retreat.

• To receive, say the words "Thank you" and observe how there is a slight opening and inflow of energy.

• Inhale slowly and imagine I am giving you the most delicious chocolate ever! Feel how you just slightly smiled, opened and received even though I wasn't even there? See. You know how to receive too.

3. RELAX SOME MORE: Just when you think you are relaxed, relax some more. To heal, the medicine has to get into subtlest parts of you, the quantum subatomic vibrational aspects of you in order to collapse old programming and bring new energies into those places. Allow the medicine to work on your entire nervous system. Open and allow the medicine to get in every cell at a DNA level. Saying the words out loud, "Relax, open, and surrender" can be helpful.

4. BREATHE: If you feel nauseous, use your breath to release nausea intentionally with each exhale. Imagine the nausea leaving with the breath. Take long slow deep breaths and stay calm. Breathing is key to relaxing. If you have a hard time relaxing or letting go of control practice taking long slow deep breaths in and as you exhale, relax every muscle in your body. Practice letting go at night before you go to bed and in the morning when you wake up and several times throughout the day. Practice what it feels like to let go on the outbreath and pause. This lets your body and your mind get familiar with what it feels like to relax and let go. See if you can actually feel an outward flow of energy leave your body as you relax your muscles. I call these surrender sessions where you just lay in bed and see how deep you can sink into your mattress, while relaxing every muscle in your body. As you do this become aware of how safe you actually are to let go.

Examples of some breathing techniques you can use:

Box Breathing: (4-4-4-4) Inhale 4 sec →Hold 4 sec →Exhale 4 sec →Hold 4 sec. Repeat. This calms the nervous system and improves focus. Be sure that you relax on both the inhale and the exhale.

4-7-8 Breathing: Inhale 4 sec →Hold 7 sec →Exhale 8 sec. Repeat. This is great for reducing anxiety. See if you can relax on both the inhale and the exhale.

Diaphragmatic (Belly) Breathing: Breathe deeply into your belly, not chest. The way you know you are breathing into your belly is if your belly extends on the inhale and pulls back in on the exhale. This activates the parasympathetic nervous system and calms you down.

Examples:

1. Use your imagination to breathe a spiral in from the top of your head down into your belly, let your belly extend and fill. Pause. Then exhale the breath down into the Earth, out and up the sides of your body, and back up to the top of your head in a toroidal like fashion. Pause. You are making the shape of an apple with your breath, moving the energy down along your spine, out, and back up.

2. Slowly inhale through the nose. Imagine the breath entering at the base of your spine. Let it rise vertebra by vertebra as your belly extends, like a slow spiral climbing

upward for a duration of 8 seconds. Hold the breath gently for 4 seconds. Exhale slowly through the mouth. Let the spiral exit through the crown of your head while the belly returns to neutral. Imagine tension unwinding upward and out for a duration of 8 seconds. Let the breath settle for 4 seconds.

Alternate Nostril Breathing: Inhale through one nostril, blocking the other with your finger. Release your finger and switch sides. Exhale through the other. Switch sides with each inhale and exhale. This balances energy and soothes the mind.

Resonant Breathing: (5-5) Inhale 5 sec →Pause.→Exhale 5 sec. →Pause.

This helps bring the heart rate down and reduces stress quickly.

Purging: Purging is very normal during the onset for some medicines, such as ayahuasca. Remember in these situations that you consented to take a purgative medicine. You chose a safe container and the setting is safe. (Right?) So, know that while purging can be intense and uncomfortable. It is safe. It can also be powerful. If you feel the urge to purge—Let it fly! You took that medicine for a reason and as Shrek says, "Better out than in, I say!"

The more you relax and let the purging come, the easier it will be. Your body knows how to release what no longer serves you. Trust it and don't resist the urge to purge. The more you can release and let go, the more you will get out of it. This is true with any medicine. Often the body will grab the gunk, (technical term there for trauma or emotional imprint) pull it into the belly, and release it with the vomit. This is a good thing. Allow it to happen.

Purging can happen during any phase of the medicine experience, not just onset.

Many types of purging: I tell my clients if you have the opportunity to purge, take it. Meaning if you feel like crying, and you have no idea why you're crying, let the sorrow and sadness come. If it's appropriate and you feel like screaming at the top of your lungs, scream at the top of your lungs. If you feel like you're going to throw up, allow your body to throw up. Sweating can be a form of release; you may also get chills depending on the medicine. Your body may shake as a way of releasing things from the tissues of the body; your mouth may make raspberry like sounds as the body releases what is no longer needed or attunes to higher frequencies. You may yawn, a lot. If any of these things happen, celebrate! Don't worry about what the facilitators might think of you. These actions and sounds are very common and normal things. Purging is any form of expelling, laughing, sneezing, crying, coughing, etc. and is HUGELY beneficial.

The Revelation Phase

After you make it through onset, you enter the revelation phase, also called the visionary phase, which may or may not be visual. This is the peak of the experience, where intense visuals, imprints, more purging, deep emotional insights and releases, ego dissolution, and a sense of interconnectedness may occur, among infinite other experiences. In the revelation phase most of the revelations happen. This is where we often experience the results of our intentions, often in ways we would never expect. It is important to continue to relax during all phases of the medicine experience and not try to control the experience.

Emotional Release: This can happen throughout the entire arc of the experience. Emotional releasing is a type of purging. Once you know how to handle an emotional release you are well on your way to clearing yourself of the shit from

98

the past. The most important thing to know about emotional release is that when you do it, be very careful NOT to attach any story to the release if possible. Attachment often happens automatically and is not a mistake—only something to notice. We will talk more about this later.

STORYTIME: *In one of my medicine journeys, I experienced a huge release of feminine rage. I felt it all well up within me and come to the surface. All the years when women were used, abused, owned, bought, sold, raped, pillaged, mutilated, and even burned at the stake came flooding in. The anger was intense, and I could feel myself blaming men and giving the rage momentum. This actually held the rage in place. It was only when I was able to witness the rage without attaching a story that cleared it from my system. I said to myself, "Rage arising... rage leaving." No story. I let the emotion well up within me and move through my body like a wave.*

We will talk more about how to process your emotions effectively in the next chapter. For now, know that if you feel emotions rising to the surface in the visionary phase, let them come.

Sovereignty: The general rule with psychedelic medicines is to set the intention and then let go of how those intentions are met. However, there are times when we can guide the medicine back to our intentions if we feel we are being taken in an unhelpful direction. For example, you may have the intention to release childhood trauma and the medicine could take you into the trauma to relive it, creating more trauma.

From what I have seen this is not helpful. Many people release trauma in loving ways without creating more trauma, and we can work with the medicines to do this in ways that are gentle, easy, and effective. The most effective healing of trauma I have seen is when an individual is shown a different perspective of the event, person, or experience and says, "Wow, that wasn't even about me. That is not mine," and then releases any stories or identities created as a result of it. We don't have to face our shadows in darkness to learn and evolve from them. We can face them in light and with love without creating more trauma.

It is okay to ask the medicine to slow down and be gentler. It's okay to ask the medicine to give you more. It's okay to say, "No. This is not helpful, please give me a different way to work with my intentions."

Turning Fear Down and Off: Another trick Hamilton teaches when it comes to navigating the medicine space is how to turn fear down and off. Anytime you experience fear, in any of the phases, just say, "Medicine, turn down fear, turn off fear, turn off darkness, and turn on love so I can heal in love." You will still have to wait for the chemicals that were triggered by fear to die down, (fear chemistry takes time to metabolize) but this is a very effective way to work with the medicine and exercise sovereignty. Just because you let go of expectations and surrendered does not mean giving up your sovereignty. This is very important. AND don't forget to call in your guides if you need them.

STORYTIME: *I worked with a client once who was heading to Peru for an ayahuasca retreat. She was scared to death that she would have to experience what she described as demons again. She was afraid things would "go dark" as it did on her last retreat. I taught her how to invoke Sanctuary, call on her guides, exercise sovereignty, and discern the quality of the spirits she works with. This empowered her and made all the difference in the world.*

As a part of my healing journey and training with Hamilton I sat with psilocybin a lot. There were times when I did not clear my space, call in my guides, or create Sanctuary. I got lazy. As a result, I got tossed. I lost my center and had no idea what was going on. One time what felt like a couple of demons came into the space. It was then I really had to get my shit together. I reinforced Sanctuary, invoked my guides, and said, "Hey, you are welcome here. You need to heal, too." They chilled out and left shortly afterwards, but that was a huge lesson for me. It revealed to me many layers about myself. It revealed a lazy side where I wasn't approaching the medicine with reverence. I wasn't connecting with the medicine or my guides deeply and I sure wasn't being intentional. It also revealed to me that I could exercise sovereignty and handle whatever those things were! I learned. Wisdom gained!

This does not make me more advanced, just more responsible for how I now sit with medicine. Just because unhelpful energies or demons come in, doesn't mean you are at their mercy.

Spirits: Many people encounter what they call spirits in the visionary/revelation phase. Yucky ones and delightful ones alike. Encounters with loved ones, spiritual guides, and God are very common. Some say there is a spirit of ayahuasca, a spirit of psilocybin, a spirit of San Pedro; it is common to believe that everything is spirit and consider spirit to be the animus of all things, that it exists in through and all around us. Meeting beings such as Jesus, Siddhartha, Archangel Michael, and other beings is very, very, common. Building a relationship with these beings, honoring them, celebrating them, and approaching them with reverence can result in more impactful and meaningful experiences. It can also be helpful to remember they are just like us. They are not better and we are not worse. Consider connecting with your guides or an ascended master as an intention and discover for yourself if this is true.

Landing

The landing phase is the gradual return to your new baseline, where the effects of the medicine taper off, revelations settle in, and integration of the experience begins. The following are ideas on how to make the most of the landing phase.

Stay Open. Continue to Receive: If your intentions were not met in the revelation phase, you can still receive answers and insights afterwards when in the landing phase. Often my clients report being in a very heart open, connected space where they are able to tap into their intuition and can ask questions and receive answers. Many medicines clear our channel or connection to the divine, enabling us to tap into our own inner wisdom. I encourage you to look within and find your own answers after any experience.

Here's an exercise I use to cultivate intuition and inner knowing. It helps me find my own answers so I am not constantly looking outside of myself for answers. In the beginning it can feel questionable whether the answer is from your highest self or ego. The more you practice this, the more you will be able to discern whether the information is coming from a place of truth and knowing or ego by how it feels and how the answer lands in your body. This is a great exercise to use after you have landed and you still have questions.

🖈 Cultivating Intuition

Step #1: Recall a time when you had a definite yes experience. Maybe someone asked you to do something with them and you responded immediately, "Absolutely!" Get in touch with that experience and remember the feeling of what it was like to have a definite and clear yes. It landed within you as a knowing in the body. This is where intuition lives. In your body. Also recall a time when you received a definite no.

Step #2: Now that you recall what it FEELS like when your inner guidance gives you a definite yes or no, ground yourself and get into your body by cultivating awareness. (That exercise you did earlier that I mentioned was so important.) In short, you become aware of the sounds in the room, then your body, focusing on your legs, releasing tension in your belly, and centering in your heart space. Become aware of you as the aware presence that resides in physical form. Good. This should quiet your mind and all the confusion and noise around the question you have or the decision you need to make.

Step #3: Bring into your awareness the question you would like answered or the decision you need to make and just wait for the answer to drop in as a knowing. FEEL your way through this; intuition is a feeling activity where the answer lands within you as a definite knowing. There is no doubt when the right answer lands.

Does your body respond with an "Absolutely!" or is it in resistance telling you clearly, "No?" What is the feeling? The gut reaction?

If you feel uncertainty or a lot of energy around your headspace, you've slipped back into your mind. Continue to cultivate awareness to quiet the mind and shift your focus back to the heart. This will enable you to tap into your inner guidance and wisdom.

You can also use the Creative Imagination exercise in Chapter 8 to imagine yourself experiencing what it would be like if you were to say yes. Then imagine what you would experience if you said no. Intuition is not a mental process but a feeling process where you focus within and FEEL the answer land within you. Whether you like the answer or not is a whole other story!

When you stay open to receiving, it is possible for you to be given information for days and even weeks or longer after your journey because the medicine may still be in your system and it's easier to tap into higher states of consciousness if you have just been there. Keep your phone handy so you can record downloads and insights into your voice memo app. You know the information is true because it lands within you as a knowing, it's like a lightning bolt from God. So, stay in the medicine as long as you can and stay open to receive more insights even after you land.

In the landing phase you are coming down from the revelation/visionary phase. Just allow yourself to be with the revelations as long as possible. Let them sink in. Rest and let things settle within you. If you had a difficult experience, try not to judge it; instead, be curious about how you feel as you land. Often people who have difficult experiences may not realize that what they experienced was a purge. Especially if they purged anxiety, control, confusion, or chaos. In order to be released these things can come to the surface to be unpacked and released.

STORYTIME: *In an ayahuasca ceremony I folded in on myself, totally lost control, and it was chaotic and confusing* *the whole time. I had no idea what happened. Then the next night when ceremony two came around I was so grounded and clear it was like I wasn't in the medicine at all. Revisiting my intentions for day one I discovered my intention was to receive focus and clarity. Day one was a purging of everything that was in the way of my ability to focus. Our intentions are not always met in ways we wish them to be!*

The Ego: Your Friendly Neighborhood Narrator

Imagine you've just returned from a cosmic joyride. Your heart is wide open, your mind is blown, and your soul is singing. You have experienced yourself as a thinking, perceiving God Nugget! But wait, who's that grumpy voice in your head saying, "What the hell happened? That wasn't real. Put those walls back up!"?

Meet your ego. It's not evil. It's just confused.

The ego is like the narrator of your life story. It loves to make sense of things, even when there's no sense to be made. During a psychedelic experience, the ego often takes a nap, which is great because you get to experience yourself beyond its constant commentary. But when you come back, it wakes up like a toddler after a nap—cranky, confused, and ready to reclaim control.

Here's the thing: don't fight it. You can't kill the ego because it never really existed as a thing. It's more like a habit—a collection of thoughts, beliefs, and stories you've picked up throughout your life. And like any habit, it can be changed.

Think of the ego as your individuation engine. It's what allows you to say "I" and mean it. It's the costume you wear loosely knowing it could never be all that you are. It's not the whole story. You are not just the roles you play or the stories you tell. You are the awareness behind them, the one who watches, feels, and chooses.

So how do you work with the ego without inflating it, resisting it, or wanting to rocket launch it to the moon?

1. Observe, don't argue. When the ego flares up, notice it. Don't engage in a debate. Just watch.

2. Use identity, don't be used by it. Ask yourself: "What if I didn't have an identity, but used one?" This keeps you flexible and open, rather than rigid and defensive.

3. Stay curious. The ego loves certainty. But growth happens in curiosity. When you feel triggered, ask: "What's this trying to show me?"

4. Redirect the mind. When your mind starts replaying old stories, gently say, "Thanks, but what else have you got?" The mind loves a challenge and it loves to be directed.

5. Be patient. The ego won't transform overnight. It's like a puppy—it needs training, not punishment.

You Have Faculties

This localization of consciousness, this thinking and perceiving God nugget called you has many faculties that bring you information and enable you to experience the universe. That's the glory of your physical apparatus.

You have two eyes that bring you information regarding what you see, a nose that smells, ears that hear, and a mouth that tastes. You have fingers that touch. These are faculties that bring you information and let you experience the universe. And you, as the nugget of thinking and perceiving, get to receive and interpret that information.

You also have a faculty called the mind that brings you information in the form of thoughts. Your job as the aware perceiver is to accept or release any information the mind brings you based on what feels true or right for you. This includes any information about identity.

This doesn't mean the word identity is a bad word. Identity provides the language and framework through which individuals can express who they are. But when the individual beingness attaches to itself a compilation of thoughts, ideas, beliefs, and perceptions based on false information or past experiences it becomes limited.

Knowing that your mind is a bringer of information and you are the receiver enables you to be really picky about what you allow into your nugget.

Ego Elasticity

Not all egos are rigid. Some are more elastic and able to stretch, adapt, and return without snapping. This elasticity determines how gracefully one navigates the psychedelic experience.

- **A Rigid Ego:** Resists change, interprets insights as threats, and may lead to anxiety or confusion.
- **An Elastic Ego:** Allows insights to flow, integrates new perspectives, and supports growth.

Before entering a psychedelic space, ask yourself, "How elastic is my ego today? Am I willing to let it stretch without breaking?"

The Role of Intention

The ego often reacts based on the intention set before the journey. If the intention is vague or ego driven ("I want to feel special"), the ego may hijack the experience. If the intention is clear and heart-centered ("I want to understand my patterns"), the ego is more likely to cooperate.

Here is a chart that can help you identify unhelpful ego activity and activities that reflect your true nature.

Important Note: Both columns arise within consciousness and are not moral judgments.

Activities of the Ego/False Self/ Separate Self	Activities of the Aware Perceiver/ True Self
Fear, Dread	Unconditional Love, Safety
Lives in the headspace	Lives in the heart space
Uncertainty, Anxiety	Certainty, Inner Knowing,
Anger, Frustration, Stress	Intuition
Difficulty	Calm
Guilt and Shame	Ease
Judgement, Lack	Peace and Joy
Self-Doubt, Worry	Acceptance, Allowance
Apathy, Resignation,	Confidence
Cynicism	Beingness/Isness
Hopelessness	Freedom
Sadness, Loneliness	Empty, Yet Full
I have to/need to, should/	I choose
shouldn't	Infinite Possibilities
Right/wrong good/bad	In Flow
The Need to Control	Human Being, Is-ness,
Human Doing Activity	Inspired action
Energy in the Headspace,	Energy in the Heart Space,
Mental Activity	Calm
Closed, Resistance,	Open, Allowance,
Contraction	expansion
Unreasonable	Wisdom
Lack, Scarcity, More, more,	Contentment, Complete
more	Lives in the present
Lives in the past and future	moment
Wants to Protect	Knows You are Safe
Stories and Meaning/False	Absence of all Story, True
Identity	Identity
Separation	Oneness

When you experience any of the emotions or compulsions in the left hand column, most likely the narrator has come online and created story. When you experience the feelings or qualities in the right hand column, you have likely tapped into aspects of your inner core or essence beyond narration.

The Ego Interrupt

When you notice unhelpful egoic activity, this is how you can interrupt the ego:

🕯 **STOP!** Take one long, slow deep breath in. Pause. Relax your muscles on the exhale. Pause. Sink into your body, witness the information brought to you and let it go. Watch it dissolve with your aware presence. Thank it for trying to keep you safe and reassure it that all is well. It's okay. You've got the wheel.

If you get hooked or triggered by the information the mind brings you or thrashes you with, CULTIVATE AWARENESS of what's happening (you're caught up in mind/ego activity). Notice the sounds in the room, the fan, the creaking walls, etc. SHIFT your attention from your headspace to your body, release your belly and focus on your heartbeat to ground and center you. Sense the aware presence that is you. This will pull you out of the headspace where the mind lives into the calm peacefulness of your inner body and beingness where peace resides.

Cultivating awareness increases your level of consciousness so you may rise above mind activity and can put you firmly in the seat as the aware presence.

The Ego Re-Entry Checklist

After the experience, use this simple checklist to assess ego re-entry:

- Am I feeling defensive or expansive?
- Am I trying to explain away the experience?
- Am I integrating or inflating?
- What story is my ego telling now?

This helps you catch ego flare-ups early and integrate insights more smoothly.

The ego as a narrator of your cosmic journey can point out landmarks but it shouldn't drive the car. You are the traveler. The narrator is there to assist, not control.

🦚 Grounding Practice for Post-Journey Integration

Sit quietly.

Place one hand on your heart, one on your belly.

Breathe slowly.

Say: "I am here. I am safe. I am integrating."

This anchors you in your body, not just your mind.

Remember, the goal isn't to destroy the ego. It's to integrate it. To let it serve you, not rule you. As you work with the ego in this way the voice of the ego can get less intense and fade into the background over time.

You are a unique expression of consciousness, a

thinking and perceiving God nugget. Enjoy the ride. And when the ego gets loud, just smile and say, "Thanks for your input. I've got this."

Let's continue with other suggestions that will help you navigate the landing phase of your journey.

More Tips to Support the Landing Phase

Capture the Revelations: When you feel you have completely landed and are compelled to get up, go straight to your journal or phone voice memo app and tell the story of what happened into your phone as if you are doing a play by play. Stay objective and non-judgmental. Capture as much information as you possibly can.

Avoid Negative Exposure: As you come out of the medicine and into the landing phase, it is recommended that you don't get on that phone for the day. Even if you're really strongly driven to it. People will say, "Oh, man, I gotta call my partner and tell them about this amazing experience." Well, you may be wide open and your partner may not be. The partner is not likely going to be able to relate and may even negate the experience. Do not make any phone calls, rash decisions, and avoid computers and screens completely, with the exception of using the voice memo function to collect data.

Nutritious Foods: Depending on the experience and medicine you can bring your favorite foods with you in case you get hungry after you land. Fruits and vegetables, watermelon, apples, and chocolate are all really, really good after a journey.

Don't Analyze: Don't try to analyze or understand the information revealed to you right away. Trust it will unfold perfectly for your highest good. Just be with it. Have an open and curious mindset. The mind tends to want to put revelations into a box. Don't do this. Let your mind just be with the multidimensional information. Let it soak in. You will have time to work with the information later. For now, just capture it and stay open.

Don't Judge: Don't shy away or avoid the revelations you might call negative. Some people's inner child comes out to play, and sometimes that aspect of themselves from the past can be pissy, annoying, or judgmental. Sometimes people feel freer than ever and it can be embarrassing. Don't judge how you acted or what is revealed to you in the medicine space. If you spent the whole time trying to control the medicine, good! How do you feel afterwards? Do you still feel the need to control? Was that a purge? If you had a hard time letting go, good! You took one step closer to letting go and may be inching towards it little by little as you acclimate to the process. Did darkness come in? Good! How did you respond? How did you face it? Did you invoke Sanctuary and your guides? What would you do differently next time? Did you meet God, Source, Universe, Spirit and shy away? Did you see yourself beyond the constructs you've created about yourself? Good! How did you deal with these revelations? These are things to be curious about, to question, ponder and ask what you learned about you. So never judge what was revealed to you or how you responded. You're healing and growing remember?

Don't Compare: Never compare your revelations to anyone else's. You are on your path, and there is only one you. What you receive in the medicine space is for you and you alone. I have found a person's revelations are almost always exactly what that person needs at the time. They just may not know how to work with the information, or pull out the reflections, the metaphors, or the revelations. That's where integration comes in and guidance is invaluable.

Ask For What You Need: Ask for what you need. Your facilitator should be there by your side the whole time without judgment hopefully holding the space of unconditional love. If you need a hand to hold, someone to talk to, or a glass of water or a blanket, allow your facilitator to care for you.

Awesome! You are now well prepared to go into sacred ceremony! You've set your intentions, learned how to navigate all phases of the medicine space, and have planned how you will capture as many revelations from the experience as possible. You know what to do if things go sideways and how to work with ego if it activates after landing. Well done!

The next four chapters will focus on what do and how to care for yourself or others after you have landed.

PART 2

STABILIZATION AND INTEGRATION

After non-ordinary states, the nervous system needs time to recalibrate, and interpretation or adding meaning to the experience is best delayed. Immediately after a journey is when people are most vulnerable to over-interpretation. Clarity often improves as the intensity of the experience fades and meaning can emerge on its own. The next four chapters will focus on how to stabilize, organize, translate, integrate, and navigate difficulties that may arise.

CHAPTER 5

THE POST-MEDICINE CHECK-IN

In this chapter we will explore how to integrate physically, mentally, emotionally, and spiritually after the ceremony is over. We will focus on how to quiet the mind, process your emotions, and work with spiritual revelations. We'll talk about the golden window where changes can be made with more ease and give you plenty of tools to move through any challenges you may face. You will receive tools to ground, stabilize, and make the most of any retreat regardless of how difficult it was, and you will learn one way to journey without medicine if this interests you.

Let's dive in!

Containment Before Content

You have many aspects that make up the totality of you. After being in the medicine, checking in with these aspects to see where you are and what might have changed can be invaluable. This creates structure that serves as a container so that things can settle before distortion or delusion can take place. Again, medicine experiences can create fragmentation. The following structure serves as a container, a consistent format that ensures you are safe, grounded, and whole before you reflect on the experience itself.

This structure is not rigidity; it is the means in which you return to coherence after mystical experiences.

Your safety always precedes any meaning you may receive from a ceremony. No matter how intense, no matter how regal or divine, insight without containment becomes fragmentation. Containment begins when you allow your nervous system to settle, your physical body to rest, it includes grounding and pacing yourself as you work with your experience and your revelations.

Here are some questions to ask yourself after each journey:

1. How are you physically? Does the physical body need rest and nurturing?
2. How are you emotionally? Are you still crying or deeply emotional?
3. How are you mentally? Is the mind busy or quiet?
4. How are you spiritually? Was new information revealed to you about your spiritual journey?

Let's go through these one by one.

Physical Integration

Some medicines, especially when taken at high doses, are so powerful the experience can feel like 4000 watts of power going into a 40-watt body. Again, it can feel like a total reset, which is good, but not always comfortable or advisable if you are not pacing yourself or honoring the limits of the body. Some people will come out of an experience and say, "I'm exhausted, I'm not feeling good at all." This is normal, especially with some medicines like MDMA. Other people might feel amazing. If you feel great, other than maybe a little tired, move on and check in with how you are doing emotionally. If you are not feeling physically well, here are some things to keep in mind that can be reassuring with tips to help.

Frequency Flu: I had one client who said he connected with God and discovered himself to be one with God and all that is...for hours. Afterwards his whole body was experiencing flu-like symptoms. That's what I call "frequency flu." It is also common and normal after prolonged intense experiences.

Some scientific models describe emotions as having different energetic or vibrational qualities. Dr. David Hawkins, for instance, conducted extensive research on emotions as energy and devised a system that rates emotions on a scale from 1 to 1000. There are low vibrational frequency emotions that give you a certain experience, such as anger, fear, anxiety, depression, and self-doubt, and you have high vibrational frequency emotions that give you experiences of contentment, knowing, gratitude, joy, and love. And a wide variety of vibrational experiences in between.

This indicates that over time and with practice, you can increase your frequency or decrease your frequency by consciously choosing thoughts and setting intentions that bring about certain feelings or emotional responses. You get to choose.

When we increase our frequency and experience unconditional love, ecstasy, or bliss in a medicine journey those frequencies impact the physical body, and it can be overwhelming to say the least. It can take some time for the body to adapt. It can feel like old circuits are being blown apart so new neurological circuits can form. Emotional imprints from the past or trauma may have been released and the body may be healing. It may feel as if the medicine is burning off the stuff we no longer need. Achiness, fever, fatigue, shock, and general feelings of depletion are very normal symptoms after such an experience.

It's similar to a Herxheimer reaction that occurs when antibiotics are used to kill bacteria. When the bacteria are killed, you release toxins that cause flu-like symptoms. It's a positive sign that the antibiotics are working, and it's also a positive sign that the medicine did some deep work with you. Knowing this can reassure you that all is well, and it's a part of the healing process.

Most people recover physically within two to four days after such an experience. Sometimes you might feel a little nauseous or queasy for the first day or two and have some trouble sleeping after taking certain medicines. This is normal. Since I started doing this work, I've had only a few people who took up to two weeks before they felt better. Each of these clients had taken synthetic medicines. This is not good or bad, it just is. For example, many medicines can deplete the body of serotonin and make recovery hard for some people. Knowing that you are depleted and need rest can be reassuring.

★ TIPS

- **Feel** – Feel your experience land in your body. Feel your body as it reorganizes its new set point.
- **Be Still** – Too much activity after a journey can be destabilizing and prevent your systems from integrating. Stillness stabilizes the nervous system after expanded states.

- **Ground** – Walk barefoot. Sit under a tree. Hold a rock. Breathe.
- **Be Silent** – Don't talk about your experience. Let meaning arise spontaneously.
- **Drink Plenty of Water** – Water is known to help flush residual medicine and toxins from your body.
- **Eat Small Portions** – Eating small amounts will help keep your digestive system running smoothly and keep the focus on recovering rather than digesting enormous amounts of food at one time.
- **Poop Daily** – Ingest plenty of fruits, vegetables, and water to keep things running properly. This is highly effective.
- **Supplements** – Take any supplements recommended by your facilitator. These will help to restore electrolytes and balance chemistry.
- **Cut Back on Strenuous Exercise** – While very light exercise, such as walking, can be beneficial, strenuous exercise may be too much. Follow your intuition and what feels right for you.
- **Bodywork** – Receiving bodywork after a medicine retreat can support the embodiment of your revelations. Whether it is craniosacral therapy, a massage, or energy work, these practices can be very helpful during the integration phase.

Be Gentle with Yourself

Be gentle with yourself and give yourself the time, space, and compassion to heal. Take gentle walks, long baths, and nurture yourself in healthy ways.

You may be experiencing a significant reset and now is the perfect time to create new patterns.

- Journal about your experience extensively.
- Listen to relaxing and enjoyable music.

- Go for walks in nature.
- Breathe deeply.
- Avoid sugar and processed foods.
- Be mindful. Be present.
- Be quiet. Be still. Silence and stillness are very effective integrators.

Grounding

After a medicine experience people often need grounding exercises to bring them back into their bodies. After a journey is the time to become aware of gravity, increase body awareness, do a whole body scan, and set your intention to land fully back into your body to integrate your new set point. How do you know if you need grounding?

- You have trouble focusing.
- You can't sit still and constantly multitask,
- You're emotional.
- You're tired, fatigued, or drained.
- You feel nervous, anxious, or overwhelmed.
- Your mind won't quiet.

📌 1-Minute Grounding Exercise

Sit or stand comfortably.

Take in a slow, deep breath through your nose, pause, and let it out through your nose, pause, relaxing and releasing tension on the exhale. Do that twice more.

Now, press your feet gently into the ground. Feel the floor beneath you. Imagine roots spreading from your feet anchoring you into the center of the Earth. Stand like this for 15 minutes.

Rest for a bit under a sturdy tree.

Bring your attention to your body: notice where you're holding tension, maybe in your jaw, shoulders, or stomach and soften and relax those areas.

Feel the weight of your body. Feel gravity.

Gently wiggle your fingers or roll your shoulders.

Bring your attention to your heartbeat and watch any chaotic ungrounded energy balance, settle, and dissipate with every beat of your heart.

As you breathe, silently say: "I am here. I am safe. I am integrating."

Connecting to earth and with nature, walking barefoot on the earth, and physical movement is also grounding. Holding crystals and heavy rocks can also be very grounding.

Neuroplasticity: There is an acute period of time post-ceremony of neuroplasticity in which we can make changes easier and in a shorter period of time. This is why so many organizations recommend dietary restrictions and downtime post-ceremony so that nothing interferes with the physical body as it acclimates to its new neurological set point.

It is important for people to clear their schedule as much as possible post ceremony to allow this neurological reset and restructuring to occur. This is the time when new neuro networks form, old habits and patterns are interrupted, and new ways of thinking and being in the world can be created. The brain chemistry balances and the body is adjusting to the atomic, subatomic, and quantum changes that occur when you work with these sacred medicines. Allow your brain chemistry, DNA structures, and physical body to settle, heal, harmonize, balance, and reorient to this new set point by getting lots of rest, eating well, and taking time to just be with the revelations.

Depletion: MDMA and other medicines deplete serotonin in the brain and can deplete the body. The ceremony itself can be exhausting, especially if there was purging, physical restructurings, healing, or God experiences. In these cases, it is even more important to rest and integrate while the body adapts and recovers.

The Golden Window

Remember from Chapter 4 after any medicine experience there is a golden window where change is easier. This is worth repeating and reinforcing. Many of us have evolved beyond habits and coping patterns, yet we are still enacting them. Many medicines interrupt these habits and patterns offering us a gift, a window of opportunity where change can happen with more ease and grace because of the pattern interrupt or neurological reset that just occurred. Think of the medicines as opportunities to reprogram your operating system and install a new one. However, if you just go home, go back to work, and hop back into life you are reactivating those old programs instead of creating new ones, you are losing a huge opportunity for growth and evolution. Take advantage of this golden window. Here's how:

Change Patterns: Be more loving, more kind, more present. Practice loving kindness. Yes, it may be awkward at first but it's a way of being that is highly enjoyable.

Delete What Doesn't Serve: Delegate or delete the things you dislike or don't want to do from your schedule and take a personal day if you need to for the physical body to integrate. Take a peek at your calendar now. Is there anything you'd like to handoff, cancel, reschedule, or delete altogether?

Incorporate Fun: What does a perfect month for you look like? Add some fun to your calendar by scheduling the things you love. Whether it's reading a book, going for a hike, playing with the kids, cooking dinner while listening to music, or taking a class. Bring in what gives you joy and eliminate what doesn't. See if you can create the perfect life for you after your medicine experience.

Social Media and Time Suck Deletions: After a medicine experience improve your cell phone experience. Look at your cell phone and if there is anything on there that is a time suck, that you find yourself mindlessly scrolling through or is distracting you from living your life, delete it. You can still access it on your laptop if you wish later, but for now consider being more present with yourself and those you love.

Self-Care: Engage in activities that nourish the body and relax you, such as taking baths, receiving massages, or listening to soothing music. Prioritize self-care practices that support your well-being before and after the ceremony.

Cultivate Supportive Relationships: Build community and relationships with like-minded individuals who understand and support your journey. Talking about your experience can be valuable and help you integrate physically if there is someone you can talk to who understands and won't negate your experience.

Nature: Again, spend time in nature, cultivating a sense of reverence and connection. Engage in grounding practices, such as walking barefoot, gardening, or sitting with trees. These are all methods that can help with physical integration.

Next let's talk about what to do if you are emotional after a retreat.

Emotional Integration

If you use sugar, alcohol, or food to soothe yourself or avoid your emotions, see if you can let them go for a spell while you acclimate to your new set point. The need to use substances to avoid emotions, manage emotions, or soothe emotions may be greatly decreased or completely gone.

Begin the transition from relying on substances to manage emotions to being with them, allowing them, feeling them, and letting them go instead.

You might be crying at the drop of a hat. This is common and many people don't even know why they are crying. It helps to know it is normal to feel this way. If you feel raw or emotionally vulnerable, the best thing to do is to let those emotions come and go like waves without attaching any story.

Being emotional post-ceremony is an indication that you are still either purging an emotional imprint or integrating an extraordinary revelation that may not be describable with words. Here is a tool I give to my clients to help them process emotions.

⚲ Emotional Mastery: The 5 Step Dissipater

Step 1: Identify the Emotion: What is the emotion you are feeling? Love? Joy? Overwhelm? Fear? If you can't describe it that's ok. Be with the indescribable.

Step 2: Locate it: Once you identify the emotion,

locate it. Where is it in your body? Is it in your chest? Your throat? Your belly? Is it all over? Does your heart beat faster, does your throat close? Does your stomach turn? Where does this feeling/emotion live in your body? Be curious.

Step 3: Feel It: Once you identify the emotion and locate it, allow it to be there. Be with it. Feel it fully. It may feel like you will die if you allow yourself to feel the emotion fully but you won't. I promise. Grief, love, fear, and pain are all a part of the human experience, and when we suppress them they can get hung up in the body. It's when we face them, feel them, and let them go that they can be released or expressed. If it is located in the throat chakra something may need to be said or expressed out loud to release it. Go on, feel it. It's okay.

Step 4: Let it Go: If done in awareness, when you get to this step the emotion is often already gone. If it's not already gone, you may have attached a story to it and got caught up in the drama or pain around the emotion. Release the story, cultivate awareness, ground in your body, and take some slow deep breaths releasing on the exhale and watch the emotion dissipate. Use your breath to move the energy of the emotion. It is very important to know the emotion always dissipates. If it feels like you are still purging after a journey keep grounding, breathing, and letting go.

Step 5: Receive the Gift: After things calm down ask questions:

What is the gift of this experience?

What am I learning?

What is the emotion trying to tell me?

What wisdom have I gained?

Wait for the answers to come as experiential knowings. Emotions tell you where you are with yourself. Emotions are always about you and no one else. You may learn how your emotions have kept you safe or made you stronger, they may teach you how you've suppressed grief, sorrow or anger, or are telling you that you are doing something you'd rather not do. They may be telling you it's time to love and fear is creeping in. The emotion may even be trying to tell you something about who and what you are. There is always a gift to be received. Always. All you need to do is ask, "What is the gift?"

If you are experiencing intense grief, can you feel it? Can you express it? Can you honor it? If you are experiencing love that has no bounds, that indescribable ineffable thing called God, Source, Spirit, Universe, Consciousness, can you soften and allow it? Explore it even? Can you let it move in, through, and all around you?

Many people find that cultivating awareness helps in these circumstances because as they focus on their heartbeat and their body they naturally ground and let things settle and move as they need to. Also consider invoking Sanctuary. It will help too. These are two powerful tools that can help with emotional processing. This is one way we cleanse the body and chakra systems of emotional imprints. When this is done, the energy can run cleanly through the central channel allowing us to function as a coherent conscious being.

If you feel raw and vulnerable after a journey, know it is normal. Prioritize self-care and give yourself the space and time to let your physical body and your emotional body acclimate to what was revealed to you.

Don't be afraid to see your crunchy bits so you can process them and learn from them. It's really not that scary. Humbling for certain, but when you shine the light on shadow it gives you compassion. I know from facing my own shadow, the things I've done, not done, said, and how I have hurt others and got caught up in ego and pretense that when I see it in others I have great compassion for them. I can relate. It is facing the shadow and all the crunchy bits that allow your becoming. Facing the shadow can result in authenticity, greater connection, and self-realization. It gives you insight into your whole self, your True Self and wisdom can be gained from it. Shadow is a gift. It tells us where we are with ourselves. The 5 Step Dissipater helps us face even the most difficult emotions and is alchemy at its best.

When you feel your emotions, understand them, and process them in gratitude for how they serve you and what they are telling you, it transforms them from something to be avoided at all costs to something of great value. You know you have used this technique properly when you experience relief or gratitude for what your emotions have taught you.

★ TIPS

1. Face it... See it... Feel it... Watch it go.
2. When a difficult emotion or trigger arises within you,

it is important to face it with heightened awareness. Don't go down the rabbit hole and wallow in it for long periods of time. The goal is not to have a crying session that lasts for hours lamenting your childhood or be dramatic in the release of the emotional imprint. The goal is to address emotions and frameworks lodged within the body from a grounded observed perspective, with the intention to dissolve them.

3. What this process looks like is: Feel it. Ground. Breathe through it. Let it go. Feel it. Ground. Breathe through it. Let it go. Feel it. Ground. Breathe through it. Let it go... It is gone. It can feel quite cathartic when you master this process; it can actually feel really good, like poison leaving your body. The breath can move energy. The regulation of all body systems are enhanced with proper breathing. Ask, often, "Am I breathing? Am I resisting, contracting, or am I relaxing and releasing?"

4. It is not unusual for the same emotion or pattern to come up a few times because the ego loves to pick back up what you've already put down. Just keep shining the light of your awareness onto the now unnecessary pattern or belief and it will dissolve over time.

5. It is not unusual to cry and not know what you are crying for. Some feelings just have no words and are indescribable. You know you are doing this correctly when you can observe the feeling move through you and out of you without giving it meaning.

Here's another way to work with emotions:

🖋 Emotions Arising Strategy

This strategy can be used when you are feeling emotional, when you get triggered or snagged by a negative thought pattern or fear itself. It can also help you acclimate to the overwhelming feelings of divinity and unconditional love experienced in the medicine space.

Step 1: Cultivate Awareness. Ground in your body and become very present with yourself.

Step 2: Identify the emotion. You may even notice where the emotion lives in your body.

Step 3: Allow the emotion to rise within you.

Step 4: Label the emotion as it rises. For instance, "raw vulnerability arising."

Step 5: Watch the emotion move through you and out of you like a wave and say, "raw vulnerability leaving."

This works the same with the indescribable or the overwhelming feelings of love we are gifted with. In this case you would say, "overwhelming love arising... overwhelming love leaving." No story. Just a pure experience and expression of your feelings.

When you can label the emotion aloud with detachment, feel it rise and fall within you, you have successfully navigated an emotion.

To clarify: we are not suppressing, resisting, or avoiding the emotion; we are watching it arise and leave. We are not attaching to it. When you get emotional, you know you've been snagged and the mind may be attaching a story, trying to attach meaning, or creating fear.

The important thing to experience is the energetic difference between getting snagged by the emotion and witnessing it.

- Getting snagged by the emotion feels like the energy of the emotion has grabbed you and taken you on the journey of a story. The energy of the emotion gets hung up within you, and it feels like you are a dog chewing on an emotional bone. The important thing to note is that you disappeared into the emotion.

- Detaching from the emotion enables you to witness the emotion without getting caught up in its energy or story. You watch the feeling move through you and out of you. Not good, not bad, not right, not wrong, it doesn't mean anything about who you are. You just had an emotional experience.

STORYTIME: *I was teaching a group of executives once and a fellow who was standing in the back with his arms crossed (obviously in resistance) said to me, "I just lost my wife who I loved dearly. What do you expect me to do with that?" I said, "Sorrow arising, sorrow leaving."*

When you feel a feeling without attaching a story, you become a human who feels deeply. When you attach a story, you become emotional and can get caught up in the drama that your mind creates.

Cultivating Awareness Is Key: I think I have said this before. ;-) Cultivating awareness is always step one because it does both: grounds you in your body and expands awareness. This empowers you to step into your seat as the observer of your experience. It makes it easier to express the emotion without getting hung up in it.

If you are crying and you don't know why, I encourage you to just cry and continue to release what is there for you. If grief arises, say, "Grief arising" and just be with it until it leaves. Then say, "Grief leaving." No story. If you are experiencing whelming beauty say, "Beauty arising... Beauty leaving." No story.

If you enter into any emotion WITHOUT a story, the emotion becomes power; the power becomes your original nature, which is love, every time. For example, anger is the energy for defense of something you love when it is threatened. If you feel hurt, sad, or depressed, and allow yourself to feel these emotions fully, you may experience a knowing that all you really want is to love and be loved.

If you enter into a feeling WITH a story, it's focused on something else. Now there is blame. You did this, and that is why I feel this—this is how you made me feel—or there is a victim identity created as "poor me" and you enter into an endless realm of action and response and drama that goes on and on.

- Feelings are not personal. For example, peace, love, joy, sorrow, and beauty are feelings. You feel them.
- Emotions are feelings with the attachment of a story. They are personal and often made by false identities that you think are you. For example, fear, worry, control, and despair all have stories attached, do they not? I am a loving person can also be a false identity when the feeling of love is attached to a story of you as a good person.
- Becoming emotional will wrap you up in the traps of the thinking mind.
- Experiencing your feelings will bring you home to yourself. Your feelings become your teacher.

Can you see the difference?

Emotional situations leave an imprint on the emotional body. Some are so strong we do everything we can to not face them. Many people believe facing their emotions is like facing death. It can certainly be scary the first time you do it. Especially if, like most people, you have experienced some kind of trauma.

Many people avoid feeling. They create these huge stories and beliefs that emotions should be avoided at all costs. But when you pull back the curtain, they are really trying to keep you safe.

The best way to handle even the most monstrous of emotional flare-ups is to allow them to happen. Once they are felt fully, they will leave. The Emotion Arising strategy shows you how to process emotions safely and with the least discomfort as possible. There are other tools for emotional mastery in my book *The Extraordinary Ordinary You,* if you feel you need additional support.

Emotional Lows Are Normal: Know that acclimation of mind and body to higher self/truths/feelings are upward movements that are often followed by what feels like downward movements of integration. Knowing that melancholy, sadness, and even emptiness are all normal after experiencing emotional highs is extremely helpful in riding out a downward period of integration. "This too shall pass" is a good mantra when releasing emotions.

The more you learn to process and feel your feelings the more they begin to even out over time. The highs are not so high and the lows are not so low and you experience more peace.

As you remove story from emotions you feel deeply and return to your innate sense of beingness, which is True Self. True Self can be a sensed feeling experience in your body that heals and harmonizes. When you cultivate awareness and let your emotions move through you and out of you, it is often the end of the emotional body, the emotional body is transformed into a feeling body. You feel deeply but are no longer emotional. Many people have found that when the emotional body settles, balances, harmonizes and heals, it reorients to who you are beyond the past and old stories you had about yourself and others. It releases the pressure to be different or special allowing spiritual insight to be reconciled with ordinary life.

Now that's worth integrating.

After you have checked in with yourself physically and emotionally, how is your mind?

Mental Integration

Is the mind quiet and calm, or is it racing? Sometimes the mind is so quiet and calm we want to do all we can to integrate that, which is often doing nothing. It may also seem like you just busted open a bees' nest and thoughts are like bees swarming all around you! While this is uncomfortable, it is normal as the mind tries to grasp and make sense of what was just revealed.

- If your mind is racing, cultivate awareness of your body, ground into your body while expanding or magnifying your awareness. This can quiet the mind. It pulls the energy and focus from the headspace where the mental activity lives, to the body where you can ground and balance and tap into your intuition. Remove any story the mind wants to attach to the experience and ground the experience in your body. The body knows what to do with it, the mind may not.

- If the mind is calm, anchor in that peace by cultivating awareness also. This can help you stay in your body while being aware of awareness itself. The more you do this, the more likely you are to hold onto your newfound peace.

Here is that exercise again. Do it now to familiarize yourself with how it feels to calm your mind and be in your body.

📌 Cultivating Awareness Exercise

In this exercise keep your eyes open and loosely focused on something in front of you. Don't close your eyes and disappear inward; expand your awareness. Practice super awareness.

Step 1: Direct your gaze down at a 45-degree angle. Listen to the sounds in the room. Be very aware of your external environment. Don't judge the sounds; see how many sounds you can become aware of.

Step 2: Next, bring your awareness to your body and where it is located in the room. Feel your feet. Feel your legs. Become aware of the weight of your legs. Feel gravity. Release your belly. Become aware of your heartbeat. Can you feel your heart pumping blood to your entire body? (Releasing the belly helps to release stress or tension and the heartbeat brings you to center. This exercise grounds and balances you.) Notice how your chest rises on the inhale and falls on the exhale. Enjoy the silent pauses in between breaths.

Step 3: Feel the aware presence that resides within that physical body. Awareness. Consciousness. Experience what some call the 'I am that I am' as a feeling sense. If your mind is active and you sink back into the realm of thoughts, just let them come and go. Resist nothing. Be curious. Tell your mind to chill out and redirect your focus back to your heartbeat.

Above the Mental Plane of Thought: Again, it is

important to reinforce that this exercise rises you above the mental plane of thought; above belief structures, ego, and emotional reactivity. You still see them, but they can't hook you. When witnessed at this level they may just disappear. I have found that nothing can withstand the power of pure consciousness. Nothing. No habitual pattern, no belief structure, and no false identity.

How did you do? What did you discover? Did your mind quiet?

Distress: Often when someone is in mental distress, it's because the mind is trying to make sense of the experience and is trying to put meaning on it. If you are disoriented or are in any form of distress after a journey, take a lot of deep breaths, cultivate awareness, and just stop. Allow your heartbeat to calm.

Can you allow yourself to not put any meaning on your experience? Can you allow the uncertainty of not knowing what just happened? This is where cultivating awareness can be very, very useful. Can you allow yourself to be empty of what you released in the medicine space? Even if it was your identity?

Cultivating awareness pulls you out of the headspace where the ego and the mental activity lies. Chaos, confusion, uncertainty, and distress can gain momentum when the mind tries to make sense of that which makes no sense. Grounding in the body quiets the mind and can bring you peace. It gives you a valuable skill to navigate the mind.

Many people have had meaningful experiences that were profound but left them unsure how to carry it forward or make sense of it. This is when nothing needs to be done. Let the mind settle. Be still. Be silent. Let the nervous system balance and stabilize. Return to daily functioning and release any idea of being special or more or less advanced than another. Do not chase meaning or try to make sense of the mystery. Instead let things stabilize before meaning is added. This is mental integration.

Meditation: Establishing a regular meditation practice to cultivate inner stillness, focus, and awareness can also help the mind integrate new states of being. Explore different meditation techniques, such as mindfulness meditation, loving kindness meditation, or guided visualizations. Be sure to stay in your body and ground at the same time you expand consciousness.

Stay Open: Stay open and in the medicine as long as possible. Continue to receive downloads, insights, knowings, upgrades, and restructurings after the journey is over. It can also be valuable to listen to your voice recording the same day to really get the information into your system and subconscious mind. Be with the information. Put it into quarantine. Ponder it. Stay open to more.

You have now explored ways to integrate physically, emotionally, and mentally. Let's take some time now and talk about how you can integrate spiritual revelations in ways that keep you expanded and grounded.

How Are You Spiritually?

After you have checked in with yourself physically, emotionally, and mentally, check in with yourself spiritually, especially if you went into a medicine experience with a spiritual intent.

If you had experiences that felt like you connected with God; saw yourself as God, with God or in God; or experienced yourself beyond physical form, are you trying to negate the experience and wiggle out of your divinity?

Are you avoiding those revelations because they threaten your current idea of self? Or even your current idea of God? Or has the ego grabbed the revelation and attached story, meaning or identity to it?

So many of my clients try to skate by or brush off their divinity. If you left your body and met what many call God, what may be asking to be integrated is a broader perspective about God and your divinity. A lot of people are uncomfortable with their divinity and will shy away from it. Marianne Williamson said once, "Our deepest fear is not that we are inadequate. Our deepest fear is that we are powerful beyond measure. It is our light, not our darkness, that most frightens us." I see this often and have experienced it myself.

Integrating Divinity: When an individual is shown a different perspective of who they are, it is so much easier to let go of patterns of unworthiness or stories of not being loved. One of my very favorite things to ask is, "So do you know who you are and what you are in truth?" Saying yes is a big step in unraveling shame and stories that they are not enough. I will also ask if there was any judgment, right, wrong, good, or bad in what they experienced? The answer is always a resounding no. So, if you have divine revelations, as you enter the integration phase, take plenty of time to let your experience sink in. Being with these revelations in silence deepens integration.

I came out of a journey like a blubbering idiot once because there were just no words to describe what I experienced as God. Integrating that which cannot be described is a task in itself. It requires us to be okay not knowing that which we absolutely know but could never know. The paradoxes abound in the medicine space! But all paradoxes can be reconciled. Can you allow yourself to know the unknowable and still stay in the mystery?

Can you allow your divinity? Can you allow others their divinity? This is integration.

One thing to be aware of is if you have a spiritual revelation of yourself as God is to you keep your ego in check. The ego loves to grab a hold of divinity and claim it for itself. A client might say, "I am God!" This is where I say, "Yes, you are and so is everyone else. So, get back down here and let's do some work." Spiritual significance is all too common in the medicine space as is spiritual bypassing. There are many people who think they are advanced who are not. There are many people who attach to archetypical energies that come into their journeys and declare, "I am a goddess, or I was Isis in a past life." There are even more people claiming to be the Christ reincarnated. This often creates more confusion than clarity. In general, you always want to ask, does this help me or does it send me down an egoic rabbit hole? Does this revelation help me increase my inner power if I felt powerless? Does it help me release deep rooted beliefs? False identities? Or is it a distraction?

It is more productive to ponder how these beings walked the Earth, to learn from them, and use those revelations to empower us in our own lives. We can use the energies and archetypical qualities to help us cultivate courage, move out of limitation and into possibility without identifying with them.

What Spiritual Integration Actually Looks Like

True integration after powerful spiritual experiences looks like:

- Increased interest in ordinary life
- Steadier emotions
- Less urgency to explain
- Less identity around meaning

- More patience
- More humility
- More embodiment

In the psychedelic spaces meaning often accelerates faster than embodiment. If this book successfully does one thing, it is my hope that it will interrupt spiritual inflation kindly and normalize any post-revelatory spiritual vulnerability.

Many people assume that after "revelation" they should feel stable, wise, or resolved.

In reality, integration often includes:

- Disorientation
- Tenderness
- Grief
- Irritability
- Loss of meaning
- Loss of community
- Identity confusion

Knowing this is normal can reduce panic, instability, and any secondary harm.

It can be helpful to talk with someone who shares your spiritual beliefs and will hold space for you to share your experience. This can help you process it. I always use the same language my clients use when it comes to religion or spirituality to prevent contaminating their experience with my preferences or language. If I have a Christian client who uses the word God, then I use that. If I have a new ager who prefers Source, I use that. Universe is getting more and more popular as a way to describe this thing that is in, through, and around all things. Spirit works, too.

I like to be nimble and flexible in my language and do not project my own beliefs onto others. If you come out of the medicine space after meeting God, Source, Spirit, Universe, it can be amazing, and the desire to evangelize can be tempting. Please be mindful that you don't project your beliefs onto others. And be sincerely curious as you explore this thing that cannot be described. When I ask my clients to describe what they experience as God, the most common descriptor is unconditional, unlimited, infinite love.

Spiritual integration can include letting the physical body and nervous system reorganize. It can include emotional processing as you acclimate to the more intense frequencies of joy and love. It can include letting the mental body acclimate to new perspectives about yourself and the divine.

The most important recommendation I can make when integrating spiritual revelations is to be with them in silence. Sit with them in stillness. Explore them with curiosity and contain any impulse to identify with anything. Allow yourself to be with the mystery without trying to figure it out, own it, or attach to it in any way.

Spiritual revelations often continue to unfold overt time and revisiting them can reveal new aspects, new dimensions, and new insights. These revelations are rarely "one and done" and the gifts they provide keep on giving for years after you might think it may be complete.

Let the meaning of spiritual revelations emerge on their own. Emergence of meaning is like a kiss from the Universe; it can linger and leaves you star struck every time.

Were Your Intentions Met?

After you are reassured that you are okay physically, emotionally, mentally, and spiritually, ask yourself if your intentions were met. Often people meet their intentions without realizing it. We sometimes think our intentions need to be met in a certain way, when in all actuality the medicine had a much better way of meeting that intention.

STORYTIME: *A client of mine set the intention to experience unconditional love. He had the belief that it was possible. In the medicine a friend that had annoyed him to no end, who had just disappeared and become homeless, came in. He saw how he had judged this friend and rejected him and taken advantage of him. He saw how as a result the friend had closed himself off into a bubble so no one could hurt him anymore. He felt a deep sense of loss. He cried for the hurt and pain of his friend and saw that he actually loved him very much. At first he was disappointed that he was not able to experience unconditional love. When I asked if that was true and to take another look at his revelation, he realized unconditional love was not what he thought it was. It wasn't rainbows and unicorns; it was kindness, acceptance, and a deep love for even those who annoy us the most.*

Here's another example of how intentions can be met in roundabout ways:

STORYTIME: *I worked with a client whose only intention was to be more joyful. She thought she would go into the medicine and experience what it was like to be joyful. The medicine, however, in its ultimate wisdom, knew she needed to clear the pain from past trauma first and she cried the whole time. After she landed, she was disappointed and said she got nothing out of the experience. With deeper inquiry and an open mind, she discovered she felt lighter, freer, and had more capacity for joy now that the pain from the trauma was gone.*

Trusting that the medicine, in partnership with you and your system, often knows what needs to happen in order for your intention to be granted requires trust and curiosity. All people experience a new set point post medicine. Let it sink in that you may have actually achieved what you wanted to achieve in a roundabout way.

Here's another example of how this works:

STORYTIME: *In one of my psilocybin ceremonies I asked the medicine to help me be of the highest service to humankind. The medicine scanned my body as if it was evaluating my abilities to serve. When it came to my heart it said, "Oh, you have a selfish heart." There was no judgment, just straight and neutral truth. This floored me because my whole life had been all about being of service. The medicine showed me that I wasn't of service to my fellows but to myself because being of service was how I navigated the desire to be a good person. It gave me significance and identity. I was crushed. My whole life...selfish. That was a tough one to face. Unraveling that became a constant process of asking why I was doing something. Was it to sincerely help another or to get a hit of, "I'm okay, right?" Did the medicine meet my intention? It did more than that. It helped me get rid of what was in the way of my intention, as humbling and uncomfortable as it was.*

Our intentions may not be met how we think they will. Be on the lookout for met intentions that may not be recognized as such.

Susceptibility

Just as you did before your experience, after a medicine experience it is even more important to be careful who and what you are exposed to. You may be wide open to outside influences. So definitely don't watch horror movies or the news. Stay away from politics or anything that could imprint or implant something into your subconscious mind. The more you can just be with the information, listen to the music, and continue to integrate and be with your revelations the better.

Always take medicine or be served medicine from someone you know and trust.

Meaning

Separating the experience from over-interpretation is a backbone of this book. The experience was real. Yes. The interpretation is provisional.

Psychedelics are not dangerous in themselves. The danger arises when meaning is attributed faster than the revelation can be integrated. Therefore, it is very important to ground significant or intense revelations, put them into quarantine, and keep them clean of any specialness or uniqueness that might trigger a "better than you or less than" pattern.

It is normal to want to feel special after meeting what some people call God, Source, Universe, Spirit, True Self. It is normal to feel vulnerable. Therefore, it is wise to avoid identity labels such as:

- Healer
- Guide
- Transmitter
- Portal
- Bridge
- Channel
- Frequency holder
- Planetary servant

While these may describe the role or function you hold, they are not identities and can be subtle ego traps that can result in spiritual bypassing and shadow avoidance. Meaning is not something that is assigned by the mind as identity, significance, or special. It is something that arises spontaneously as a knowing. It is not a mental process.

The psyche often reaches for meaning because it seeks

meaning. But meaning is nothing if not embodied. Instead of assigning meaning, shift from meaning to presence and ask instead:

- What it felt like
- What it disrupted
- What it did or did not resolve

Presence transmits and integrates more than interpretation. Silence is THE greatest integrator and moments of not knowing are sacred. Moments when you stop and allow the nervous system to settle are healing. Moments where nothing dramatic happened but something settled is integration.

Give yourself permission to stay grounded.

Structure: Any experience that reorganizes meaning must be held in such a way that prevents identity expansion. The Revelation Integration Method Fundamentals creates the structure, the container in which meaning can be reorganized safely.

When structure is missing, meaning can:

- Inflate the experience
- Recruit identity
- Look for purpose or a mission
- Externalize authority
- Accelerate behavior

If an experience makes you feel assigned, chosen, or responsible for others' evolution, pause. This is a sign that meaning is exceeding integration capacity.

When structure is present meaning can settle, humble and integrate slowly. A good question to ask is, "How does this change how you eat, sleep, speak, work, or relate?" If an insight does not improve your patience, boundaries, kindness, and stability, it has not integrated yet.

Structure is the container that determines how meaning is applied. Two people can have the same psychedelic insight.

- One integrates.
- The other destabilizes.

The difference is not insight. It is the structure in which the revelation is contained. This is the beauty of the Revelation Integration Method. It does not seek meaning. It provides structure and clarity. Structure is not glamorous. It does not feel expansive. It often feels boring to the part of the psyche that wants meaning. That's exactly why it works.

Here are some other questions that can help with meaning. When in doubt ask:

- What happened?
- What meaning did you make of it?
- How are you choosing to live now?

Meaning making is intensified after altered states. Even healthy minds can over-conclude under those conditions. So be gentle with yourself if you have put meaning on something that wasn't there. I've certainly done it...more than once! Humans are meaning making machines. So, after any medicine experience get into the habit of grounding. Stabilize all aspects of your being: Physically, mentally, emotionally and spiritually. I recommend reaching for silence, stillness and humility often, it is these things that allows meaning to emerge on its own accord.

Journeying Without Medicine

I was able to journey without the medicine after a medicine experience and can still do so today. This is something I teach my clients, if they are interested. This is also an amazing exercise for emotional restructuring and helping your body acclimate and integrate the higher vibrational frequencies.

Plant medicine journeys frequently reveal our multidimensionality and we can experience different aspects of ourselves. These medicines give us glimpses into who we truly are beyond the negative thoughts, limiting beliefs, unruly emotions, and ego activity. But what if we don't need plant medicines to experience this? What if we are already multidimensional beings able to access who we are without psychedelic medicine?

⚘ Journeying Without Medicine:

This exercise may not be as intense as a medicine experience, but it can help you tap into other dimensions of yourself and help you access information nonetheless.

Many people have been entrained to fear, anxiety, scarcity, doubt, guilt, judgment, shame, etc. and resist feeling good. This exercise helps us release that resistance and adapt to the higher frequency emotions such as safety, gratitude, joy, freedom, abundance, and love. It can also help unwind false identity and integrate True Self as you get more and more familiar with the high frequency attributes of True Self and who you are beyond your thoughts, beliefs, and emotional constructs.

Allowing yourself to experience high frequency emotions and levels of consciousness can teach you how to enter into a journey like state without plant medicine. It can also provide emotional restructuring and frequency adaptation, without psychedelic medicine.

The following exercise is adapted from a meditation I discovered in the book *Althar the Crystal Dragon* by Joachim Wolffram. This exercise is most effective right after a medicine journey while the medicine is still in your system.

1. Settle and Cultivate Awareness of Your True Self: Sit quietly with your feet flat on the floor, your spine straight, and your palms face up resting comfortably on your thighs. Shift your attention from your headspace to your body. Become aware of your energy. Watch any chaos settle. Increase your awareness of your body. Feel your feet, your heartbeat, and your chest rise and fall with the rhythm of your breath. Turn up the dial on awareness so that you are super aware of the sounds in the room, the fan, the creaking walls, and most importantly, the true essence of you.

2. Become Aware of Safety: How safe are you right now? Be curious about safety. What does safety feel like? When you feel safety imagine an old thermostat dial used to turn up the heat and imagine that you are turning that dial all the way to magnify what it feels like to be safe x1000. Imagine you are being held within the arms of loving mother. Safe. Stay here as long as you like.

3. Become Aware of Gratitude: Once you have explored and magnified safety, become aware of gratitude. If your ego is active and saying, "This is a bunch of shit," just ignore it and focus on the small things you have to be grateful for. Think of the simple things like ice cream, the roof over your head, and a good meal. Be curious about gratitude. What does gratitude feel like? When you have the feeling of gratitude, magnify it x 1000 so you are really vibrating in alignment with gratitude. Gratitude can be the gateway to these higher frequency feelings and true self-realization.

4. Become Aware of Joy: When it feels natural, next become aware of joy. What is joy? What does joy really feel like? When you have the feeling of joy, turn up the dial and magnify the feeling of joy x1000! Let a smile cross your lips and really allow yourself to feel joy magnified times a thousand! Stay here as long as you like.

5. Become Aware of Love: When it seems natural, become aware of love. What is love? Be curious. What does love feel like? Where does it live in your body? When you have the feeling of love, turn up the dial on love and magnify the feeling of love x1000! What does it feel like to experience unconditional love without any reason, with no meaning, no expectations, or attachments to outcomes? Experience love without restraint, open your heart, let it fly!

6. Become Aware of Freedom: When you are called to it, next become aware of freedom. What does freedom feel like? What does it feel like to be able to go where you want to go, experience what you want to experience, and express all that you are? If you need to stir up the feeling, think of a time in your life where you felt free. When you have the feeling of freedom, turn up the dial and magnify freedom x 1000! Allow yourself to spread your wings and fly!

7. Become Aware of Wisdom: When the time feels right, become aware of wisdom. What is wisdom? What does wisdom really feel like? When you have wisdom, turn up the dial and magnify it. Become aware of all the things that have happened in your life and how they brought wisdom. From this life and even past lives think of all that has happened that has brought you wisdom.

8. Bliss: Now combine all these feeling states together to feel bliss! Turn up that dial and experience bliss. Really allow yourself to experience bliss! Stay in this state as long as you are called to. It's not a holding; it's like you are just about to have an orgasm!

9. Other Feelings: If you are called to spontaneously bring in other feelings like beauty, peace, contentment, or others go for it!

10. Embody the Feelings: Don't jet out of your body when you do this; stay grounded in your body. This helps the body adapt and heal through these higher frequencies. Allow your body to adapt to the vibrational frequencies of these feelings by staying aware of them as long as possible and carrying the awareness of them with you as you go about your day.

These feelings can become more available to you over time; you simply have to be aware of them.

You can go in any order that calls to you. If you feel like jumping from safety to wisdom, do that. There is no right way or wrong way. Stay in your body at all times so you experience being both grounded and elevated.

If you have an emotional release and start crying tears of sorrow, suffering, joy, or beauty, let them come. If your body starts to shake or move in different ways, just allow it to do what it does. It is part of the physical body letting go of old frequencies and adapting to new frequencies. You may also go into the visionary space and have a journey like experiences without medicine.

Not being able to surrender, needing to control people or situations, fear, worry about what people think, fear of judgment or rejection, fear of not good enough, guilt, and shame are all lower-level ego activities originally created in an effort to keep you safe. These are things that can cause resistance to feeling good. Thank the ego for its good intention, then elevate yourself to the higher levels where there is only love. When you get more comfortable with the elevated emotions, they displace the lower emotions and dissolve old emotional imprints and patterns. Be patient and let whatever arises come to be processed.

Note: It is normal to experience ups and downs and highs and lows that will eventually even out over time. Eventually you won't need the extreme highs because constant peace just becomes a natural side effect of healing. It is normal to experience emotional releases, intense moments of realization, and levels of expanded states of awareness. The goal is not to disappear and jet out of our physical existence, but to embody these higher frequencies and bring them here. As the saying goes...As above so below!

Another thing that can give you a journey-like experience is listening to the music played at a retreat while you lie or sit in stillness. Play the journey music in the background and surrender to the bed or the chair. Relax and let go as much as possible, even do a full body scan releasing any tension you find. This can put you into state dependent learning and enables you to go back into the experience without medicine. Journal about your experience for integration.

This is a good exercise for people who are addicted to or are entrained to feeling bad. These individuals can go into the medicine space and experience joy and love and an open heartedness and may not know what to do with it. Afterward, they need to be taught how to feel good. This exercise can do that.

Let's continue our exploration of things to consider immediately after a sacred medicine ceremony.

Don't Make Any Rash Decisions

It is often wise to pause in the weeks following a retreat. You might misinterpret what you're shown and add meaning to it that's not there. Just capture the information and stay open. Be neutral and objective. Be curious as you work with your revelations. Some people come out of a journey and say I'm changing my name. I'm divorcing my wife. I'm doing this and so on...Whoa, whoa, whoa, whoa, whoa, whoa, whoa, let's just sit with the information before you do anything.

Many medicines can literally blow people apart, in a good way. The neurological reset is just one way our system is disrupted. The Default Mode Network (DMN) is a network of brain regions that is responsible for thinking about ourselves and our personal identity. Psychedelics reduce DMN activity and has been correlated with experiences of ego dissolution, which can lead to shifts in self-perception and potentially help break negative thought patterns and rumination associated with conditions like depression and anxiety. This can lead to the feeling that the "false self" is disappearing, creating a sense of unity or connectedness with everything.

After being blown apart like that it is wise to integrate, which is to be in stillness, to let things settle before making any big decisions. Please, allow things to settle back into their new set point before you make any dramatic changes.

Quick Recap: Let's take a moment and review what we have covered so far.

- You learned that the Revelation Integration Method is a map of healing.
- You discovered how to set an intention.
- You created your own intentions and discovered the core intentions that fulfill many intentions at once.
- You started an intention journal.
- You documented your starting set point.
- You learned how to prepare for a medicine experience in detail.
- You received instruction on how to navigate the medicine space safely.
- You received emergency tactics on what to do if things go sideways by reinforcing Sanctuary and calling on your guides.
- You learned how to catch yourself and check in physically, mentally, emotionally, and spiritually afterwards to work with any post journey instability.
- You received powerful tools to help mitigate fear, process emotions, work with ego, ground, quiet the mind, let go, and receive. (Cultivating awareness is the

foundation to all of these tools.)

- You learned how to capture as much information, or as many revelations as possible from your medicine experience.
- You learned how to journey without medicine.

Wow! Look at us go!

Next, let's dive into how to work with the revelations themselves.

CHAPTER 6

THE POST-MEDICINE REVELATION ORGANIZATION

In this chapter we will discuss methods that you can use to organize and work with what was revealed to you in the medicine space so your mind, body, and spirit can adapt to the information. You will learn how to stay focused on the revelations, how to integrate difficult journeys, and how to safely face those crunchy bits and pieces you may have kept tucked away. You will learn how to extract the self-realizations, how to identify any directives, how to receive any metaphors or reflections, and how to tell if your intentions were met or not. You will also learn how to work with joint transcriptions if you journeyed with a partner.

Imagine that you have just returned home from a retreat. You are letting everything settle within you. You are exploring how you are physically, emotionally, mentally, and spiritually different. You are curious about your new set point, and you want to make the most of the medicine experience by integrating as much as possible.

The following are ideas and suggestions to help you do just that.

Talking: Talking about your experience is part of the integration process. Having someone to confide in that you trust to help you process your revelations can be invaluable. If you don't have anyone to confide in who will just listen without interjecting or projecting or putting meaning on anything, consider hiring an integration guide. If they see you avoiding something they will redirect you back to it by asking you to say more about that particular revelation; if you are not sure what to make of the experience you can explore it together. I find asking questions is the best way to help someone integrate because it allows them to discover their own answers and insights.

If you are working with an integration guide, I recommend scheduling the post call within 48 hours or as soon as you get home from the experience. The sooner the better. The reason for this is if the ego feels threatened by the experience or was shut down in any way, it can come back online and try to negate the experience and say things like, "That didn't happen; it wasn't real; it was just a hallucination; close down your heart, it's not safe!" Reassure the ego that all is well. The ego wants to keep you safe and an open heart in its book may not be safe. Continue to reassure it that all is well. You've got this.

Meeting with your guide as soon as possible gives you the opportunity to anchor in or ground valuable information before it can get distorted by the mind or ego. You want to be able to reinforce the valuable bits and interrupt any fear so you feel safe to make the changes or shifts you intended.

A guide can be invaluable as you enter the integration phase because they can often see things you don't. They can tell you to chill out and be curious about your new set point.

If you don't have anyone to talk with, continue to ground, breathe, center and begin the process of capturing as much information from your experience as possible.

Capturing the Revelations

Whether you decided to use the voice memo app on your phone or journal about the experience after you landed, there are some really cool ways to work with the information for maximum impact and integration. But you need to have the data first. Think of the revelations as data that you are plugging into your new operating system.

- **Journal:** If you journaled about the experience after you landed, keep journaling until you feel you have captured everything of relevance. Then type it into a Word or Google document. Stay open to capture any further insights and realizations as you go.
- **Transcribe:** If you talked and were able to capture what you said in a recording, like the voice memo app on your phone, you will want to transcribe everything that you said into a Word or Google doc and continue capturing downloads or insights as you go.
- **Listen:** Keep listening to the recording, if you have one. It can help integrate the energy in the body and can also facilitate more releases. When you can listen to the transcript in neutrality, especially if it was one of release, you know you are complete. Listening can help you stay in the remembering of it.

Group the Revelations into Themes

Once you have captured all the information from your journey, group the information into themes. The mind can loop on the same topic as it tries to work through something. For instance, mom may come in for a bit, then you may move on to your partner, then back to mom. Cut and paste all information regarding mom into one grouping so you have all the revelations regarding mom in one section. This will make it easier for you to receive the revelations. If it doesn't make sense to organize it into themes because there was only one theme, don't worry about it. Leave it as it is.

Working with the revelations this way exposes you to the information a second, third, or even fourth time, which can help your mind and body acclimate to the information that was revealed. It helps reprogram your system to the new information and reinforces the old information as no longer relevant. Stay alert for more downloads, self-realizations, directives, and metaphors as you organize the revelations, and remain curious about how you feel for two weeks or longer after being in the medicine.

If you traveled the universe, create a theme for that. If you met God, released anxiety, puked up the past, met with an angel, received a restructuring or a healing, cut and paste each of those topics into themes. Grouping the various revelations into sections can help the mind organize and make sense of the revelations. Especially if you looped and your mind was trying to work through something.

Looping: Looping is when the mind plays with something like a cat with a catnip toy. It doesn't want to let it go! Your mind may leave a subject then return to it again and again. This can be both helpful and not helpful. It is helpful when the mind is trying to work through something. Therefore, capture as much data from the looping experience as possible. Is there a reflection, a mirroring, or a metaphor for your life at play here? Do you loop on things like that outside the medicine space? Sometimes we loop because the information is so important we need it driven into us repetitively.

Looping can be unhelpful when you've received the information, and the mind won't let it go. A good facilitator can interrupt looping if they are aware of it. If you find yourself looping and you want out, take a few deep breaths and tell the mind to chill out. Cultivate awareness. This can work both in and out of the medicine space.

STORYTIME: *In the journey I mentioned earlier where I had oral surgery, I was so amazed by what was happening it was hard to believe. In the medicine I kept saying to myself over and over again, "Dani, do not doubt this healing." I was looping on the same topic over and over again to really get what was happening into my subconscious mind. (I can be quite dense sometimes.) In another journey, the medicine revealed to me that "I was in my knowing" but that wasn't enough for me. I wanted to know the unknowable. I kept saying, "I want to know. I want to know," in between acknowledging that I did indeed know. It was quite frustrating. This is an example of how the mind can loop on something as a way of working through it.*

Trauma: When people release trauma, it is not necessary to go digging back into the experience to capture the data unless you are called to. If you let go of something and the last thing you want to do is journal about it, don't do it. That can create more trauma. Sometimes it is enough to ask, "How do I feel about that life event now? Am I complete with it?" It is not uncommon for clients who have released trauma, sexual abuse, physical abuse, emotional abuse, mental abuse, family lineage patterns, and so on to see the event from a different perspective. They find they are neutral to the event and are ready to move on with their lives. Some who face it may continue to release stored emotions relative to the event after the medicine experience is over and emotional processing assistance can be invaluable. Often when it comes to trauma, it is best to face it and see what arises. Again, when you can talk about the trauma with neutrality, you know you are complete with it.

Avoidance: When people say, "Ooh, I don't want to listen to my transcript or journal about the experience," they may be avoiding important information about themselves. This is okay. Sometimes we are not ready for some revelations and a year later we may be able to listen to the recording. Never pressure yourself to do something you don't want to do. But be very aware of why you are avoiding it. Is your ego being a bitch, or are you really not ready for this next leap in your own evolution?

If you feel you are avoiding something that needs to be seen, something that could be of great value, I advise you to channel courage and create the time to face what was revealed from the witness perspective. Try being objective, even pretend that the transcript is not yours so you can at the very least capture the information.

Remove Judgment: Again, never, ever, EVER judge what is revealed to you in the medicine space. People will often judge their experience or compare it to what other people experienced. All experiences are valid. All experiences are beautiful. All experiences are useful and contain within them gold nuggets, reflections of the self or your life that you can learn from. Every time you catch yourself judging, let it go over and over and over again to the best of your ability. You do this by redirecting your focus from judgment and comparison to curiosity about your own experience. Curiosity is the antidote for judgment.

STORYTIME: *I was working with a gal who went into the medicine space and saw herself as a shining sun. Free, light, and divine. When she landed, she immediately compared her experience to her friend and assumed her friend's experience was better. She said she got nothing from the experience. She had a pattern of FOMO. She spent much of her life in fear of missing out or being left behind. As we integrated, she realized that seeing herself as a sun was incredibly valuable and the feelings in her journey as free, light, and in divinity was exactly what she needed to feel more secure in herself and less at the effect of others.*

Stay Focused on the Revelations: Often times people will talk about how they felt after the experience rather than the experience itself. It's also very important to focus on what was revealed to you in the experience, whether your intention was met, as well as how you feel afterwards. You might have left your body and experienced who you are beyond the physical form and try to skip over it or trivialize it when what you are really being asked to do is step into who and what you really are. Staying focused on the main revelations helps you integrate and see different aspects of those revelations.

No Good or Bad Revelations: There is nothing that could be revealed to you about yourself in the medicine space that you can't deal with. There is no good or bad. Just lessons learned and layers of the self to unpack. How you acted in the medicine; whether you lost control or held your shit together is a revelation itself to ponder. Whatever happens in the medicine space, whether it be "good" or what some people call "bad" is a revelation. Even if the facilitator screws up royally and demons enter the room, you get to unpack how you responded and take responsibility for you. It is important to put all experiences and revelations into quarantine, especially what we would call the "bad" ones. Once in quarantine you can look at them like a Rubik's Cube and ask questions, such as, "What did this experience teach me about me? Is the experience mirroring something to me about me? Is it reflecting something to me about my life? Is it a metaphor for something?"

Think about a medicine experience you might have had that did not go so well. Did you play the victim role? Did you blame the medicine? Did you lose your shit because you took too much? Did you try to control the experience and not let go? Did you ignore the revelation because you weren't ready to face it? These are powerful reflections of you. So many people want the good experiences and avoid what we would call the bad ones, but there is gold in them when we are ready to face them. When you approach integration this way, with curiosity, and a willingness to witness even your crunchy bits, it's is an opportunity to learn, grow, and evolve.

Face the Crunchy Bits

Going through the journal entries or transcript can be a raw and vulnerable experience. It's where you may face those aspects of yourself that are crunchy. The selfish, judgmental, and insecure parts. But once you understand the integration process and feel safe facing all of your bits and pieces, you'll be more eager and excited to face the next crunchy bit, then the next one, then the next one. Hold a neutral, compassionate, non-judgmental space for yourself as you go through this process. You're healing, and this is what healing looks like. Allow yourself to be humbled and be kind to yourself as you go through this process.

Meaning: As you go through your revelations be careful not to add meaning where there is none. This includes over identification with a revelation. For instance, if Jesus came in and had a chat with you, be very careful that you don't add meaning to the experience by assuming you are special because of it. Better to take the wise words of a master and integrate those into your life.

Purging: As you are exploring your revelations keep an eye out for purges that you may not recognize as such. Purging happens frequently without our even being aware of it. Often times someone will have a difficult experience in the medicine and not know what to make of it. Those experiences are often purges.

Denial: Sometimes information will come through and you might brush it off without looking deeper. For instance, people will say, "There was nothing that was shown to me that I didn't already know." To which I reply, "Was it a deep knowing or an intellectual concept?" You might have known it intellectually, but after the ceremony, is it more embodied? Now do you know, like you know, like you know from the core of your being?

Everyone has a new set point coming out of a medicine experience. It may be very subtle or extremely profound.

Spiritual Bypassing: Many people will take another journey before the first one is complete. This is literally spiritual bypassing and can result in a person taking journey after journey and getting nowhere. Don't do this. How do you know a journey is complete? After you have spent time with your revelations, taken action where insight provided direction, gone through your intention journal to see what is complete and what is not, and have reached a plateau. Reviewing your intention journal can clearly show you what is complete and where you still have work to do intuitively. You will just know. Don't use the medicine to escape, get another hit, or avoid something. Use it to catalyze you forward and help you face something when you need help.

Triggers: If reviewing a revelation triggers you, there is something important there for you to explore. The trigger is the teacher and its always about you. If you are resisting journaling about your experience or listening to your recording, the ego may be threatened. This means it's more important than ever to face those revelations and be curious about what's there for you.

When you are willing to look at triggers, what they represent and how you respond to them, you may have new insights into yourself and a pattern that may no longer be serving you. The trigger can often be transmuted by looking at it, seeing it for what it is, and letting it go.

Distortions: What we would call the bad experiences often involve fear, unworthiness, guilt, shame, judgment, comparison, greed, control, resistance, avoidance, addictions, trauma, etc. I call these distortions because they are all either stories about something that happened in the past, something that may happen in the future but never does, or judgment of a now moment. When we cultivate awareness and rest in the infinite now moment, we are free of all of these. One way to understand distortions is to think of them as low vibrational patterns we inherited from our parents and the world around us. These are the programming of our youth many of us are deactivating and reorienting to broader perspectives.

When distortions come up in the medicine space, they are often coming to the surface to be released and healed. Let them come. Stay alert to how you feel afterwards. Was facing them in the medicine space enough to drop them or at least loosen the pattern?

Negative thought patterns, limiting belief structures, unruly emotions, and the ego activity are all an old, outdated operating system that sucked then and still sucks now. We know how to release these distortions. It used to be a mystery. Today more and more people use awareness to dissolve the illusions of fear and the irrational patterns of doubt, guilt, or shame just by becoming aware of them and letting them go over and over again until they are gone. These individuals have made it easier for us. What one does on behalf of themselves they do on behalf of the collective. Like ending a family lineage of physical abuse. At some point a member will stop it and say, "No. This ends here. I will not pass this on to my kids."

There are many benefits to cultivating awareness and increasing our level of consciousness. When a distortion is exposed to pure consciousness, it just dissolves. I have found that nothing can withstand the power of pure consciousness. Nothing. I believe I have said this before. ;-)

Once you have the journal or transcript complete and you have captured all the revelations and organized them into themes, it is time to roll up your sleeves and start exploring all the data you have captured.

What To Look For

Self-realizations: These come forth in medicine space in the form of "I" language. Examples are, "I am a good mom." "I love my husband so much." "I need to be more present with my child." People often report self-realizations coming from their higher self. Like they are coaching themselves. These are very important to pay attention to. Make a list of any self-realizations you had in the medicine space.

Directives: These often come through in the medicine space in the form of "you" language. For example, "You need to let go." "You know." "Just be." "Surrender." "Be nicer to your partner." These are very important to integrate because they come through the medicine loud and clear, like a thunderbolt from God. Many people report the directives coming from their higher self or Source itself. Directives are strong and succinct.

STORYTIME: *I was in a mushroom journey once and the mushrooms told me to "Temper it." I was shown my impatience, and how sometimes I could be too direct with my clients. I knew that was a directive that definitely needed integrating! So, I practiced slowing down, softening and being more presence until I felt my approach was tempered. Sometimes I succeeded and sometimes I failed miserably. This is another example of how insight, or directive can become embodied when practiced over time and with patience and compassion.*

🕯 **STOP** now and make a list of all the self-realizations and directives you have received.

These are powerful and when sat with can give us direction on how to live, be, and act in ways that are congruent with our highest self without ego inflation or getting stuck.

Metaphors: Sometimes revelations will appear metaphorically. People may come up to a wall and break it down. When I ask what the wall represented they say, "The protection around my heart." If you notice metaphors being revealed to you, these can be of great value, especially if you moved through something into freedom and an open heart. Integrating that metaphoric experience afterwards might be acclimating to and adjusting to having an open heart. You might be clumsy and awkward at first. This is normal as you integrate and learn to love in new ways.

Reflections and Mirroring: Did the medicine reflect something to you about yourself? What is it showing you? Like looking in a mirror, the medicine may be showing you something about yourself that needs to be seen. Reflections can be wonderful and they can be challenging as well. For instance, if you spent the whole journey trying to control the experience and could not let go, is this a reflection of how you live your life?

Make a list of any metaphors or reflections revealed to you in the medicine space.

It is important to ponder the reflections and ask questions such as, "Was what I experienced a purging experience? Do I still have that need to control now?" You have a new set point, remember? Other reflections may include aspects of your personality; for example, did fear, anxiety, or helplessness come in? Look at these reflections and see if they are still active patterns after you have landed. Many patterns can be interrupted without our knowing it happened.

Mirroring shows us aspects of ourselves, our lives, or others that we may need to see. For example, if your ceremony was all about fear, can you look at this as if you are looking into a mirror and see that fearful aspect of yourself? How often are you fearful in your life? If you spent the whole time basking in love, how big a role does love play in your life? These are valuable insights, and while some may not be comfortable, they need to be seen in order for us to move past them or integrate them at a deeper level.

I love questions and ask these often: What is this mirroring to me about myself? How do I feel about this now? When did it arise? How did this serve me? Do I still need it? Is it gone? What would life be like without this?

Intention Completion

- **Completion:** As you go through your revelations, look to see if you achieved what you set out to achieve. If you set the intention to release unworthiness, did you do it? If so, and you feel like you are worthy beyond a shadow of a doubt, anchor that in. If weeks later you still feel worthy then you are complete! Yay! You set an intention and completed it! If this was a video game you would get a gold star or an upgrade! But still stay alert so it doesn't creep back in without you knowing it.

- **In Process:** If you set the intention to release unworthiness and you are still carrying some doubt about your worthiness the intention is not complete, it is in process. Make notes about this in your intention journal. Is your new set point more worthy than you were before? Did the medicine dislodge it a bit? Is this something to keep working on as you move forward?

Once you have determined if your intentions were met, then move on to the revelations themselves.

Revelation Completion

Completion: Completion regarding each revelation means there are no threads on it. You received the information, and it is done. For instance, is the selfishness the medicine showed you gone? Yay! Again, give yourself a gold star for facing something that needed to be seen and embodying what it means to be free of selfishness. The medicine can help us

168

release and let go of some incredible blockages, but it's up to us to not pick them back up or let a pattern sneak back in. If you let something go and it's completely gone weeks or months later; and you know like you know like you know that pattern is gone, you are complete.

In Process: If the selfishness is still present, how present is it? Is it less than it was before? Or do you still have some work to do? If it is still there it is in process. Keep after it knowing over time it will disappear as you ask for and adapt to a more giving heart. If it was revealed to you that love is all that matters and you have no idea what that looks like after you land, that revelation is in process. If it was revealed to you that nothing matters and everything you thought matters doesn't, allow that revelation to be in process. This means to explore it. Play with it, be with it and look for synchronicities or signposts that help clarity unfold. Just be, let go, and love are directives that usually take some time to implement in ways that feel right for you.

Implementation: It's up to you to implement and work with the revelations that are in process. For instance, did the directive to play more get implemented? Are you more playful? Is the pattern of judgment being whittled away bit by bit with awareness and letting go? Are you tempering impatience using grounding and breathing techniques? Are you using mirror work to develop self-trust and self-love?

You can tell if you are not complete with something by sitting with the revelation and feeling your way into it. For example, if mom came into your journey and you saw she did the best she could, and you forgave her for not being there in ways you wanted her to be, you released resentment and forgave. After you land and journal about your experience, ask yourself, 'How do I feel about mom now?" If resistance or resentment comes in, you know you are not complete. If you feel neutral and nothing arises, or you feel peace, you are complete. Then move on to your next revelation.

The goal is to get complete with everything that was revealed to you in your medicine experience and work with what is incomplete towards completion. The medicine is not doing it for you. You are using it as a tool. If you reach a stuck point and you need the medicine to nudge you forward that is a good use of the medicine as long as you are not expecting the medicine to do the work for you.

- When an individual integrates a revelation and is complete with it, they no longer question the information. It feels complete to them. They will often report not being triggered by things that triggered them in the past. They feel more centered and at peace.
- When a revelation feels incomplete, the individual will report still having some threads on it; they may still be triggered by the pattern. They are still working through it.

 Update Your Intention Journal: As you go through your revelations, mark off the intentions you have completed and the intentions that are still in process. Also journal about what you can do to continue to work with the revelations that are incomplete. Sitting with the ones that are incomplete in silence and stillness is a great way to continue to receive information about them. You may gain insight as to what next steps or no steps can be taken. Updating your intention journal is very important and can help keep you motivated and moving forward.

Joint Transcriptions

Some organizations work with couples in the medicine space to open the heart and improve communication. When couples come together in this way, it gives them the opportunity to experience what it's like to communicate with each other without getting triggered or being defensive. Their defensiveness is often reduced greatly and they can talk about anything. They report it is as if there is no such thing as vulnerability. I have couples record these sessions so they can listen to the recording and go through the topics discussed to ensure they both feel complete. You can follow the same process as is outlined for the individual, only you do it together as a couple.

If you and your partner decide to go into the medicine space together with the intention for greater ease of communication, record the session. Then listen to that recording and transcribe a little bit every day together. Have one person be in charge of the recording and the other person type it up. And anytime either of you has a question, stop the recording and talk about it. You learned how to communicate openly in the medicine space, it showed you how. Now is the time to practice it outside of the medicine space.

Above all, the most important thing for you to remember is what it felt like to be open and safe to say anything. Remember the honesty, the openness, the laughter, and the lighthearted way you engaged with each other and practice bringing that into your daily life. If you experienced open heartfelt communication once, you now have that reference point and experience to draw upon. You can then anchor that new communication style into your lives in loving ways outside of the medicine space.

Now that you have captured your revelations and

organized them into main themes, documented the self-realizations and directives, and reflected on the metaphors, reflections, and mirroring that may have occurred, as well as noted what is now complete and what is in process, it's time to continue to work with them for greater embodiment.

CHAPTER 7

POST-MEDICINE INTEGRATION TOOLS

The information in this chapter is intended to take the integration process one step further so that your revelations land in your life in ways that enhance your relationship with yourself, those around you, and life itself. This chapter offers a tool kit that can give you the confidence to know, like you know, like you know how to handle anything that comes before you. This is everything that I know, a brain-dump so to speak, of all the tools I've used over the years. Take what resonates, play with it, adapt it, use it in a way that feels good to you. Leave what doesn't resonate. We all have our own artistic ways in which we work with our revelations. My way is not the only way. Not by a long shot. This chapter will also help you anchor in what is complete so an old pattern doesn't come creeping back into your life. That's what this chapter is all about: Tools.

Let's begin.

Self-Realizations and Directives

After you have journaled about your medicine experience and cut and pasted everything into main themes and pulled out all the self-realizations and directives, you want to spend as much time with the revelations as possible. You revisit them to let your mind get used to the revelations; you acclimate to the new information or set point. Yep! You integrate!

I feel self-realizations and directives are the most important revelations to integrate because they give us a place to go. They tell us what's important to integrate.

Word Search Tool: If you are unsure and can't find any self-realizations or directives, use the word search tool on Word or Google documents to see what words from your journey were used the most. I once searched a transcript of one of my clients' journeys for the word love and it came in 853 times. This person was obviously integrating love! ChatGPT can also come up with some interesting interpretations, but be sure they resonate and always take any AI tool with a grain of salt and a heavy dose of discernment.

Okay. Once you have your revelations, realizations and directives, let's play with them a bit. Let's create truth cards and mantras.

Truth Cards

Truth Cards take all the self-realizations and directives you gain in the medicine space and puts them onto index cards for you to sit with, ponder, acclimate to, align to, and integrate into your life. These can be the most important revelations that you want to remember and integrate. It is one thing to have a self-realization and another thing to embody or integrate it.

Truths cards remind you of who you are, how you want to be, what you want to express or experience, and what's important to you. These are the insights revealed to you in the medicine.

1. On the front of the card is the revelation, directive or self-realization.
2. On the back of the card is the action step you will take to anchor that revelation into your life.

These cards act as triggers or reminders and help activate, integrate, and anchor the insight within you. The more energy and creativity you put into remembering and applying your revelations, the more they will become a part of your life.

Choose your words carefully so you experience a positive feeling or a sense of empowerment in your body when you read them. Consider using the same language you experienced in the medicine space if it feels right. Some of my clients feel truth cards should always be worded in the positive. For example, instead of "I am not unworthy" they write down, "I am worthy." Using present terminology can be also helpful. For example, instead of "I am going to love myself." You could say, "I love myself" The language you used in the medicine space I feel is most powerful and am okay letting go of these constructs and writing down what feels good to you. I had a directive come through loud and clear to "Stop avoiding." This was firm and a clear directive.

When I created a truth card for this directive on the front of the index card I wrote "Stop Avoiding." And as I colored it and created it, I infused the energy of courage and empowerment to set boundaries and face what I was avoiding. On the back of the card I wrote my action steps which were: Create boundaries. Speak your truth. Face the discomfort so it dissipates and transmute the feelings of discomfort. Hold my vibration coherently so I am not at the effect of others.

This may not seem very clear to someone else; it is very clear to me. That is the most important thing. Play around with the language so that it feels good to you.

With the truth cards, you're encoding the vibration of the message on to that card. Every time you look at that card, it should trigger a feeling response that aligns you to what you experienced in your journey, not inflate ego or a sense of significance. Allow yourself to feel solid in your power without inflating your identity.

When you are creating a truth card, doodle on it, color it, get some paints or markers and have fun with them, and really infuse that card with the feeling of the experience that you had in the medicine space. Invite your kids, if you have them, to join you when you create these. They too may have an insight to integrate.

Here's another example, if the medicine revealed to you that "You are in your knowing." On the front of the card write: You are in your knowing. On the back of the card write down the action steps to integrate this revelation. In this case action steps might be to:

- Trust your intuition
- Stop and listen
- Meditate to quiet the mind and calm the interference
- Practice being more present

Often the action is no action. You may have received the revelation that it is time to just be, heal, or allow. This is when the action step would be to practice non-doing and being. Action steps for these might be:

- Rest and take naps
- Meditate more

- Get comfortable being still
- Practice being quiet and not talking

Leave these cards laying around your house, in your car, at work, or on your desk as reminders.

When you feel you have fully integrated an insight into your life you can throw the card away.

Mantras

You can also create a mantra using the most powerful words that came through for you. For instance, if your whole journey was about learning to trust yourself and you told yourself throughout the whole journey to just trust and let go, you could create a mantra like this: *Trust. You are safe. It's okay. Let go.*

If the big revelation was to let go of control, you could create a mantra like this: *It's okay. Release control. You got this. Allow.*

Mantras bring relief. They can mitigate and dissolve fear. They can help you align to authenticity instead of ego. They can help you reprogram your entire operating system.

You see, words carry information that some call codes that trigger biological responses. You can feel the results of your words. For example,

- Say the words "Thank You." Imagine a time when you received one of your most favorite gifts and say it again. "Thank you." Did you feel an opening and an inflow of energy? Keep saying it until you do.
- Now say, "No," and feel the results of that. Feel how it is sharp and short.

The important thing to remember when you create a mantra is that you must FEEL the results of the mantra. You can't say the words without feeling them and expect anything to happen. You must elicit a feeling response. This is the reprogramming.

By definition, a mantra is "a word, phrase, or sound repeated to aid concentration in meditation or to reinforce a specific mindset." It originates from Sanskrit, where "man" means mind and "tra" means tool—so a mantra is essentially a tool for the mind.

How Does a Mantra Work?

When you have thought, it releases chemicals that give you a feeling response. When you say a word, it does the same thing. This is how the body works. It is how you create with thoughts and words. We'll go more into this later, but for now, when you create a mantra, you are stirring up feeling responses in the body to let go of the feelings you no longer want and bring in the ones that you do want. Mantras that help you just chill out are the best. Once you have learned to chill, then it can be nice to bring in the big guns of joy, love, and freedom. But hey, who am I to limit your choices?

How can a mantra be used?

1. To Increase Focus & Meditation – Repeating a mantra helps quiet the mind and improve focus, making it easier to enter a trance or meditative state.

2. To Align Vibration & Energy – In many traditions, certain sounds (like "Om" and "Aum") create vibrations that align the body's chakras and energy systems.

3. To Affirm & Reprogram – Positive mantras (e.g., "I am loved" can reinforce beliefs and reshape thought patterns.)

4. To Increase Coherence – The rhythm of chanting a mantra can synchronize the breathing, mind, and heart, promoting coherence and relaxation, and

reduce stress.

5. To Reinforce Realizations & Directives – To reinforce realizations and give energy and momentum to directives.

When I was struggling with unworthiness, I wanted more peace so I used the mantra: *Peace. Trust. Truth.* Let go. I repeated these words several times a day, especially when the thought pattern of I can't or who am I to do that? arose. Some days I really needed trust and other days peace really helped me quiet my mind. Just by saying the word "Peace" my body responded. Just by saying the words "Let go" my mind relaxed. This helped me deactivate the old pattern and create a new one.

What would you like to reprogram with a mantra?

Some words are like codes that trigger a relaxation effect on the body, which helps us release and let go. Other words can affect us adversely. Say the word "hate" and you will understand what I mean. Words carry vibration and information we can align to. We can feel the effects of our words. Mantras can be used to interrupt negative thought patterns, old belief structures, or behaviors that don't serve and to create new ones that do. Think of it as de-programming and reprogramming your system for more joy, love, compassion, or whatever you want to experience just through saying words.

Voice Memo Recordings

Another way to integrate your revelations, especially the powerful ones you captured in a recording, is to take that recording and re-record the parts you want to integrate most into another brief memo for you to play later. This way you don't have to listen to the whole recording to get to the most impactful part when it is needed.

Listening to yourself declare that the trauma from your

youth is gone keeps you from picking it back up. In a journey I said, "I am everything and nothing and everything and nothing!" I was so excited when I said this that I wanted to remind myself and my ego, that yes, I am everything and I am nothing. To me, this meant there is no identity, no significance attached to the everything, and at the same time I am nothing special. Period. Without this recording it may have been easy for my ego to identify with "I am everything" and forget the "I am nothing" part. (The ego doesn't like being nothing, but it does adapt to being nothing over time.)

The more you listen to those voice memos, the more you can attune to them and embody them. If there's a lot of silence in the recording, there is a function in most phones that skips silence. So, if there are long blocks of silence between speaking, it can make going through the recording a little bit easier. Some people find listening to the silence relaxing and they can tune back into the state they were in when they were in the medicine.

Letter Writing

If you had a beloved come into the medicine space and you saw how much you love that person, write them a letter. Tell them how much you love them along with any other revelations they may need to hear. It is not uncommon for parents to see how much they love their kids and the directives are often, "Let them be. They've got this." If I had a letter from my mom or dad telling me they loved me I would still have it today.

If your partner came in and you saw that you were a jerk and need to show them more love, say you're sorry. Show them more love. An insight is only as valuable as your follow through. Take what comes into the medicine space and implement those revelations here. That's why you took the medicine, right?

Another way letters can be helpful is if you are not on good terms with the person who came in and you purged some trauma, anger, or frustration but there still feels like some of those emotions are still stuck within you. Letter writing can help you release what's still there. This person can be alive or deceased. It doesn't matter.

STORYTIME: *I was going through a rough time. I was holding onto a lot of anger towards my mom, who was a strict negative reinforcer. Nothing I ever did was good enough and saying I was angry is putting it lightly. I hated her. I knew this was not healthy and wanted to get it out of my system so I sat down to write my mom a letter. She had already passed away, but that didn't matter. I called in her presence and used my imagination to picture her right in front of me and I let her have it. As I wrote the letter my hand scribbled furiously, "Why was it never good enough?! Why? No matter what I did it never measured up. Why? What did I do that was so bad?" I cursed a lot and swore like a sailor at her. I called her a few choice names. This may sound horrible and you may judge me; so be it. It was how I felt and I didn't want to hold it in anymore. When I was done, I felt like a weight had been lifted. I crumpled up the paper and threw it away.*

About a week later I did the same thing. I called in her presence and imagined she was sitting right next to me. The anger came but was not nearly as intensely and as I scribbled the anger died down and I started to cry and wrote, "Why? Why couldn't you have just loved me the way I wanted to be loved?" and when the tears stopped falling and my hand stopped writing, I crumpled up the letter and threw it away.

A week later I returned to the process and called my mom in again. When I started writing, there was no anger.

The sadness came and as I rocked myself back and forth, I realized that my mom did the best she could. Now I knew this intellectually, but the emotional hairball stilled lived within my heart. This process helped me dislodge it. I saw that there was no way in the world she could have loved me the way I wanted to be loved because she never knew how. She grew up practically raised by Catholic nuns. Negative reinforcement was all she knew. The sadness was gone and all that was left was understanding.

A week later I sat down with paper and pen again, and when I called in my mom's presence and sat with her, my hand stopped writing. I expected to purge some more. But no anger came. No sadness came. The understanding was there and then what came in was the galling realization that she was my greatest teacher. Yep. I couldn't believe it. If she hadn't been the bitch I thought she was, I never would have had the hutzpah to say, "Oh I will show you!" My whole life was one big, "How about now? Am I good enough now?" that drove me and drove me to be better than I was. It was the "I will show you attitude" that empowered me to go back to school, start a business, write a book, and be the best version of myself. I was a bit pissed at this realization and it took me a couple weeks to integrate that one. Mind you, there was no medicine involved in writing any of these letters. Just my ability to imagine her right in front of me so I could let her have it and get what was on my chest out.

A couple weeks later I sat down again. I called her in and imagined she was right there with me and nothing came. No anger, no sadness, nothing. As I waited to see what was next, I felt this huge inflow of love, and my hand started writing as if she was writing to me. It said, "I too can wear a mask and play a role. While I never loved you the way you wanted me to in life, I am here with you now and my arms are around you whenever you need them." I lost it and bawled my eyes out.

Now whenever I think of my mom I feel only love and appreciation for the role she played in moving me forward.

If there are letters that need to be written to your parent, whether they are alive or not, write them. Don't give the letter to them. That is not what this is about. Writing the letters is not to set them straight, although it may feel that way. They are for you to get clean with you. Period.

If you are wrapped up in some drama with anyone in your life, puke it out on paper. Then you will know exactly where you are with yourself. You will see on paper where you may be stuck in rage, righteousness, or are acting like a dog chewing on a bone unwilling to let something go. You may be caught in a victim story; it doesn't matter what the drama is about. The letters are for you to release those stored up emotional hairballs so you can move on with your life. You may even see your part in the drama and be compelled to apologize. I know in my heart I would have been a lot lazier if it wasn't for my mom.

I hope you will receive the gift of an honest emotional release like I did.

Is there a letter that needs to be written to someone in your life for YOU to get clean?

★ TIPS

- Call in the essence of the person with whom you wish to get clean. Feel their presence.
- Be fully present. Cultivate awareness and ground in your body.
- Sit at the paper with pen poised and just write whatever comes up.

- Let your emotions fly.
- Don't judge anything. Get petty. Get it out.
- Crumple the letter and throw it away.
- Keep writing weekly or as often as you are called to until you feel you have expressed and released what is inside of you.
- Do not hold onto your emotions or pick them back up after you let them out. Use the emotional processing tools from Chapter 5.

The situation was what it was. It is over. You can make peace with it if you are willing. You can receive the gift that situation gave you, if you are willing. Are you willing?

Letter writing is a great tool to use when someone came into your journey and you still feel something is incomplete. Letter writing can be done before a journey, after a journey, or just because it calls to you.

Word Cloud

Are you artistic? Have AI take the top ten words in your journal and create a word cloud image. This is an image composed of words in which the size of each word indicates the importance of it. The larger words are used more and are the primary words to integrate.

Mirror Work

One of the most common things I see over and over again is people trying to integrate self-love. In the medicine space they feel overwhelming feelings of love for themselves but then when they return home the old patterns of self-flagellation can come creeping back in.

Taking time alone in front of a mirror to get to know yourself is very helpful in building self-trust and integrating self-love. Mirror work is weirdly confronting, extremely intimidating, and a bit embarrassing. It is also profoundly healing.

Mirror work tests your ability to be with yourself. Only when you can be comfortable in your skin can you be in authentic relationship with the world around you. If you're not happy with you, or you rely on that other person to make you happy, you may manipulate the relationship. There might be conditions, expectations, or attachments. It's good to spend time alone. Not to be lonely, but to be comfortable with yourself.

Mirror work is the antidote for self-deception, and humans are so prone to deceiving themselves!

Mirror work is a method originally developed by author Louise Hay as a way of getting in touch with the inner self. The primary purpose of mirror work is to develop self-acceptance, self-care, and a more meaningful relationship with yourself. This is a tool you can use when you ask HOW do I integrate directives such as, "Love yourself. Trust yourself. Just be with you."

In front of the mirror, there is no hiding. You may be able to hide things from others but you can't hide them from yourself. In front of the mirror, you catch an intimate and sometimes painful glimpse into the relationship you have with yourself. A mirror reflects immediately where you are stuck with yourself and where you are open and accepting. It clearly shows you what thoughts you have about yourself and what you would like to change.

Mirror work can make us feel initially uneasy because it exposes our inner critic in plain daylight. Suddenly everything we feel about ourselves, that we might not be aware of, comes to the surface. And if you haven't developed a compassionate relationship with yourself, you might be prone to believing all the nastiness with which your thinking mind or inner critic thrashes you.

When you do mirror work, you might notice strong feelings coming up. Sometimes you may feel sad, emotional, or tender without knowing exactly why. This often happens because you are seeing a younger version of yourself—the part of you that learned how to survive, feel, and make sense of the world early in life. This is often called the inner child, but it isn't separate from you. It's simply a real part of your own experience showing itself.

As you look into the mirror, you may notice these feelings rising to the surface. Nothing has gone wrong. You don't need to fix anything or make the feelings disappear. Just staying with yourself—breathing, noticing, and allowing what you feel, can be deeply healing. When you give yourself permission to feel without judgment, those younger parts naturally relax and feel safer. Over time, this helps you feel more whole, grounded, and at ease with who you are.

You may also experience a connection to your soul or spirit. The eyes are the windows to the soul as the old saying goes, and mirror work can give you direct access to that deeper part of you. Sometimes you may need to work through sadness, anger, insecurities, and self-resentments before you can sense your deeper inner presence emerge.

When you do mirror work:
- Play some calm soothing spa-like music with no vocals.
- Don't have anything on your agenda and be free of distractions.
- Prepare some nourishing meals.
- Sit in front of the mirror for long periods of time.
- Allow yourself to feel your emotions fully. Use the 5

Step Dissipater for emotional mastery that you learned in Chapter 5.

- Trust that you can handle whatever arises with the skills you have learned so far.

When you do mirror work, accept and acknowledge the emotions that come to the surface. It's normal and okay to feel angry or upset. If you feel the need to cry, let yourself cry. The pain of all the negative thoughts and limiting beliefs stuffed down in the past may come bubbling to the surface. Often the emotions we feel during mirror work are from childhood, particularly if they are intense.

You may witness the angry part of yourself that is all pissed off because you haven't done what you said you would do or you just can't stop doing, doing, doing. Allow yourself to experience this anger. You may experience a wide variety of emotions. For example, if you feel ugly, allow yourself to feel ugly. Don't resist it, but don't wallow in it either. If you feel uncomfortable in your own presence, you can affirm, "It's okay to feel uncomfortable." Just be with whatever arises.

You may witness shyness. You may witness the hurt aspects of yourself that you inflicted. Many of us treat ourselves much worse than we treat other people. It is a normal part of mirror work for the need to apologize to arise.

Be gentle with yourself. It's very important that we forgive ourselves. You may learn that given all of your negative beliefs about yourself you've done the best you possibly could. In the end, you may even come to realize that there's nothing to forgive, seeing how you were hardwired by your parents and those around you.

Don't deny anything. The point isn't to be disingenuous; the aim is to allow whatever is present to be there. Self-love and compassion may just naturally bubble to the surface over time. So much healing work can be done by simply looking at yourself in the mirror.

Mirror work is the number one integration tool I recommend for integrating self-trust and self-love.

Anchoring

Anchoring tools can also help you embody the information revealed to you in the medicine space. Anchoring involves repetition and consciously pondering the information in such a way that the mind and body adapt to the information so it becomes your new normal. Here are some examples of ways to anchor a revelation:

1. Practice Embodied Repetition

Repeat the revelation while engaging the body. For example, speaking an insight out loud while walking, dancing, or doing the dishes. The mantra you created earlier is an example of a way to repeat an important revelation while you go about your day.

Another example of embodied repetition is pairing a specific posture or gesture with a concept. For example, placing your hand over your heart while affirming self-love. If the king, queen or goddess came into your journey to nudge you out of feelings of powerlessness, consider taking on a superhero posture to embody and practice setting boundaries.

You can put a pile of paperclips on your desk, and every time you notice them, move one from one side of your desk to the other while you remember your revelations and feel the insights land in your body. Anything you can do to return to the revelation while doing something with your body is a positive thing.

2. Breathe in Your Revelation

Use your breath to anchor a revelation into the nervous

system. On the inhale, mentally repeat the phrase that came to you in the medicine space. Such as, "I am so right here. I am so present." Then on the exhale, imagine it settling deeper into your cells. Using your breath in this way regulates the autonomic nervous system, making the body more receptive and calmer—ideal for integration.

3. Walk and Speak Your Revelation

If you are a mover and a shaker and don't like to be still, you can repeat your revelation aloud while you walk. For example, "I trust my inner guidance."

4. Use Touch to Anchor a Revelation

Each time you say a revelation to yourself or out loud, press your thumb and middle finger together. This helps you builds a physical trigger for recall. For example, if you experience anxiety or fear and in the medicine space and you said repeatedly, "I am safe. I am free," say this while you engage the two fingers. You can use this touch point to dissipate anxiety or fear when it arises, helping you embody safety and freedom.

5. Shift Your Posture

Did the medicine reveal something empowering? Stand tall, press your shoulders back, angle your chin up. Hold the posture for 60 seconds while mentally repeating the revelation. Postures of openness, joy, humility, and quiet presence can be powerful integration and embodiment tools.

6. Grounding and Repeating a Revelation

Place your feet firmly on the ground. Say the revelation while pressing your heels into the floor. Feel the earth below you, feel your feet or walk barefoot as you contemplate your revelations. For example, "I belong here. My gifts matter. I matter. I am loved."

7. Anchor a Revelation into an Object

Some people love this. I prefer anchoring a revelation into

the body directly but sometimes we need tools to remind us to get something into the body. That is where the power of an object comes in. Assign a revelation to an object (like a stone, a ring or bracelet). Every time you touch it, recall the revelation and feel the feelings it invokes.

Anchoring the Abstract: In the medicine space there are many self-realizations or directives that can seem abstract. Integrating the abstract can sometimes be challenging. For example, common directives I see are "let go of control," "let go of fear," "let go of the past," and when the person returns from the medicine space they ask, "How do I do this? How do I let go?" If we don't know what that feels like in the body or have a clear action to take, it can stay fuzzy and frustrating.

As an embodied experience letting go becomes real when you actually feel it happen in the body. Take a moment right now and:

- Soften your jaw.
- Drop in your shoulders.
- Take a deep breath in. Pause. Release the breath with a sigh. Pause.

Did you feel your muscles relax?

You just did it! You know you let go when you feel an outward flow of energy leave the body and the muscles soften. If you can relax your jaw and pause between breaths, you can let go. Practice letting go many, many times throughout the day. You will find it amazing what chooses to leave your body with the out breath. This is how your programming from the past or those repetitive ways of thinking or being can be released.

You are practicing letting go as a skill, not just a concept. For example, when you inhale you may feel the grip of whatever it is you need to let go of. When you exhale you feel the release. It is tangible and experienced. You can also watch to see what softens within you as you do this. So, while letting go starts as an idea, it becomes real the moment you feel the shift in your body, your breath, or your actions. It's less about effort, more about allowing.

Here are some more ways to work with embodying the most common revelations:

1. "Just Let Go" Action Step: Every time you feel tension or the need to control rising, take a deep inhale, raise your shoulders, then exhale fully and drop them. Whisper: "Let go." Let it be an embodied command.

The fear that arises when we consider letting go of an old way, whether it is depression, anxiety, control, judgment, guilt, unworthiness, or fear itself, can be intense. The first time you try to let go of something, the mind might come in and tell you that you are not safe to let it go. It might question who you will be if you let it go. Reassure your mind that you are safe. Tell it to chill out. You're healing, remember?

2. "Just Be" Action Step: Set a 1-minute timer, sit or stand still, feel your breath and body without doing anything. Say softly: "Being is enough."

Humans are so busy going, going, going, and doing, doing, doing that stopping for a moment can be extremely uncomfortable. We have become human doings not human beings. When you stop for just 1 minute and live, it gives you the courage to try for 2 minutes next time. When you stop, all the things you have been avoiding may come to the surface. Let them come. Write down in your journal what comes to the surface when you allow yourself to just be. It's ok to be uncomfortable. Cry, get mad, feel anxious. Let it move through you and out of you without attaching any story.

3. "Nothing Matters" Action Step: When caught in overthinking, step outside and look up at the sky for 30 seconds.

Ask, "What really matters right now?" Let spaciousness and zooming out remind you of what really matters to you.

This is a common revelation for people who love to put meaning on things or attaching things as identity. It doesn't matter how much money you have, the size of your house, or the car you drive. All the things that we think matter don't. It doesn't matter how clean your house is, what you look like. All the things you do so people will like you don't matter. On your death bed you will never say, "Geez, I wish I would have had more stuff." Nope. It's peace, love, kindness, and joy we all wish for and think the stuff will give it to us. But it doesn't. This is a revelation that is asking you to reorient your priorities. It is asking you to stop, zoom out, and consider what matters, then experience those things. Don't just think about them; experience them.

4. "Love More" Action Step: Choose one moment each day to place your hand on your heart while making eye contact with someone (even yourself in the mirror). Say silently: "I am safe to love." You can take this one step further by hugging someone and telling them you love them.

Often what is revealed is how much we love those around us and that we need to express it more. Tools to help you open to love and express love are very important. It takes courage to love. We fear that if we express our love we will get rejected so we create these walls around our hearts to keep us safe from disappointment or rejection. While this may seem safe, it limits the love and joy we experience in life. So, know, in the beginning expressing love is awkward and uncomfortable until you acclimate or integrate what it means to love and be loved and express love. Be awkward. Be uncomfortable. Love is worth the expression.

Reframing

Other common realizations and directives include: I'm okay, just be, you are safe, let go, relax, chill out, heal, trust, just breathe, I'm free, stop thinking, open, receive, how can I serve? Be yourself, release it all. Just be. I am that I am.

Core medicine space realizations can be so deeply true and yet are often met with resistance when it's time to live them. Reframing is a powerful bridge from "I can't" or "I don't know how" to "Maybe I can try it this way."

Here are some examples of how gentle, grounded reframing can help integrate some of these insights or directives when the mind resists:

Medicine Message: "Just be."

Resistance: "I don't know how to just be."

Reframe: "Maybe I can I sit for 30 seconds and feel the air on my skin. That's being. Just being doesn't mean doing nothing—it means not fighting this moment."

Medicine Message: "Let go."

Resistance: "I can't. It's too hard. I don't know what that means."

Reframe: "What if letting go is just one exhale? Perhaps I don't have to let go of everything. I can just loosen my grip a little right now."

Medicine Message: "You are safe."

Resistance: "I don't feel safe."

Reframe: "Am I safe? Hmm...is anyone going to hit me over the head or run me over? Maybe I can consider I am safe?"

Medicine Message: "Trust."

Resistance: "But I've been hurt. I don't know how to trust."

Reframe: "Maybe I don't have to trust the future—just this present moment."

Medicine Message: "Heal."
Resistance: "I don't know how. It's too much."
Reframe: "My body knows what to do. Maybe healing just means being honest with what hurts."

Medicine Message: "I'm okay."
Resistance: "But I don't feel okay."
Reframe: "Maybe I am still okay underneath the feelings. Can I be okay for now?"

Medicine Message: "Just breathe."
Resistance: "It's not enough. Breathing won't fix this."
Reframe: "Breathing won't fix it, but it will support me while I walk through it."

Medicine Message: "How can I serve?"
Resistance: "I don't know how."
Reframe: "Service might be as simple as being kind to myself and others today."

Medicine Message: "Be yourself."
Resistance: "I don't know who I am."
Reframe: "Maybe being myself means being honest about not knowing yet. Maybe I can explore who I am without needing to define it today."

These reframes honor the resistance without making it wrong. They offer a path forward through the doorway of small, doable shifts that can bring the revelation into your daily life.

Future Forecasting and Imagination

Future forecasting is taking a revelation and using your imagination to explore what life would be like if you integrated it.

Olympic and world-class athletes know very well when they use their imagination and direct their daydreams and visualize themselves performing an event and winning, it increases the potential of them actually achieving it. There are numerous studies that prove those who imagine the end result are most likely to achieve it. This is future forecasting a positive end result.

If world-class athletes use imagination to obtain their dreams, why can't you use it to integrate?

How is Imagination Used?

You could use imagination to integrate many things, such as:

- If your partner, friend, or family member is sabotaging you, and the revelation was to just love them, you could imagine how you will stay in a loving peaceful state regardless of their attitude.
- You could imagine yourself saying "no" with grace, kindness and self-confidence if it was revealed you need more boundaries.
- If you are uncertain about life purpose, and something like "Your purpose is in your being" was revealed to you, you could imagine what that would be like; to not do, but to be your purpose.
- You can imagine loving who you are and what it looks like to express that love to others.
- You could imagine what life would look like if you implemented your directive to play more.

- If you were safe to be, do, or have anything, what would that be like?
- If it was a rough journey and you got tossed you could imagine how you would behave in the space if that happened again.

Using your imagination helps the mind acclimate to new information. Anything revealed to you in the medicine space can be played with using imagination to get the mind on board. Anything!

How Imagination Works

Okay, so how does this work? Your brain truly doesn't know the difference between what's real and imagined. It will encode what you visualize as a real memory, and it only takes 30 seconds!

Think of it this way, when you imagine your favorite food, you salivate. There is a clear, tangible physical reaction there. The brain doesn't know the difference between you imagining that you are eating your favorite food and you actually eating it. When you imagine your favorite food, the taste, smells, and texture, you create a situation with your brain that increases your chance of getting that food by 100 percent. You are 100 percent more likely to take the 'inspired action' of going to get that food.

So why not imagine yourself as you saw yourself in that journey? Unconditionally loved, connected to all things, and completely at peace and worthy just as you are. Yep. Just as you are.

The cool thing about imagination, is that you already have a reference point, a remembering of what you are wanting to incorporate or embody from your journey. When you activate the memory and imagine yourself walking through the world as you saw yourself in your journey, you are more likely to adapt to it and integrate that new way of being.

The more you imagine, (or remember in the case of your journey) the more your subconscious mind believes that this is 'really happening'. Using this method you can change your relationship with yourself from one of self-loathing to self-love. You can change your whole self-image using this method. You can also imagine what it would be like to not have a self-image or identity, but to express as an individuation.

How You Do It

Before you get cracking at this, it is important to know that you have to believe it to be effective. If using imagination to integrate isn't working for you, then you're missing one of the following elements:

1. **You must know exactly what you're integrating:** Imagination only works when you know in exquisite detail what you want to integrate. Take a moment now and remember as many details as you can regarding what was revealed to you in your last journey. If it was unpleasant and you purged, remember how you felt afterwards empty of it. Explore that emptiness. Is it really empty? Imagine how that revelation can enhance your life, give you, peace, assist your ability to just be, or quiet your mind. If the journey was wonderful can you imagine bringing more wonderful to your life?

2. **Desire:** You have to sincerely want to integrate it. Put your hand over your heart and ask yourself, "Do I really want this?" If the answer is no, reframe it and play with it until it feels good to you or let it go. You may not be ready to integrate. That's okay. Use imagination

to explore what you do want and can do.

3. **Belief:** You have to believe it can happen for the revelation to be integrated. If not, you are in conflict. "I want to release this need to control but don't know who I would be without it." Use imagination, "What would it look like if I let go of the little things first?"

4. **You must feel worthy to receive it:** This is the most common missing ingredient: feeling worthy enough to actually accept and integrate what was revealed. You actually have to receive it in your imagination.

As children we learned early that we are judged by our performance. Whether we cleaned our rooms, did well in school, or shared our toys, these actions are what may have deemed us worthy. Only if we fulfill certain criteria that are set by our parents and the world around us did we feel worthy to receive.

When we grow up, we are taught that going to college and getting a good job is something we need to achieve to be worthy. If we don't have those papers, we are somehow unworthy.

Then, there is the all-pervasive need to look good and not look bad. To have the perfect body, get in shape, and eat the perfect diet so then we can be worthy of receiving love and acceptance. If we somehow manage to convey the illusion of perfection, or achieve these goals, the next goal is to make more money, be more successful, and get the newest cell phone. The list of things to acquire to be worthy goes on and on. It never stops. There is always a newer car, a bigger house, more money to make, and something about our bodies to be dissatisfied with.

Using this old and outdated methodology to measure worthiness keeps us running in circles, forever chasing some lofty goal. We never stop to take a breath or to feel into our true presence—the I Am that lies within each and every one of us. So, let's bust that belief right now.

You are worthy, every single bit of you, just as you are.

Let that sink in.

Okay. Let's continue.

Focus on the Outcome: When you practice imagination, your focus must be on the outcome of what integrating a revelation looks and feels like. Not the process or how it will unfold. Let's say in the medicine you saw that it is time to sell your company and be free, and you experienced that freedom. Your focus must be on the feeling of having it already done and the feelings it invoked. So, as you imagine your company already sold, call on those feelings and that outcome and trust that when you set your intention to do something it is done. This means being willing to shuck and jive if something other than what you expect comes along.

Here's another example: Let's say in ceremony you self-realized. You experienced yourself and the 'I Am' presence permeated in through and all around you. You feel you can finally say, "I know who I am. I know what I am." Then you land and have to go to work on Monday. You can use imagination to explore doing that job and living your life from this new expanded perspective.

There is a Zen Buddhist proverb that says, "Before enlightenment, chop wood, carry water. After enlightenment, chop wood, carry water." This emphasizes that enlightenment doesn't change the fundamental realities of life, and that even after achieving spiritual awakening, one still needs to engage in everyday tasks. It highlights the importance of mindfulness and presence in daily activities, regardless of one's state of mind.

Here's another example of how imagination can be used

to integrate: You set your intention and go into the medicine space and got spanked. Maybe you took too much, forgot to invoke Sanctuary, and could not stay grounded. Maybe in a group ceremony you got loud and interrupted everyone's process. Use your imagination to imagine yourself next time breathing, grounding, calling on your guides, invoking sanctuary, and maintaining sovereignty while you build a relationship with the medicine.

Imagination is awesome! In many ways it is how we create.

Take Inspired Action: When you use your imagination you may at some point be inspired to take action. Physical action is required to successfully embody many realizations. The key to taking action is to take only inspired action. You will know it when it hits you. You will be compelled to get up and take action. When this happens, get up and take action! Say, "I love you." Smile. "Kiss your partner." Give words of love and appreciation to your parents. Reassure yourself that it's okay to let go of control. Those were your directives, weren't they?

Gratitude: When things start to line up, acknowledge the process. The significance of practicing gratitude is well known. It is the energy of receiving.

Really Feel it: You have to feel like you've already achieved your directive. Bring your imagination to life as if watching a mental movie. Concentrate your thoughts with laser-like precision and indulge all your senses. Really imagine what it would be like if you already completed your directive. Savor it! Get so immersed in your imagination, that you give yourself goosebumps. The more goosebumps you get, the more effective this process will be!

Feel All Your Emotions: Many people think integrating what you want is focusing only on the good feelings. This is not true. We must allow ourselves to feel all our emotions. Even the uncomfortable ones. So, if sorrow, sadness, or grief arise, let them come...and let them go. Allow yourself to be a human who feels deeply. Often as we allow ourselves to experience joy, love, and deep presence, they bring the gunk of the past to the surface to be released. This is part of the healing and cleansing process.

Revisit It Throughout Your Day: Reconnect with your revelation at regular intervals throughout your day. It doesn't have to be long; 30 seconds is more than enough to let insights mature through revisitation. Re-reading, re-speaking, re-sensing the revelations can reveal new aspects you hadn't seen before.

Remove Desire: Wanting and longing will only get you more wanting and longing. Once you align with your revelation, consider it done. Don't create a separation between you and the revelation. That will prevent you from embodying it. Imagine it now, in fullness and get on with your day knowing it is done.

Creation Basics

Let's talk briefly about the basics of creation. This is important because after a medicine ceremony is the perfect time to align to your visions in order to bring them into the manifest world. When you understand that on the level of consciousness all matter is frequency and this frequency manifests in different ways, you understand the process of creation. Nothing can be created on this plane without a conscious intention to bring it forth. As mentioned, a conscious intention is a choice and for it to manifest you must put some emotion behind it. You must believe in your intention and know like you know it is done.

There are three aspects to how we create.

1. Intention: A choice or decision to experience or express something. Don't limit or pigeonhole yourself by intending to do or experience things you don't enjoy or something you think you should choose based upon dogma or doctrine. Often we choose unconsciously without realizing it. Remember an intention is a combination of attention/focus, emotion and action in coherence. So, what are you intending for your life? What would you like to focus on, feel good about and take action towards?

Note: Remember that an intention is a decree. Mean what you say and say what you mean and know that you are the master of your life and you do it through intention. Remember the movie with Harry Potter? For his magic wand to work he had to come into alignment with his intention. He needed to believe in himself and what he wanted to bring forth. If he didn't, the wand did not work. Pretend you are Harry Potter with a magic wand and have some fun with this! Truly, what is your heart's desire?

2. Self Awareness: Once you are solid and have set your intention, you can then cultivate awareness so you know whether you are in alignment with your intention or not. You will know by how you feel. If you are in alignment, you feel good. If you feel lack, self-doubt, if you feel separate from your choice or there is fear in your field, you are out of alignment. Self-awareness is key.

3. Vibrational Alignment: When through awareness you find yourself out of alignment with your choice, bring yourself back into alignment. Again, you know based on feeling; feelings always come first and mechanics second. If you feel confident and in your knowing that you are on path to fulfilling your intention, you are probably in alignment. If you feel lack, self-doubt, or separate from your desire, fear, or ego is active in your field, you are most likely not.

You bring yourself back into alignment by shifting focus, consciously choosing to change your feeling state, and take any action that is congruent with your intention. You can cultivate awareness, repeat your mantra, process an emotion, revisit a truth card, listen to your journey music, or shift focus to something that feels good. Imagine that, changing how you feel just because you can. These are examples of what coming into alignment with your intention may look like.

You have a magic wand, and just like Harry Potter, believing in yourself (coming into alignment with your intention) is key.

Important: It is your intention that determines what is created. Once you choose, stay focused on that choice, not the lack of it and don't change your choice, that confuses the universe and you may get a mixed response.

If you choose as a result of a medicine experience to let go of selfishness and release fear, the last thing you want to do is focus on fear and selfishness. No. Focus on the feelings that releasing those things will give you.

When you go into the medicine and experience yourself as loved beyond conditions, in that moment the medicine transforms low vibe emotions, such as unworthiness or loneliness. After you land, you can do the same thing simply by remembering the experience and using imagination to stay above any discord or drama by constantly reactivating that feeling of unconditional love.

The issue most people have is they align to separation between where they think they are and what was revealed. "I experienced this thing, but now I don't have this thing. I want this thing." That just gets them more lack and more wanting.

It is important to emphasize that more abundance can't be created. It is inherent. It just is and already exists. When you intend abundance and say, "I am choosing abundance." This is when you have to align to the abundance that is here right now. As long as you are in the "I want to, I need to, I should or shouldn't" you are screwed, because you are keeping yourself separate from what is. But when you rest home in your true nature, you come home to the abundance and love that is already there.

When someone shares that they are awakening and experiencing more peace and love and want more abundance, what often needs to shift is their language. The wanting, the calling in, the belief in separation from abundance is what creates the lack. Believe me, I know! I've spent years stuck in the story of lack.

- I don't have it: scarcity and separation.
- I want to create it: I have to work for it to exhaustion. No.

Abundance is. It is what exists in the absence of the ideas of I don't have it, don't deserve it, shouldn't have it, it's bad, guilt, shame, or whatever programming that happened.

We do the same thing with health. You can buy all the green juice, do all the red light therapy but as long as you are keeping yourself separate from health, as long as there is a belief in separation between who you really are as whole, complete and healed, and who you think you are as unhealthy, true health will elude you.

We live in a world of story and a history of not enough and separation. When you let go of the old programming the body can heal and you may experience abundance, health, and vitality simply by recognizing what is already here.

I think it was St. Francis of Assisi who said something akin to, "The you that you are looking for is the you that is there in the absence of the you that you think you are."

Another way to put it is to release what we are not and acclimate to who we are. We create the separation between where we are and what we think we need and in the process we create lack and scarcity.

But it is all right here. It's like there's always somewhere to get to until you realize there isn't.

As long as you think there's somewhere to get to you will be in separation. That's okay. True compassion is to let everyone be exactly where they are now. If you don't know your path, then not knowing your path is your path now. There's a suffering that comes with, "No, I should know my path. What's my purpose?"

What if you could allow yourself to receive what's already here beyond fear, anxiety, or neediness?

Can you imagine it? Creation just for the sake of creating, not because you have to or need anything, but because you choose to align to what is already within you.

That's undistorted creation at its finest!

Let's continue and explore more tools found in your integration tool box.

Pattern Interrupts

When an old pattern arises, see it for what it is then exhale it out, swipe left, flick it off your shoulder, do anything you can to face it and let it go. Don't ignore it or avoid it. Face it. Pause. Watch it dissolve. Then redirect your focus to the new program you wish to install and activate that. This is especially effective post retreat.

For instance, let's say your partner is standing at the sink doing dishes and you have the desire to go up behind them and hug them. Fear creeps in. You recognize an old pattern of fear of rejection. You face the fear, watch it dissipate, then flick it off your shoulder, and go in for the love anyway. You have just interrupted an old pattern and began the process of creating a new one.

Pattern interrupts can be of great value to you while you integrate. As you work with your revelations you may be tempted to create meaning where there is none. Maybe you saw a Roman helmet come in and you have no idea what it means. If you have a pattern of identifying with things, you may want to attach a story that you were a Roman soldier in a past life. This creates a false identity that could take you down a rabbit hole of false identity and significance.

The greatest tool for pattern interrupts is truth. Plain and simple. Ask, "Is that true? Was I really a Roman soldier in a past life?" Then wait and see what drops in.

Grounding my clients in truth is one of my super skills. I learned how to do this when I read Byron Katie's book, *Loving What Is*. This book is extraordinarily valuable for those doing medicine work because it is way too easy to get delusional.

After a medicine journey people might say things like, "Nothing happened. I got nothing from the experience" or they will say things like, "I'm here to save the world," or "I am the only one." People love to create story and add meaning where there is none and Katie's methodology can get to the core of the insight in four simple and easy questions. I highly recommend her book.

Here are the four questions briefly to get you started:

Byron Katie's The Work

"The Work" consists of four questions and a turnaround. The four questions are:

1. Is it true?
2. Can I absolutely know that it's true?

3. How do I feel when I think that thought?

4. Who would I be, what would I experience without the thought?

The turnaround is a way of experiencing the opposite of the thought that one is believing. For example, the revelation "Love more" can be scary and the thought, I am not safe to love may arise. This can be turned around to "I am safe to love."

Using this methodology you can ponder how each turnaround might be truer than the original thought. The only way to know The Work is just to do it.

Take a moment now and write down the top negative, self-defeating thought or limiting belief your mind likes to thrash you with. Feel free to get petty and just dump it all out.

Now, hold that thought up to some scrutiny. Put it into quarantine and explore with curiosity these questions:

1. "Is what you have written down true?" Try not to get too mental about this question. This is an experiential exercise of finding the truth, not a mental exercise. If you believe it to be true, hold onto it and continue with the following questions.

2. Because our minds can be devious, we need to ask this a second time: "Can you ABSOLUTELY know that it's true?" Don't get caught up in the truth-ness of it. If you wrote down, "I am fat." Ask, "What does it mean to be fat?" and you will get at the heart of your self-defeating thought or limiting belief.

3. "How do you feel when you believe or think that thought?"

4. "Who would you be, or what would you experience without the thought?"

INTEGRATION: Really take your time here. Who would you be without that thought you wrote down? True or not true, who would you be? What would you experience?

These questions give you a beautiful glimpse of what lives behind your thoughts. When you explore your thoughts with curiosity, practice discernment, and do The Work, you will have many aha moments, and finally say, "OMG, I get it!"

Now experience the turnaround. This involves projection, judgment, and opposition. While we like to think we don't judge, we all do it and often. What we judge in others is usually a reflection of ourselves, and if what we judge does not exist within us, our judgment is telling us that we are still judging.

What turnaround is available to you? Think in oppositions or redirect the thought back at yourself in a different way.

Examples of Turnarounds: I am not worthy becomes I am worthy. He is a jerk becomes I am a jerk, or he is not a jerk. I am not lovable becomes I am lovable. I can't do this becomes I can do this.

The Revelation Integration Method, again, is about receiving information regarding yourself in any medicine space. These self-realizations, self-knowings, self-exploration, and self-reflections are extremely important, and being able to discern what is true and what is not is paramount in your ability to move beyond unhelpful patterns.

Always be on the lookout for delusion. Always ask, "Is this true? Does it serve me? Or is it a distraction?"

If you had a hard journey and the layers revealed to you about yourself are crunchy and hard to face, you must face them if you want to move beyond them. Asking the question, "Is this true?" can humble you when you need humbling. It can temper you when you need tempering. It can also help you move through shadow and integrate your divinity. Facing shadow is the way.

The truth helps you face distortions so you can move

beyond them. The truth helps you integrate those aspects that you might shy away from. The truth enables us to grow and learn and align to broader perspectives.

REFLECTIVE MOMENT: It is important to question truth. I was once told that a truth is only true if it is always true. A truth does not change. Ponder this for yourself. You may have your truth, and Sally may have her truth, but if that truth changes, is it true?

Artful Integration

For those reading this who love artistic expression, there are many ways to integrate artistically. You can create a mandala, paint a picture, create a crystal grid, or draw the sacred geometry you saw. If you love to be creative, go for it! One of my clients wrote a poem in the medicine space, another wrote a song. Someone I know wrote a one man show! The sky is the limit! Art is a wonderful tool that can aid integration.

Integrating an Open Heart

Often when people have experienced an open heart and pure unconditional love in the medicine space, they come out so full of love all they want to do is share with their beloveds how much they care for them. Then when the fairy dust wears off they may find themselves in this awkward space of, "I don't know how to do this. I don't know how to maintain this." It feels really weird because the ego kicks back in and tells them, "Hey! What are you doing? Why is your heart so open? It's not safe. Shut it down! Red alert!" Integrating an open heart takes courage. It's awkward. Uncomfortable. And fear of rejection is a thing. Here's how I gave it a go:

STORYTIME: *I made myself the promise once that I would* *keep my heart open for the whole day, no matter what. It was during the summer and I was grocery shopping, walking through the produce department and I was smelling all the fruits and all the vegetables. I was practically making love to the vegetables! The produce manager noticed me and said, "Hey, did you see the black watermelons out front?"*

And I said, "No, are they really black?"

And he said, "Come on, I'll show you."

So, he took me out front. The watermelons were this deep dark green on the outside and bright red on the inside. He told me they were really sweet and said, "Do you want one?"

And I said, "Yes!"

He picked one out for me and asked, "Have you tasted the peaches yet this year?"

And I said no.

He said, "Come on!"

So, we went inside, he cut open a peach and he handed it to me, and it was so good, and my heart was just wide open. I was having the time of my life. And then all of a sudden, he said, "And the Rainier Cherries are in too…"

Out of nowhere my heart shut down and my mind created a story that he was going to ask me out and I would have to reject him. "Run," said my mind, "run!" Immediately I said, "No, thank you. I'm good. I really have to go." And beelined it out of the produce department. As soon as I got out, I took a couple of deep breaths, and I said to myself, "Dani, don't be a coward. You go back there and you keep your heart open." So I went back. I went up to him and I said, "I just want you to know how much I appreciate the work that you do and the joy that you bring to your job."

And he launched into a 15-minute diatribe about how he had nine lives and had lost three of them already. And the whole

*time he was talking, my heart was opening and closing! My
mind kept saying, "Oh, he's going to ask you out! You're going
to have to reject him."*

*Finally, he said, "Well, thank you so much. I've enjoyed talking
to you, but I really have to get back to work." And he went on
his own way.*

He never asked me out. I freaked out for nothing.

My point for telling this story is to give you an example
of what living with an open heart can be like in the beginning.
This example has helped many of my clients have the courage
to try it themselves. The heart can be opened on command.
Through intention. Try it right now by thinking of something
you love. Soften your forehead, release your belly, and think of
love. Did you feel it?

CHALLENGE: Spend the entire day with an open
heart. This doesn't mean you have to say yes to
everything; it doesn't mean you don't discern what
you will or will not do. If you say no to something you
say no with the qualities and feelings of openness and
kindness. When you say yes, you say it with openness
and kindness.

Right after a medicine experience is the most valuable
time for people to acclimate to having an open heart. When
your heart has been blown open and you have experienced
unconditional love, there is nothing like it. This is the time
for you to maintain that openness, to acclimate to love and an
open heart.

Sometimes an integration tool isn't an exercise or a
meditation. Sometimes it is a process of implementing an
insight in ways that are right for you.

Let's close out this chapter with one last tool. One last exercise that can bring clarity.

Your New Set Point

Imagine with me that you have journaled like crazy about a medicine experience. You organized the revelations into main themes, pulled the self-realizations and the directives, and created truth cards with action steps on the back. You made a mantra and maybe wrote a letter to someone you love or want to get clean with. If you were really gutsy maybe you did some mirror work. You went through all the revelations with a fine toothcomb and you pondered them, you contemplated them, and you know what is complete and what is not complete. You now have your new set point.

Congratulations!

At this point the medicine may call you back. Beckoning you to take one more step up that spiral staircase of evolution. If this is the case, take what feels incomplete and use that to create your intentions for the next ceremony. There is a reason it's called medicine. It is there to help you move forward, to get complete with what feels incomplete.

If you feel called to do so, repeat the exercise you did to establish your starting baseline. Then you can compare where you were with where you are now. It is a fabulous way to track your progress and the activity of the mind.

For 15 minutes do the cultivating awareness exercise I gave you earlier (become aware of sounds in the room, your body, release your belly, tune into your heartbeat) and then pay very close attention to your thoughts. When a thought about the past pops in, write that thought down in the column under the past. When you find yourself judging or observing the now moment, put that in the middle column. When you find yourself fantasizing about the future place that fantasy in the future column. When your mind is quiet and calm do nothing. Write down any negative thought patterns, limiting beliefs, habitual ways of being, or egoic patterns that arise.

Past Memory	Present Judgment or Observation	Future Fantasy

Compare your results with your starting baseline. Is your mind quieter? Are there more moments of no thought? This information can go into your intention journal so you can track your progress.

You are using your intention journal, aren't you?

Let's do a quick recap of all the tools you have learned so far.

Your Toolbox Recap

Mental Mastery Tools
Cultivating Awareness
Truth Cards
Byron Katie's The Work
The Ego Interrupt
Mantras
Anchoring
Reframing
Future Forecasting and Imagination

Emotional Mastery Tools
Cultivating Awareness
Emotional Mastery The 5 Step Dissipater
Emotions Arising Strategy
Journeying Without Medicine
Letter Writing
Mirror Work

Physical Body Mastery
Cultivating Awareness
Body Response Awareness Exercise
Letting Go/Relaxation Exercise
Grounding Exercises
Receptivity Exercise
Journeying Without Medicine

Tools for Personal Choice, Sovereignty & Relating
Cultivating Awareness
Boundaries Redefined
Expectations Vs. Agreements

Future Forecasting and Imagination
Creation Basics

Spiritual Mastery and Integration

Cultivating Awareness
Cultivating Intuition
Sanctuary
Journeying Without Medicine
Integrating an Open Heart

At some point you will be asked to let go of all tools. But that's a story for another book.

For now, know that integration occurs when an insight changes your behavior. Integration happens when the revelation settles into the body; when understanding no longer needs rehearsal and when nothing needs to be done to remember because the system has reorganized. Integration shows up as a steadier nervous system, quieter compulsions, different choices made without effort and fewer internal contradictions.

Integration is the rewiring that prevents collapse back to habit.

When someone knows how to integrate, they can take that into their daily life. For instance, imagine you are at a grocery store, you have an interaction with a grocery clerk and you get triggered. When you get home, you can ponder the event to see which layers of yourself were revealed to you during that interaction. How did you respond to the situation? Are you happy with the quality of your response? If your emotional response was not equal to or way out of proportion to the event, your ego was most likely triggered and a story was created. Sit with that, ponder it, let the mind see it from a different perspective. Take responsibility for it. Learn from it. What wisdom did you gain? This is how we heal.

You have now seen the full arc of a medicine experience from intention to integration completion. You are now familiar with one methodology that may help you release what you inherited that is not yours, that may help you heal and acclimate to who and what you are little by little, step by step, medicine journey after medicine journey.

Now let's look at some common difficulties people face and how to work with those difficulties.

CHAPTER 8

NAVIGATING DIFFICULTY

In this chapter we will look at some of the difficult experiences people have. Because you are reading this book, I am assuming you are taking psychedelic medicine in one form or another. If this is the case, you are bound to have a difficult experience. Knowing this can help you prepare and navigate such experiences. I will share what I have seen to be the most common difficulties and give you some ideas on how to navigate those difficulties, from overwhelm and dark visitors, bad trips, and new set points to the trap of expectations. We will talk about common revelations, situations, and experiences that can create suffering and what to do if they arise.

Frequency Flu

In Chapter 5 we talked in depth about frequency flu.

Whether you believe this to be a thing or not, if you feel cold- or flu-like symptoms after a medicine journey, please take the time to rest and let your body recover. Psychedelic medicine, breathwork, and intense meditation can affect your whole body-mind structure. This is even more true when the experience takes us so deep that it feels like it is approaching the very blueprints of our human composition. When I take medicine I invite it into every cell in my body. I ask for the changes that will help me move forward. These changes can manifest as feelings of being whole, complete, and totally healed. Upon landing from these experiences we need to give the body a chance to catch up to these experiences. The body can also react by feeling depleted and/or achy, and it is not uncommon depending on the medicine to experience headaches, unpleasant body symptoms, and emotional turmoil.

What Helps: I urge you again to take the necessary integration time to rest, allow yourself to just be with the revelations and information gleaned from your experience. Let things settle, let your body adapt, heal, and find a new balance. Nourish your body deeply. There is simply no way to avoid the downward phase of integration. However, when you know the downward phase is normal, the less you battle with it or resist it. You know that this too shall pass, and over time, the downward phase gets easier and less intense.

As the body adjusts, notice the impulse to resist or label what is happening as "wrong." Instead of creating a story about discomfort, bring awareness to the sensations as they arise. Feel the tiredness, the ache, and the emotion without judgment. Let them be. Allow discomfort to be a part of your healing and evolutionary experience.

Fear

Some individuals experience fear or overwhelm before, during, or after a journey, especially if they are new to medicine work. This is very normal and natural.

What Helps: Cultivate awareness. Breathe in deeply and breathe out long and slow. Relax with every out breath. Relax, let go, and relax some more. Reassuring yourself that all is well can be very helpful. Use Maestro Hamilton's approach and turn down fear by saying the words, "Medicine, turn down fear. Turn on love." I found this to be very helpful. I've used this to help clients turn down depression and anxiety as well. Cultivating awareness is huge here because you get to witness the fear or anxiety leave. It's really cool. You can actually witness the chemicals that are released through fear dissipate. If you are not using medicine, you can still tell the body and the mind to chill out and turn down fear and it will respond. The body is very responsive once you learn to take the wheel and feel the results of your words. Use the 5 Step Dissipater and Emotions Arising strategies to mitigate fear.

Fear of Death: As we increase our level of awareness of who we are beyond form, as we disidentify from our physical body, fear subsides naturally and we can allow the True Self signature that is us to permeate our body. Fear is slowly left behind as we integrate ever changing, ever evolving, broader perspectives of who we are. Over time you may come to realize that there is no death, only a new beginning.

According to Buddhist tradition, Siddhartha Gautama (the Buddha) intentionally allowed the body to cease, without confusion, fear, or attachment. From a spiritual perspective, this is said to be possible because the Buddha had fully realized non-identification with the body and mind. With no clinging to sensation, identity, or becoming anything, there was nothing pulling consciousness back into form. Death was not something that happened to him, but something he entered knowingly, as a natural completion rather than a loss.

In Buddhism, this is considered the ultimate expression of integration: total clarity, equanimity, and release. Pretty cool, huh?

For the rest of us facing fear of death, it can be helpful if we are willing to shift our perspective on death. Near death experiences, people who swear deceased loved ones are near, and the fact that people leave their body in the medicine space all the time are good indicators that death is also an illusion. So, turn down fear and explore other perspectives. What you find just might astound you.

Fragmentation

Fragmentation after a psychedelic medicine experience can occur when the intensity or insight of the experience outpaces the nervous system's capacity to organize it. A person may feel expanded, disoriented, or split between who they were before and what they glimpsed during the experience. This can show up as difficulty relating to everyday life, swings between meaning and confusion, trouble sleeping, emotional volatility, or a sense that ordinary reality feels flat or unreal. The challenge is not that the experience was "too much," but that its material has not yet found a stable place within the person's existing psychological, relational, and embodied structures.

What Helps: What helps is slow, grounded integration rather than further stimulation. This means prioritizing nervous system regulation (sleep, stillness, food, gentle movement, time in nature), talking through the experience with a skilled, reality-oriented support person, and translating insights into small, concrete changes rather than sweeping conclusions. Writing, gentle reflection, and allowing meaning to unfold gradually help prevent fixation. Most importantly, the person can learn to let the experience inform life without redefining identity around it. Integration succeeds when the insight becomes quieter, more ordinary, and expressed through steadier behavior rather than continued intensity.

Ego Inflation

Ego inflation after a psychedelic medicine experience can arise when powerful insight, unity, or significance is interpreted as evidence of special status, unique destiny, or elevated understanding. The person may feel chosen, superior, or uniquely awakened, and begin to see others as less aware or "behind." This often shows up as increased certainty, reduced curiosity, dismissal of feedback, or an urge to teach, correct, or redefine identity around the experience. While it can feel expansive and empowering at first, ego inflation subtly narrows perception, weakens relationships, and replaces humility with rigidity—moving the person away from integration and toward separation.

What Helps: What helps is grounding insight back into humility, relationship, and ordinary responsibility. Integration here means treating the experience as information, not identity. This involves deliberately returning attention to daily tasks, listening deeply to others, seeking honest feedback, and noticing where certainty has replaced openness. Working with a therapist, guide, or trusted peer who is willing to gently challenge interpretations is especially important. Over time, the insight is allowed to mature into compassion, patience, and behavioral change rather than self-concept. When ego inflation resolves, the experience no longer needs to be defended or proclaimed—it simply informs how the person shows up more responsibly and relationally in the world.

Agency

Giving up agency after a psychedelic medicine experience can occur when surrender, trust, or dissolution is misinterpreted as a permanent state rather than a temporary experience. A person may begin to feel that decisions should be guided by forces outside themselves—medicine, signs, guides, or "the field"—and hesitate to take responsibility for choices, boundaries, or direction. This can show up as passivity, indecision, difficulty asserting needs, or deferring authority to experiences, symbols, or other people. Over time, the individual may feel less capable, less grounded, and more dependent, even while believing they are being guided by something wiser than themselves.

What Helps: What helps is consciously reclaiming authorship of one's life while honoring the experience as informative, not directive. Integration here involves re-centering decision-making in practical reasoning, values, and embodied discernment. Small acts of choice—setting schedules, making commitments, stating preferences—help restore confidence and agency. It is also important to reflect on insights with someone who emphasizes responsibility and autonomy rather than mystical authority. When agency is integrated, surrender becomes a skill that can be entered and exited when appropriate, rather than a default stance. The intuitive experience then supports self-trust instead of replacing it.

Trust in Reality

Loss of trust in ordinary reality can occur when the

psychedelic experience feels more vivid, meaningful, or "real" than everyday life. Afterward, work, routines, conversations, and responsibilities may feel flat or artificial by comparison. This can lead to disengagement, restlessness, or a quiet grief that something essential is missing. The person may struggle to care about practical matters, interpreting the contrast as a sign that ordinary life is somehow false or less valuable.

What Helps: What helps is slowly re-investing attention in the tangible and relational world. This includes maintaining routines, showing up to commitments even when motivation is low, and noticing small sensory details—meals, movement, nature, conversation. Meaning is rebuilt through participation, not comparison. Over time, ordinary reality regains depth as the nervous system settles and the experience is integrated into life rather than held apart from it.

Boundaries

Boundary confusion can arise when experiences of unity or openness blur healthy distinctions between self and others. A person may overshare, take on others' emotions, feel responsible for healing people around them, or struggle to say no. The sense of interconnectedness can unintentionally override discernment, leading to exhaustion, relational strain, or loss of personal clarity.

What Helps: What helps is re-establishing clear interpersonal and emotional boundaries. This means pausing before sharing, noticing when "yes" is automatic rather than chosen, and practicing saying no without justification. Time alone, journaling, and reflecting on what actually belongs to oneself versus others can restore balance. Boundaries do not negate unity; they allow connection to remain sustainable and respectful. We will talk more about boundaries later.

Emotional Flooding

Emotional flooding can happen when the experience opens unresolved grief, fear, or trauma without fully resolving it. Emotions may surface unpredictably, feeling raw, intense, or difficult to regulate. The person might feel overwhelmed, tearful, anxious, or irritable without understanding why, especially if they lack tools for containment and pacing.

What Helps: What helps is prioritizing nervous system regulation and emotional containment. Containment doesn't mean suppression; it means processing them in digestible increments that are comfortable. In ways that won't leave you feeling raw and vulnerable. This includes sleep, regular meals, gentle movement, time in nature, and reducing stimulation. Talking with a therapist or integration-informed support person can help metabolize emotions gradually rather than all at once. The goal is not to process everything immediately, but to allow feelings to move through in tolerable doses. Having said this, emotional flooding can be cathartic when you know how to handle it. I have had experiences when I purged and cried for a good two hours. This emotional flooding taught me how to breathe through the release, not attach any story and master the Emotions Arising strategy for processing emotions. Sometimes emotional flooding can't be helped. In those situations, reach for the 5 Step Dissipater or Emotions Arising strategies.

Meaning Fixation

Meaning fixation occurs when someone repeatedly returns to the experience trying to extract a final message, explanation, or hidden truth. The mind stays preoccupied with interpretation, symbolism, or "what it all means," often replaying the experience internally. This can prevent insight from settling and keep the person mentally tethered to the past rather than present life.

What Helps: What helps is shifting from interpretation to application. Instead of asking "What did it mean?", the person can ask, "How does this change how I treat myself or others?" Limiting rumination, writing once and then stepping away, and grounding attention in current tasks helps the experience become embodied. Meaning deepens when it is lived, not endlessly analyzed.

Spiritual Bypassing

Spiritual bypassing can arise when the language of acceptance, oneness, or transcendence is used to avoid pain, conflict, or psychological work. Difficult emotions, relational issues, or trauma may be dismissed as illusions or "already healed," creating a split between spiritual concepts and lived reality. This can stall growth while appearing mature or enlightened.

What Helps: What helps is bringing honesty back into the body and relationships. This means allowing discomfort, acknowledging anger or grief, and engaging in silence when relating to others. Listen instead of speaking. Let go of the need to be right, enlightened, or awake. Instead of pretending that you know, can you admit that perhaps you may not know? Mirror work can humble a case of spiritual bypassing because you can't hide from yourself. Asking, "What am I avoiding, feeling or addressing right now?" can be clarifying. Integration is not about rising above humanity, but about inhabiting it more fully and responsibly.

Too Much Medicine

During my training to become a clinical herbalist one of the things my teacher taught me was to start with very small doses and titrate up. When I started my training with Hamilton he recommended the same process: to explore the medicine and find the least most effective dose. I started out microdosing and slowly increased my dose of psilocybin to a level that was comfortable for me. This enabled me to acclimate and get to know to the medicine. Now I know the doses that enable me to work with the medicine in ways that are right for me.

Starting out with smaller doses and working your way up helps you build trust with the medicine and can help you find the amount that is right for you. This can decrease dramatically one's experience of overwhelm and a bad trip.

Many people are taking what is called a "Hero's Dose." I don't see anything heroic about taking so much medicine that you have to hang on for dear life. That just seems dumb. I recommend starting small and increasing your dose slowly to a level that is perfect for you.

Everyone is different. What is perfect for me may be too much or too little for you. The intensity of your experience depends on how the medicine was grown or processed, how strong it is, and how your body metabolizes the medicine, just to name a few important factors.

What Helps: To avoid taking too much medicine, start out with a small dose and increase to your comfort level to get to know the medicine and avoid unnecessary discomfort. Ensure set and setting make you feel safe and that you trust the facilitator and the process. If you are working with a facilitator, have a conversation about dose to give you a sense of safety and trust. If you do take too much medicine or the small dose that you usually take all of a sudden becomes massive (this does happen), breathe deeply and slowly, ground yourself, center yourself, invoke

Sanctuary. Invoke your guides. Relax and ride it out and breathe your way through it. At the very least you will have a cool revelation at how you navigated that dose effectively! It only takes getting tossed a few times before you realize you are not completely at the effect of the medicine. It's like riding a surfboard, the more you balance, focus, breathe, and stay relaxed the better the ride.

Intensity

The intensity of a psychedelic medicine experience is often mistaken for truth because everything gets turned up at once: the nervous system, emotions, meaning-making, and perception. When sensory clarity is razor-sharp and feelings arrive with absolute certainty, it can feel like whatever is happening must be capital-T True. The brain is very persuasive in these moments; it can equate intensity with importance. But intensity measures the volume of an experience, not the accuracy or longevity of its conclusions.

Intensity is excellent at breaking rigid patterns, interrupting denial, and cracking things open. It loosens old narratives and widens perception. What it does not do well is build a stable life. Intensity opens the door; it is not meant to be the foundation you move your furniture onto.

What Helps: What helps afterward is intentionally separating intensity from meaning. Integration means giving the nervous system time to come back online before making declarations, life changes, or spiritual resumes. Write insights down, then revisit them in a grounded and centered state, with curiosity and discernment to see what still makes sense. Talk them through with grounded people who live in bodies and pay bills. Ask how the insight actually translates into lived reality. The most reliable truths tend to stay relevant after intensity fades; distortions usually demand urgency. As a rule of thumb: intensity spikes, truth holds. A useful question is, "Does this insight require me to be special, advanced, chosen, or finished?" Psychedelic spaces are full of powerful experiences, beautiful symbolism, emotional catharsis, and moments of deep coherence—but integration isn't about preserving the peak. It's about asking, what still functions when the intensity is gone?

Unruly Inner Children

I have seen more than a few people connect with what we call the inner child. When people land after such experiences they may be embarrassed about how they acted. This can be humbling and show you exactly what kind of relationship you have with yourself and your past. Unruly inner children are not separate from us. They are the part of us that learned how to survive, feel, and make sense of the world early in life. It's simply a real part of your own experience showing up as an inner child to show you where you might be denying that that aspect of you.

What Helps: Be gentle with yourself. If your inner child came out strongly in a journey, chances are this part of you may not have had a voice. It may have been ignored, suppressed, or maybe forced to put childhood on the back burner while you grew up fast. Look at the experience with curiosity. What is this revelation showing you about yourself? Treat this aspect of yourself as you would have liked to be treated back then, with love, acceptance, and kindness. Be compassionate and consider doing some mirror work to get in touch with the deeper aspects of yourself. Inner children do grow up and can be healed and integrated when we give ourselves time and space. Only you know what was needed back then. Can you give that to yourself now?

Be careful not to create a new identity around the inner child, like "my wounded child" or "my broken past." Instead, focus on the awareness that witnesses it all, and the spaciousness in which these younger parts appear in order to be healed and integrated.

Dark Visitors

This is one of the most interesting phenomena that I have witnessed and experienced. When we choose to take medicine, meditate, or do breathwork, we open ourselves to the unseen and the unknown. Often people report encountering what they call demons or dark, evil energies in and out of the medicine space. These experiences can be frightening and difficult experiences to navigate, but once you do it a few times the less scary they are. I can only speak on how to handle these types of encounters from my own experience and the experiences of those I've worked with.

STORYTIME: *After a medicine journey I was back home and had just crawled into bed when I noticed a presence in the room with me. It was dark. It was evil. It was just there. The first time this happened I sat upright in bed and faced it. I said, "Hey, I see you. What are you going to do? Hit me over the head?" My heart was beating like crazy. Soon after it went away. The second time this happened I had two demon-like energies come into the psilocybin medicine space with me. I was startled at first then invoked Sanctuary and called on God and my guides to be right there with me. Then I said to these two buggers, "You are welcome here. You may heal in this space with me." It was like they sat right in front of me for a bit, then disappeared. Again, this does not make me more advanced, just more responsible for how I face fear.*

I have worked with veterans who spent their whole life fighting dark energies and "the dark forces." When they fought these energies, the battle never ended. The fighting just gave them more energy. When they stopped fighting and just faced the energies, they went away. Someone I know asked their demons to stand guard over him while he journeyed and they did. Another one wrapped his arms around the demon and it turned into love. There are more and more reports of people putting down their swords and approaching these energies with love in Sanctuary.

Hamilton Souther has had more experience working with these energies than anyone I know, and I am truly grateful for how he approaches them today: with love and compassion and intent to help them heal. Sanctuary provides a safe space for all of us to heal. Demons included.

What Helps: Call on God, Source, Spirit, Universe. Invoke your guides. Face them and tell the medicine to turn down fear. Reinforce the space you are holding as one of unconditional love. You may welcome them to heal with you or tell them to leave, whichever feels more comfortable to you. I believe these energies need healing just as much as we do. They influence us in unseen ways and offering them Sanctuary seems like the right thing to do.

The Trap of Perfection

Life is always as it is. The mind calls it "good," "bad," "perfect," or "imperfect," but those are labels. Beneath the labels, this moment simply is. In that sense, reality is always whole, complete, and perfect because it cannot be other than what it is right now. The mind imagines a perfect version of life and then struggles when reality does not match it. It says, one day, everything will be right, and then I can relax. But that day never comes because the mind always finds something else to fix.

The ego loves the idea of perfection because it promises a future moment when everything will finally be "right." This keeps people chasing something better, something different— always postponing peace and joy. Peace is only ever found by accepting the present moment fully, whether it matches the mind's version of "perfect" or not.

People are also not perfect. Expecting them to be different than they are sets you up for disappointment. Always. It's like saying, "Can you change who you are or your behavior so I can be more comfortable?" It doesn't work. All you can change is you and how you respond. It is better to ask, "What is my response saying about me?"

What Helps: If you are getting caught up in perfection, know that in reality, nothing is ever perfect. Everything that exists on this planet either evolves or dies. It is the nature of reality. It is ever evolving. That's what makes it perfect. Once we understand this, once we realize that we never get it right and we never get it done, we can let go of the idea of perfection and free ourselves to enjoy the human experience. Then when we fall, we can laugh like we did as kids, brush ourselves off, and get back on the ride!

Give yourself grace as you integrate. Some days you may move three steps forward and other days you may fall two steps back. Allow yourself to be imperfect. Allow others to be imperfect. When you stop demanding perfection from yourself, others, or life, you discover a deeper isness. You see things as they are, not how you wish them to be.

Bad Trips

I believe bad trips occur most frequently when people don't

properly prepare themselves and their space for a medicine experience. When we don't set intentions, clear our space, call in our guides, and treat the medicine as sacred, things can go awry and we can become susceptible to negative energies and influences. Bad trips happen when we don't do our research and suddenly find ourselves in the medicine while our facilitator is curled on the couch watching YouTube videos instead of holding space. Bad trips happen when we take the medicine in a negative frame of mind, when we are exposed to negativity, or when we take it recreationally or in environments where we are at the effect of others. Bad trips happen when intending to release trauma and instead of letting go we get entangled in it and the drama around it; the list goes on and on.

What Helps: Learn from them. Bad trips can also be good trips in disguise. They reflect back to us what we did right and what could be done better next time. The less seasoned you are in the medicine space the more likely you are to have a bad trip. If you do medicine work enough you will have experiences that are uncomfortable. Most of my "bad" trips were when I got too cocky and needed a universal bitchslap to remind me to take medicine work seriously. Other times the medicine was trying to teach me how to discern between helpful revelations and revelations that distracted me from my healing and spiritual path. The medicine was also teaching me to discern between trustworthy spirits and unhelpful ones. Always approach medicine with a deep reverence, love, and a big dose of discernment knowing you may be tested.

Trickster Dynamics

Remember, the medicine experience is happening inside of you. It is not outside of you. Trickster energies destabilize, test, and reveal where you are not in alignment, holding boundaries, or may be giving up agency.

The trickster is not evil. It often emerges to test you. To see if you will collapse into darkness or pull you toward the "you are special" narrative. It often suggests that you are unique, chosen, and to be secret about your specialness. They can feel convincing, immersive, and relational.

These trickster dynamics often appear when the psyche is exploring power, identity, and meaning. They may present as voices, visions, archetypal figures, or symbolic encounters that flatter the ego or create urgency. A key giveaway is when pressure is applied and you are told to do something and do it now or do it fast. Trickster dynamics also demand, exclusivity ("don't tell anyone"), or convey a sense that you must act, obey, or step into a special role. When discernment is online, there is often a subtle bodily signal that something feels off. You may experience tightness, agitation, or loss of grounded clarity.

Trickster dynamics are not inherently bad. They often arise precisely where growth is happening. They challenge us to strengthen boundaries, self-trust, and discernment. They expose where we are vulnerable to ego inflation, authority projection, or meaning-making that outruns integration. In that sense, they can be powerful teachers—if they are recognized for what they are.

The danger comes when these experiences are taken literally or given authority. If you experience anything that feels:

- Dark
- Manipulative
- Inflates identity
- Places someone above others
- Suggests you have exclusive access to truth

It's time to kick in discernment, investigation, and

curiosity. When no discernment is present, confusion, dependency on the medicine, or repeated chasing of validation can follow.

What Helps: What helps most is discernment anchored in sovereignty and investigation. Stay grounded. Ask questions. Notice pressure. Pay attention to your body. Anything that demands your obedience, secrecy, or superiority deserves scrutiny. You never need to give up your agency, autonomy, or critical thinking in the medicine space and as mentioned before, not every insight is useful. Not every revelation is meant to be acted on. Integration means learning to say no, to pause, and to choose clarity over drama.

The goal is not to avoid these experiences, but to meet them without surrendering authority over your own life. When insight supports humility, responsibility, and grounded action, it tends to integrate well. When it asks you to be special, chosen, or finished, it's time to slow down and reassess.

The Human Doing

After a medicine experience you just had a neuroplastic event and your idea of yourself may have been challenged. Which is the perfect time to create new habits, new patterns, new ways of being in the world. That is why you took the medicine, isn't it? If you avoid this very important golden window (two to four weeks post event) you are losing a prime opportunity to break old, embedded patterns and create new ones. If someone goes right back to their daily routine after a medicine experience, the chances that they just pick back up all the old habits and patterns they just interrupted is very high.

I see this happen a lot with people who go, go, go and never rest until their head hits the pillow at night. This is the human doing who has yet to learn how to be a human being.

234

What Helps: This challenge can be faced by clearing your schedule after your retreat so you have time to evaluate your new set point. If it is uncomfortable to just be with yourself and the information, do it anyway. Let the discomfort come. Start with just one minute then increase the time you allow yourself to be still. Let any discomfort move through you and out of you like a wave. Practice the 5 Step Dissipater and Cultivate Awareness; these tools will help you to be more and more comfortable with yourself and stillness in time.

A New Reality

One of the things I see frequently with executives, industry leaders, and business owners is that they create a business while they are at one level of consciousness, and then they go in and have a big medicine experience, and after they land, they hold a new level of consciousness. They see where they were greedy, where they ignored their partner and their children, and how they drove themselves to avoid unworthiness. After their journey, they have a new reality, a new set point.

When they return to work, they must deal with their company that was created at a lower level of consciousness. They are now faced with evolving their companies, relationships, and idea of self.

What Helps: The best way to evolve an outdated creation is to restructure it by letting go of any previous expectations and creating new agreements.

This is how:

Expectations vs. Agreements

There are many ways that we engage with our fellow humans.

One way is to have expectations. Expectations lead to

disappointment and lower quality relationships, goods, and services.

Another way is to create agreements. Agreements evolve how we relate to others, and the quality of the goods and services we create is higher.

Business Expectations: For instance, leaders often have expectations of their people and will walk around expecting certain levels of job performance. They expect quality and certain quotas. I know I did. Then there are the employees themselves trying to live up to the expectations of the leaders and often resenting them because most of the expectations have been unreasonable. The executives I've worked with, when they were willing to pull up their sleeves, found they either didn't have enough staff or their people were over worked or were in resistance to the expectation itself.

STORYTIME: *When I owned my wellness center my employees were not getting their chart notes done. I huffed and puffed and walked around the office all pissed off because my employees were not meeting my expectations. While this made me feel superior and significant, I was actually being quite cowardly. I was a coward because I didn't go to them directly; I just complained about it for a while first. Then one day I sat down with one of them and asked, "Why are these not getting done?"*

That was when she said, "You're not giving us enough time in between clients."

So, I said, "If I gave you an extra ten minutes between clients would that do it?"

The reply was, "I could be in agreement with that." Boom! A lightbulb went off and that was the beginning of a business based on agreements and not expectations.

If you walk around with expectations and others don't

live up to them, you are disappointed. If they do live up to the expectations, you might say, "So what? That's what I expected."

When you have expectations you are choosing either disappointment or boredom. When you say, "I expect this of him, or I expect that," it's cowardly. If I am a true leader and an employee is consistently late, that's on me because I lack the courage to take responsibility for a team member who thinks it's okay to stroll in late.

People do not look forward to living up to expectations. They don't like it if you have expectations. Think about this for a moment. How do you feel when someone has an expectation of you?

Doesn't feel good, does it? Now imagine sitting down with someone and creating an agreement. Feels different, doesn't it? This gives you both the opportunity to express what you can and cannot do, which is stronger than an expectation. You agree on what is possible.

Medicine Expectations: This is a big one. I have clients all the time who set their intention and go into the medicine space and come out disappointed because they didn't get what they wanted. They didn't get what they expected.

How could anyone expect what might happen in the medicine space? It's impossible!

STORYTIME: *A client went into the medicine with the intention to release her feelings of not being lovable. When she landed and I had a conversation with her, she reported nothing really happened. The other people at the retreat had amazing experiences. One rode a dragon, another met their deceased parent, and another one had a conversation with Jesus. As I continued to ask questions and poke and prod, we discovered that she experienced what she described as oneness* *with everything. When I asked, "So, if you experienced oneness, what was it like?" She said it was pretty amazing, like being in the arms of God. I replied, "So how do you feel about being unlovable now?"*

She said, "Wow, I guess it's almost gone. I thought I would be really struggling to release that." She didn't realize taking a joyride into oneness was what was needed to experience being loved. It wasn't what she expected.

Let go of your expectations. Stay open and surprised at how the medicine works with you beyond your idea of what should be. Expectations lead to disappointment, not to mention they are very limiting. Period.

Family Expectations: Are you walking around disappointed in your spouse or kids? Bored with them even? Family can even be more challenging than your work relationships because expectations are higher.

STORYTIME: *I was in a relationship once where I would cook and I would do the dishes. This really bothered me. I had an expectation that if I cooked, he should do the dishes. So I walked around the house in resentment. It was cowardly of me because I didn't have the courage to outright say, "Hey honey, can we be in agreement that if I cook you'll do the dishes and vice versus?" The expectation was unreasonable because he didn't even know it was there! Expectations are reactive, fear-based, and cowardly.*

After you have returned home from a retreat is the best time to release expectations and instill agreements with those around you. You can say something like, "I know I have engaged in this pattern before, but it's not serving either one of us. Let's sit down and create some agreements together." Agreements are co-creative and courageous; they are more fun than walking around with expectations that can lead to anxiety, stress, disappointment, and even a sense of betrayal.

"I expect you to make me feel romantic and attractive; I expect you to make me feel appreciated, loved, and celebrated for bringing money home. I expect you to feel this or that."

Expectations are like cancer. People expect others to make them feel the feelings they think they should feel. Expectations are what lead to fights, judgments, and arguments with another human.

If you had no expectations, you would not have anything negative to say. What if you went home and had absolutely no expectations of anything or anyone in your home? What pleasant surprises would you encounter?

Do the members of your family actually have good intentions? Is there good will? Do you have good intentions? Underneath your crunchiness, do you really mean well?

What would happen if you let go of expectations with your partner and kids?

How would it feel if they let go of expectations of you?

Self-realization comes to those who are willing to release expectations of what should be for what is.

Imagine you are returning home from a powerful medicine ceremony. You saw what works and what doesn't. You released the resentments and expectations of the past and want to navigate your loved ones, your employees, coworkers, or kids differently.

You can start by creating agreements.

Agreements: Human beings don't like breaking their word and most people will do their best to honor their agreements. People generally keep their word. If they don't keep their agreement, you can have another conversation and ask why they are not in integrity with their agreement. You can ask, "If you give me your word, will you keep it?" If they break their word, then that person may not be a good employee or partner. The times they don't keep their agreements are such wonderful opportunities to say, "Let's look at our basic agreements with each other." This is mature. The best agreements within all relationships are:

- Can we agree to be kind to each other?
- Can we agree to be honest?
- Can we agree that the other person intends no harm?
- Can we agree to have fun?
- If you don't like a situation, create an agreement that fixes it.

The beauty of moving from expectations to agreements is you take responsibility for your happiness, for your financial wellbeing, for your health, and for your energy level. It's back to you. It's not on anyone else anymore. You are the only one you can work on anyway.

Agreements can be invaluable when integrating medicine experiences in which it was revealed to you to, "Stop nitpicking. Let go. Just be present." Creating agreements covers the details of daily life, the details of who does what and when, it sets the tone and the foundation for how you will communicate. This frees you up to be present and take the next right action step, which is usually a much higher quality action.

Let's continue on our journey into the challenges people face and solutions that help.

Apathy, Resignation, Sloth

Another challenge I see clients face is immobility. They lack momentum, inspiration, energy, and even the will to act on some of the directives revealed to them in ceremony. Sometimes it is because they have learned how to "just be" so well that they don't want to leave the bliss of their couch. At other times it is because they are avoiding the next expansion that is calling them forward.

Once you have landed from your medicine experience and retrieved the revelations, there are four main things that will try to sabotage you:

- Thoughts
- Beliefs
- Emotions such as fear
- Ego

Awareness enables you to witness these things. Once you have witnessed them, they will often dissipate right before your eyes, IF you are aware. Awareness brings you to center, to neutrality.

Neutrality is great. It's a wonderful place to pause, to heal, to rest. It's similar to resting in the void/nothing because it can feel really good. It can also lead to boredom, loneliness, apathy, or resignation if you attach a story to it. This is where many people get stuck. They take this beautiful directive to just be and use it as an excuse to not live their lives.

This can be a tough pattern to break because the energy is so low. Think of the energy of depression and that is what we are working with here. How do we, when we lack momentum and fire, take action on revelations like "enjoy your life, play with your kids, love your partner" when we can't get off the couch?

How is this self-conquest to be made?

What to do: You Cultivate Awareness. Then you activate your will. Awareness is the observer. Will is the mover. But what moves you from one to the other?

After awareness, there is a threshold moment—a breath, a decision, a spark. In that moment, you don't need energy.

You need a decision. One tiny immediate action that signals you have activated your will.

- Stand up
- Touch your heart
- Say "I choose now."

These anchors will in the body, not just the mind. Will begins with one step, not a full on plan.

You activate your will when you say, "No, mind, no. Stop bringing me shit. Go get me something better." You activate or engage your will when you face and swipe left on the thought of unworthiness, when you face fear and watch it dissipate before you, when you breathe and come to center, or when you choose a better feeling thought.

Awareness and activating will are essential for following through on your self-realizations and directives. You reshape yourself through the power of your will.

- Cultivating awareness brings you to center.
- Will is the energy and momentum that is your driving force to bring forth what you wish to create, express, or experience.

Sure, small consistent actions strengthen willpower, but it's not just taking action that has the greatest impact. It's not just sticking to routines or building self-discipline; it's also mindfulness and awareness where you recognize and manage your impulses and courageously override them.

Whether it is kicking a sugar habit or growing a company, it is your ability to exert self-control and restrain your impulses that activates your will. You absolutely can let go of negative thought patterns, ego activity, and all the awful stuff your mind brings you. You can stop being a pushover.

You can also be courageous enough to say no to the donut even when everyone else in the room is indulging. If you really believe a donut or a negative thought is stronger than you are, Byron Katie the shit out of that belief by asking is it true? Is it really true? How do you feel when you think that thought? Who would you be without it? Then cultivate awareness. By now you should know that tool by heart, but here's a brief summary followed by a way to activate willpower.

Cultivate Awareness

- Boom! Sounds in the room: Become super aware of your external environment.
- Boom! Body: Feel your feet, legs and gravity, release your belly, and become aware of your heartbeat, your breathing, your body. Redirect your focus over and over again to your heart and inner beingness.

This exercise will quiet the mind and ground you in the body. This shifts all the energy from the headspace where the chaos and compulsion live to the body where you can rest in neutrality. The mind quiets and the impulse dies down.

The key is not to fight apathy but to bring presence to it. In that presence, the heaviness dissolves, and the next step often becomes clear and without effort.

If you need to, you can then activate your willpower:

⭑ Activate Willpower Exercise

Take three deep breaths. Use your imagination to picture a huge boulder in front of you that represents everything that gets in the way of that one thing you want to experience. Look at it like you are going to obliterate it with your eyeballs. Pull your shoulders back and lift your chin. Now walk up to that boulder and push it out of the way.

Now, get off that couch and go do the thing.

If you experience resistance or the boulder comes back, use your imagination to evaporate it, blast it with fire out of your eyeballs, blow it out of the way with your hurricane-like breath.

Anything that will give you the feeling of empowerment. Get creative. Imagination is the language of will. You see it, you feel it, then you move.

Will is not discipline. Discipline is repetition. Will is ignition. Will is what gets you off the couch. Discipline is what keeps you moving.

This practice trains your mind to release hesitation and take action, strengthening your will over time.

What is one thing you have been wanting to do, but just can't seem to do it?

Is it time to do it?

This book is not about talk therapy. It will mean nothing if you don't actually use any of these tools I give you.

Speaking of tools, here's another challenge people face, with tools to gain confidence.

Setting Boundaries

Directive such as "Stop putting everyone else first. Take care of you..." can come across crystal clear in a medicine experience. But then implementing that directive when you land can be tough. This is one of the more common revelations that requires courage and activating will to implement. It also requires emotional mastery to release the guilt that arises when you start saying no after years of saying yes.

What to do: Create a boundary.

To make this easier, let's redefine what a boundary is and how to create one.

Boundaries Redefined

Traditional Definition: The traditional definition of boundaries includes drawing lines, creating division, setting limits and rules of what we are and are not willing to tolerate from ourselves and others. Traditional boundaries stir up feelings of resistance and separation. There is a "No, YOU can't do that" energy.

Redefinition: In the context of you as a free will creator, the word "Boundaries" is used in a specific way that is different from normal daily usage. In this case we look at boundaries purely from the perspective of personal preferences, personal choice, and personal responsibility that provide structure to how we express ourselves, engage with, choose to respond to, and experience people and the world around us. There is a distinct and important energetic difference between the two definitions. The redefinition has an "I CHOOSE" energy.

Boundaries from this perspective eliminate good/bad right/wrong or judgment and are accepting of different levels of awareness, personal choice, discernment, and personal responsibility as we move through life. Boundaries are made up of two parts:

1. Choice. How we choose to respond, not respond, express, create, or engage with the world around us.
2. Personal responsibility. All persons are responsible for their own choices and experiences.

Let's dive into these a bit deeper.

Personal Choice: How we choose to respond, not respond, express, create, or engage with the world around us is up to us. Each individual is responsible for their choices. In

245

this way no one can be blamed for the choices we make. No one is a victim or perpetrator, and all parties are responsible for their own choices and experiences. Since you're accountable for only your feelings as they arise and actions in response, you don't blame others. When you're blamed, if you don't feel responsible, instead of defending yourself or apologizing, you may say, "I don't take responsibility for that." Or "that's not about me." You don't assume responsibility for or obsess about other people's thoughts, feelings, beliefs, and problems.

Personal Responsibility: All persons are responsible for their own choices. It is also each individual's responsibility to regulate their own thoughts, feelings, beliefs, ideas, memory, story, imagination, desires to express or create that arise and subside within consciousness. Personal responsibility also includes owning the times your choices or responses may have impacted others or yourself adversely as opportunities to gain wisdom, be authentic, and apologize where needed.

Boundaries, in this context, is choice. We are free to choose at any given moment how we respond to a thought, emotion, idea, person, situation, or event. We also choose what we want to experience and how and when to express ourselves in the world.

There are high-quality choices and low-quality choices.

- The more fully present you are when you respond or express yourself, the higher the quality of that expression, regardless of whether it is something you are saying or creating. When you invite conscious awareness into the present moment, the quality of that decision/response/creation is more likely to be a high-quality choice, contribution, or experience.
- Conversely, if the ego presence is high—and you note feelings of fear, anxiety, doubt, guilt, shame, judgment,

or negativity—the quality of the experience, choice, or contribution is low.

When Are Boundaries Needed? Anytime you experience resistance to doing something, experience an emotional trigger, or are uncomfortable with something, someone, or a situation, a boundary is asking to be made. When you encounter resistance, it is a beautiful gift that tells you it may be time for a new choice or perspective. Resistance is an opportunity to be aware of and transcend triggers, negative thoughts, limiting beliefs, or behavior patterns we have outgrown.

The Trigger Is the Teacher: When we experience a trigger, it is an opportunity to cultivate awareness, take a deep breath, and let go. This is self-mastery. Then when the chemicals released from that thought or situation die down and you are not defensive, you are more likely to choose a more effective, kind, and meaningful response. You stop reacting and you start choosing. The trigger is always about you. Always. It teaches you where you are and are not setting boundaries; being patient, kind, or compassionate; or choosing something different. Your response to anything teaches you about yourself.

When you are triggered and react, often the reaction is colored with defensiveness, anger, frustration, or judgment. The need to be right and not wanting to be wrong is costly. You may be right at the cost of your relationship; at the cost of intimacy, love, or connection. There are not many people who want to love and connect with a know-it-all. Boundaries, in this context, teach humility and personal responsibility.

Examples

Example: If a thought arises within you that creates resistance, fear, or judgment, it is an indication that the thought may not be in alignment with what you value. You can choose to buy into that thought as true or discern it as false and release it. Either way, you acknowledge your choice and take responsibility for the results of that choice. Note that the thought arose within your consciousness, and your level of conscious awareness correlates directly to the quality of the choice you make.

Example: Someone yells at you, and you experience feeling attacked. Whether real or perceived, the feeling of being "attacked" is merely an invitation. How you choose to respond creates your experience. You can choose to counterattack and engage in battle or be quiet and non-responsive and hold a grudge (passive or direct), or you can choose not to engage and walk away. You can also choose to engage with compassion, curiosity, and inquiry. Again, note that your level of conscious awareness directly correlates to the quality of your choice/ response and the quality of your experiences in relationship.

Example: If I you are paying bills and experience fear or scarcity, the resistance within you indicates that the emotion is not in alignment with your true essence, which is infinite and unlimited. You can choose to buy into that emotion or discern it as false and choose to respond in a more productive way by acknowledging that all is well. "Things have worked out in the past and they will work out again." You alone are responsible for how you respond. Once again, the level of conscious awareness you bring to the experience correlates to the quality of your choice and to the quality of your relationship with money.

Example: You are asked to do something you don't want to do. You tap into your knowledge that boundaries are an individual phenomenon, that there is no good/bad right/ wrong or judgment, only different levels of awareness, personal preference, and self-responsibility as we move through life.

You ponder your choices: a) You can say, "No, I choose not to do this, I'm going to do something different." b) You can do that thing anyway and be miserable. c) Or you can shrink, hide, and avoid the situation entirely and not choose at all.

There are many choices that can be made in any situation. The level of conscious awareness within you directly correlates to the quality of your choice and experiences.

RECAP

- We get to choose how we express ourselves in the world. We also get to choose whether we engage and how we engage with others. The level of awareness that is present and the discernment we exercise when we choose determines the quality of our life, the quality of people we engage with, and the quality experiences we have.

- It is each individual's responsibility to regulate their own thoughts, feelings, ideas, and emotions that arise and subside within consciousness. In this way all parties are responsible for their own experiences.

★ TIPS

1. Resistance: Anytime you experience resistance you are most likely out of alignment with a choice. If you encounter resistance, something is asking to be looked at and a new choice made.

2. Discomfort and Resentment: Are indicators you have created a story, taken on a victim identity, are not setting a boundary, or are not in alignment with what you desire. If the situation requires a decision, cultivate awareness and focus on your heartbeat; this helps ground you so you can make a centered quality decision based on intuition instead of an ego reaction.

3. Allow Others Their Perspective: If you are in an uncomfortable conversation with another person, don't take it personally or judge the individual. Allow them their expression and opinion, regardless of the level of consciousness/ego behavior in the other. When you react, you are being drawn into lower levels of consciousness. When you are in choice, you reside in higher states of consciousness. Give up the need to be right and be present. If the ego gets triggered and you say something mean or lose patience, don't beat yourself up. You just slipped into an unconscious reaction. It's not who you are. Take responsibility and look forward to the next opportunity to practice keeping your mouth shut.

4. Stormy Emotions: Can be difficult to navigate. Allow yourself to feel the emotion fully, then let it go without attaching any story. Emotions truly want to be felt then let go. You won't die. I promise. Use the 5 Step Dissipater and Emotions Arising strategies to manage any guilt that may arise when you say, "No."

5. Other's Reactions: Other people may get upset when your inner compass says, "Yes" or "No." Choosing what you want can be stressful in some situations. Know the discomfort is brief and you will experience relief afterwards. Know what arises for them is theirs and what arises for you in response to your boundary is yours. Choosing how to balance self-care, work, play, and family can seem selfish or stressful. Again, know the discomfort you and others feel is brief and you will both adapt.

6. Quality: There is a difference between a high-quality "No" and a low-quality "No." When faced with a yes or no choice you can say, either "Fuck you," or you can say, "No, love." The choice and the experience you receive as a result is up to you.

📌 Boundaries Worksheet

Project yourself into the future and imagine a situation where you may be called upon to make a decision, respond to a situation, or set a boundary. Then come up several choices in how you will handle the situation.

Situation that needs a boundary:

What might arise (worst-case scenario)? Example: They may get angry, judge me, and not engage with me further.

What might arise (best-case scenario)? Example: They may understand, accept, and respect my decision without blinking an eye.

What choices do you have available to you? How could you choose to express yourself or respond to navigate each of the above situations?

What have you decided? Will you set the boundary?

How will you handle the thoughts/emotions or responses that may arise?

How will you feel after the experience?

Is this choice a good choice for your highest wellbeing and the wellbeing of others?

Identity Crisis

Another challenge that arises frequently is identity crisis. This can happen when you have let go of so much you feel empty, or what was revealed to you about yourself was more intense than you thought you could handle. At times, a deep journey dissolves the boundaries of who you thought you were. The old roles, beliefs, and self-definitions fall away, and what remains can feel like emptiness. The familiar self can vanish, and the mind, seeking control, may call this a crisis.

The few emergency calls I typically get are when clients have been so blown apart they no longer know who they are or what is real. They feel lost, empty, alone, and they don't know who they are or how to navigate their life. But, what if this emptiness is not a loss at all, but a birth? A space of pure potential where the deeper self can emerge? Beyond the changing masks of identity, there is a timeless presence, the I Am, which is not bound by the stories of the past or the expectations of the future.

Sometimes people will experience themselves as a king, a queen, or of royal blood and come out of the experience wondering what to do with that. Curiosity is the antidote for any fear, judgment, or uncertainty around identity.

Here's an example of how to work with revelations around identity using the Revelation Integration Method Fundamentals:

- **Revelation:** What was revealed to you about identity?
- **Safety:** Were you and are you safe? Did you choose wisely the facilitator, environment, and medicine? If you don't feel safe, get help. Period.
- **Receptivity:** Are you open to receiving deeper insights regarding the revelation? Are you receptive to information about identity that is other than what you thought? Beyond ego attachment?
- **Discernment:** What is the source of the revelation? Is it a quality revelation or are inner trickster dynamics coming into play stroking the ego? Is the revelation helpful? Does it instill more agency, inner sovereignty and help you let go of limitations and deep rooted beliefs? Or is it a distraction? Food for the ego?
- **Curiosity:** Put the revelation into quarantine and ask questions. How can this revelation serve me and my life now? How can I apply it? How can it help me function? What feelings or qualities can I take away from this in grounded, yet humble ways?

- **Investigation:** Investigate the quality of the source of the revelation and the revelation itself. Does it feel congruent? Aligned? Or distorted and low vibe? If you discovered you are nothing, investigate that. What does it really mean to be nothing and is nothing really empty?

- **Translation:** Raw revelation often arrives as symbolic, somatic, or imaginal. What could this be symbolizing? What can it represent, reflect, or restructure about your idea of yourself? If you saw you are a king, what qualities of a true king can be translated to your everyday life? Did you need that boost of power to step into life more fully?

- **Adaptivity:** This is when you allow a revelation to land within you and acclimate to a new perspective or idea of self. If you saw in a journey you are a goddess, what qualities will you keep from that experience and how will you adapt to those qualities over time?

- **Embodiment:** This happens when you fully embody and integrate a revelation and it feels like it has settled within you. Not as an idea, not as an identity, but as part of your being and how you walk your path.

- **Continuation:** You can then evaluate your new set point and explore what's complete and what is not. If you are stable and you still have questions regarding identity, you may take it to the medicine again and ask for clarity. Ask the medicine to be gentle.

What to do if the crisis is intense: Ground. Center. Balance. Invoke Sanctuary and cultivate awareness to stay in your body and out of your head. When disorientation arises, slow down. Breathe consciously. Rest your awareness in the body, in the present moment, in the stillness. Remind yourself that you are on a planet in a solar system moving around a wonderful universe. You are right here, right now, in body. Good. Keep grounding, keep breathing, and stay open to receive further insights. And of course, get help if you need it.

STORYTIME: *One of my clients had an identity crisis after she visited the void in the medicine space. She freaked out. We grounded her in her body and had her explore the void and being empty of identity to see if it was really something to be afraid of. Two weeks later she enjoyed being empty so much she didn't want to do anything; she was so at peace. I asked, "Are you ready to start learning about creation and how to bring things forth from the void?" (which I call the point before creation) and she said, "No, I think I'm just going to stay empty for a while longer."*

Ego Death

It can feel really good to be empty of identity or it can be scary. This can also be called ego death. What is called enlightenment, in many ways, is what happens when we let go of everything that we think that we are so that we can experience that which we truly are. And when people get to this space, it's often described as nothing, yet something at the same time. Nothing, but yet something that is difficult to describe.

The integration processes many people are experiencing now is transitioning from the false self/ego structure to allowing the emergence of True Self. This can be a wonderful, uncertain, scary and joyful process that involves acclimating to a new idea of self, not as identity but as individuation. It can also lead to an inflated ego, an identity crisis, or difficulties where everything you thought you were collapses so your True Self can come through.

I work with many people who are at this phase of their journey, and the feeling of being lost, yet found, not knowing who they are, yet sensing something indescribable within can be challenging to integrate.

Identity crisis on the spiritual path is guaranteed at some point or another. It occurs when we are willing to face all aspects of ourselves and let go of what is not us. When people have an identity crisis, I celebrate them, and while they look at me like I am crazy, it reassures them that they are okay. When we don't know who we are, we are closer to knowing who we are than ever before. We must die to the false self for the true self to be known.

Once identity is released, even the identity as a spiritual person, we can acclimate to and integrate who and what we really are. Sure, people will flop back and forth for a while. That is completely expected. When you find yourself striving to be pious or good, watch out. That's the ego wanting to attach to an identity as spiritual, significant, or better than others.

What to do: Be curious. Cultivate awareness and see if you can just sit in stillness without having to be or do anything. Pat your body to get you back into your body and out of your head. Stay super aware and alert. Look at your experience of ego death with curiosity. What is it like not to have an ego? See what the ego or false identity does as it comes back online. Does it want to negate the experience or attach to an identity as superior or better than? Does it shrink? If so, don't fight it or resist it. Send it love and compassion and continue to explore the aware presence that is in witness of the ego.

Delusion

Psychedelic medicines, such as psilocybin, ayahuasca, or 5-MeO-DMT, can open doors to profound healing and insight.

Yet if approached irresponsibly, without respect, humility, or integration the mind can quickly turn revelations into new illusions. The wise ones put all revelations into quarantine and are willing to change their interpretations again and again. The ability to translate raw revelations that occur symbolically, somatically, or through imagination into language or action steps that improve how we relate is a learned skill that requires discernment. Without discernment delusion can and does happen.

Delusion is so rampant it is considered normal. So how do we spot it and better yet, prevent it?

In general:

• Be on the watch for a heightened sense of self-importance or superiority over others. No matter what you experienced, your extraordinariness is no greater or lesser than anyone else's. Period.

• Watch for beliefs that are not based in reality. You may strongly believe something that is false or exaggerated. You may feel convinced of something the mind presents as absolute, yet truth does not shift with time. It is not threatened by inquiry. If it changes tomorrow, it was never ultimate truth to begin with but perhaps a metaphor to help you on your way.

• Watch for misinterpretation. The symbolic or archetypal imagery encountered in journeys is often misunderstood, leading to rigid, literal translations instead of reflective or metaphorical insights, solidifying what was meant to open and expand you.

• Watch for identification with archetypical energies. Identifying as the goddess, the king, or the healer can awaken inner strength when you need it, yet if you attach to the role, or claim it as identity as better than, it becomes another mask.

When lessons or insights from the medicine are not sat

with carefully, pondered with curiosity and a willingness to see all perspectives and when the question is not asked, "How does this benefit my life or help me move forward?" they can solidify into delusional belief systems or false identities causing detachment from reality or difficulties functioning in the world.

This can manifest as the individual sitting in the corner alone and isolated, without a job and unable to function in 3D because no one understands they are in the fifth dimension. It doesn't matter how many dimensions an individual is aware of, what matters is how they are functioning here in this one.

How To Prevent Delusion

If confusion or grandiosity appear, return to the now. Ground. Breathe. Become aware of your body and notice the breath moving in and out. Feel the earth beneath you, the aliveness of this moment. Insights have their place. But who you truly are, the awareness in which insights appear remains untouched, beyond all stories.

Rather than rushing to declare, "This is the meaning! This is who I am now!" pause. Ask questions such as, "Is this helpful? How does this serve me? Is this true? Is it even real?" can prevent delusion. Question. Question. Question everything!

Ask, "Will it bring more presence or joy into my life, or is it pulling me into another story?" Allow insights to rest in stillness before you give them power. Pondering, contemplating, and exploring revelations help you discern a revelation's validity and avoid delusion. Putting revelations into quarantine can ground you and the revelations, preventing the development of rigid or harmful beliefs.

Mindful reflection and cultivating an open but discerning mindset allows one to explore the revelations offered by the medicine while avoiding attachment to potentially distorted ideas. Always ask if the revelation is helpful, "Is it helping me clear something from the past? Is it helping me heal? Is it showing me who I am in such a way that it enhances my life and increases agency or will it be a distraction and lead me down an unhealthy black hole?"

Unworthiness is a delusion that humanity knows all too well. It is one of the biggest delusional patterns people are working through right now. The idea that we are somehow unlovable or unworthy needs to stop now. Who can say we are unworthy? Who can say we are worthy? Worthy of what? The whole idea of worthiness is a construct, old, outdated and in serious need of some reprogramming.

INVESTIGATION: A key fundamental of the Revelation Integration Method is investigation. It investigates and differentiates between egoic attachment and authentic insight to avoid distortion and delusion. You investigate the quality of the source of the revelation and the revelation itself. Not all revelations are benevolent.

Watch for experiences where the ego may be tempted to attach to it and create story about how special you are or that this is the first time such a revelation has ever happened. The mind loves to attach importance and meaning to experiences. Yes. I am here to pop your bubble in the most loving way and tell you that you are not as important as your mind thinks you are. Investigation, with a good dose of humility goes a long way when approaching revelations, especially what we would call the good ones. Again, yes you are unique, there is no other being like you in the universe. You are beautiful. This does not make you better than or less than anyone else. When you can ground the most beautiful revelations and embody the feeling it gave you without significance, or identity; meaning will arise on its own and you are on the right track.

Losing Touch with Reality

People working with psychedelics can experience their idea of reality loosen. The world in which we live is what many call an agreement reality, a mental overlay, a world of thought, interpretation, and story. A world of constructs. When people say someone has "lost touch with reality," they usually mean they have lost touch with the co-created agreement reality we live in.

The mind labels, divides, and names. It creates identities: "me" and "you," "success" and "failure," "worthy" and "unworthy." It builds religions and governments, cultures and civilizations, even the concepts of time and space. Much of what we navigate; roles, identities, and even time can begin to feel constructed when viewed through altered states.

When we mistake these agreed upon constructs for reality itself, suffering begins. Conflict arises because one mental world collides with another. Each person defends their version of reality, not realizing it is only a thought-form.

On a larger scale, humanity collectively agrees on certain illusions: nations, currencies, hierarchies, even the idea of separation. These agreements shift over centuries, but the underlying tendency remains: the mind, although well intentioned, often mistakes its stories for truth.

Beyond all constructs lies the simple, undeniable fact of being. The feeling of this moment. The aliveness within you right now. This is reality before the mind names it. Before we call it "the universe" or "God" or "me." It is the stillness out of which everything arises. Science is still trying to figure it all out, label it and put it into a box. But those of us who know, well, we just know.

Psychedelics often strip away the mental overlay. For some, this is liberating. For others, it is frightening because the mind's familiar world dissolves, and with it, the sense of who we think we are. To wake up is to see that behind every thought, every creation, every identity is a vast, still presence that existed before the story began.

Remember from before, what is true is always true. When you take away all impermanence, what remains? That just might be ultimate reality.

Thank you for exploring that with me.

Now let's continue on with what to do if you come out of a journey and your whole world has crashed around you.

What to do: Feel the weight of your body. Notice your breath moving in and out. As you breathe, focus on the sensations in your feet and legs. Feel gravity right here, right now. Become very body aware. This will ground you and center you in the present moment. If confusion arises, return to the now moment: You are here. You are alive. You are in a body on planet Earth, right here, right now. Period. Reassure yourself that you're safe. You did your homework; you are in a sacred trusted space that you chose. Breathe through the experience. Sit with your experience non-judgmentally and let the experience move through you naturally, rather than trying to control it or understand it.

Revisit the Revelation Integration Fundamentals to integrate revelations about reality.

Revelation Integration Method Fundamentals:

- **Revelation:** The revelation is the reason you took the medicine. Now you are receiving information about reality. Cool! Breathe!
- **Safety:** Safety is primary. Ensure you are in a safe

location and get professional help if you need it. Continue to ground and breathe. This is where a good integration guide can ground you and help you explore and begin to integrate the experience.

- **Receptivity:** Receptivity involves being open to what the medicine has shown you, no matter how challenging or ineffable it may seem. Remain open to receiving insight about reality even though you may have no clue what is happening in the moment.

- **Discernment:** Shift from the headspace into the heart space and feel into the revelation. Does it feel real, valuable, clear and pure?

- **Curiosity:** Put the revelation into quarantine and ask questions. How can this new perspective about reality help you navigate this one?

- **Investigation:** You investigate the quality of the source of the revelation and the revelation itself. Investigate the new perspective on reality. Does it resonate? Does it feel true? Do you integrate the insight or just be with it and see what emerges?

- **Translation:** Raw revelations about reality often arrive as symbolic, somatic, or imaginal. Sometimes words cannot come close to translating these experiences. Yet, while some things cannot be translated, but they can be felt, adapted to, and embodied. Can you feel the experience without having to name it or understand it?

- **Adaptivity:** Revelations about reality help us shift perceptions and adapt to new ways of perceiving reality. This is often a feeling process more than a thinking process where we let go of old constructs and adjust to new ones. Are you willing to shift your perception of reality over and over again?

- **Embodiment:** This happens when we embody the insights of a journey into our very being. This can take time. Revisiting the revelation by listening to your recording, reading your journal and feeling the feelings you experienced in your journey are helpful ways to embody a revelation. Embodiment happens when the mental, emotional, and physical body come into coherence and alignment with a revelation.

- **Continuation:** Continuation involves evaluating your new set point, what's complete, and what is not. Then taking what is not complete into the next journey. Revelations about reality may need more time to settle before you take the next journey. Lots more time! If you need to, you can also take questions about the nature of reality to the medicine for clarity when you are stable and ready.

Professional Help: If identity crisis or loss of reality seems prolonged (lasting long after the medicine should have worn off), get help. Especially if you feel that you or someone you love is a danger to themselves or others. Psychedelic hotlines are available 24 hours a day people are trained to help navigate crisis. https://firesideproject.org/hotline.

You can also contact me or one of my trained guides through my website. https://www.daniellebrooks.com/

At its core, this challenge of losing touch with reality can be identified by looking at how it affects the way we live and engage with others, how we live and work together in community (unity). The danger here is when one isolates oneself (separation) and puts up walls, creates stories and identities that are not helpful or conducive to growth and evolution.

Trauma, Addiction, and Mental Health Issues

Psychedelic medicines can heal trauma, interrupt addictive patterns, and resolve the root cause of many mental health issues, especially delusion and unworthiness.

Having said this, given the potential risks associated with psychedelic therapy, it's crucial to undergo a thorough medical and psychological evaluation by qualified facilitators before participating in a psychedelic medicine ceremony. It is your responsibility to check with your doctor before you participate in any medicine work.

You and you alone are responsible for yourself.

Certain medicines are contraindicated when used with psychedelics, just like with pharmaceuticals, when two medicines are combined they must be considered carefully. Being aware of medicine indications and contraindications empowers you to take medicine responsibly and intentionally.

There are also physical health contraindications, such as cardiovascular conditions and neurological disorders, just to mention a couple. If psychedelic medicine work is something that interests you, find a qualified and experienced facilitator who can work with you and be honest with them.

The breakdowns in mental health I have seen arise usually because someone was on certain medication or had a certain condition, such as psychosis, that they did not disclose to the facilitator. If you choose to take medicine, work with a qualified practitioner responsibly, intentionally, and with great respect for how the medicine can affect you.

The Downward Phase of Integration

Sometimes when you ride the upswing of the integration phase it can be fun, exciting, and expansive as you come to know yourself in ways you hadn't taken into consideration before. But then when you are faced with the downward curve it can get crunchy. This is usually when you face those aspects of yourself you would rather not see. But you must see them in order to move beyond them.

There is no work-around when it comes to the downswing. It can't be bypassed. But when you face it without judgment, with compassion and awareness the downswing can actually be exciting because you know where you are and what to do to prepare for the next upswing. Even if you don't know what the next upswing may have in store for you. It's like the contraction before the expansion when you face what needs to be seen in order to move through it. Losing a job or ending a relationship can be examples of the downswing. Knowing that you are just going through a cycle helps you navigate it.

What to do: Trust. Know this too shall pass. It always does. Use the tools in this book to master your emotions, quiet your mind, and allow yourself to just be in the downward phase. Silence and stillness can integrate what fear and uncertainty cannot.

When People Don't Integrate

When people don't integrate and they go back to the medicine for a second journey without integrating the first one, sometimes they will receive similar revelations. It's like the medicine is saying, "Hey! I'm trying to tell you something." So if you are not doing the work, or you're skipping through it and you're just paying lip service to it, you may not reap the benefits from the experience. This often happens when people have what they call a "bad" journey and they don't want to face or work with what was revealed to them. They only want the "good" journeys. The person who has just come out of medicine and wants to go right back in is not integrating.

Medicines may interrupt a pattern or release an emotional imprint, they may help us see things from a different perspective, they may give us the unconditional experience of love, but it is up to us to acclimate to that love, to maintain that perspective, and to not pick back up what we laid down. The medicine doesn't do the work for you. It can act as a huge catalyst for certain. It can create huge opportunities for healing. What you do with that information, experience, or revelation afterwards is completely up to you.

I have seen many individuals go into the medicine and experience themselves as whole, complete, and utterly loved unconditionally by their creator only to go home and go back to their routine as if nothing happened. They return to their unworthiness and comfortable patterns that were created in the past.

When no integration is done, the next step up the spiral of evolution is ignored. There is nothing wrong with this as some people may not be ready for the next step. But typically, this is why people take medicine. They want the next step.

A good integration guide will inspire clients to integrate the current step before taking the next step. A great integration guide will hold their clients accountable for their growth and facilitate the safety that is required for them to make a transition from identity to individuation and from false reality to true reality.

Fast and Slow Integrators

Some people are fast integrators and some are slower. Some revelations integrate immediately and some take years and even lifetimes to process. Everyone goes at their own pace.

STORYTIME: *Old people are really fun. I had an 85-year-old I guided through a medicine experience and he was just a hoot.*

He was screaming at the top of his lungs having a heyday with the medicine. When he came out, he was open, in love, and just wanted to play and laugh. He was a fast integrator because he was so ready to "drop the shit" and let go of everything. When we went through his journals and talked about the main themes of his journey, everything was already complete. Literally, I asked him, "How do you feel about your deceased wife?"
He said, "I love her with all my heart."
"How about your second wife?"
"I love her, too."
He had received the revelations and was ready to move on and implement his directive which was, "Just have fun." A month later he refused to take on any drama or move back into the seriousness that had crept into his life. He was still playing! He was a fast integrator.

Change Can be Challenging

In general, as you evolve, things that used to be fun but are no longer in alignment with where you are now may be less fun. It is very normal not to enjoy alcohol like you used to. It is also common to see relationships that were fun differently. Drama, problems, and gossip are no longer fun because you are in a different place. You have a new set point.

It's also normal for many people who have struggled with their weight their whole life to work through feelings of unworthiness and experience they no longer need to feed, soothe, or avoid anything with food.

It is normal to spend more time alone than be around people and situations that no longer resonate. If you are willing to open to the possibilities of meeting others at your set point, this is possible for you...if you don't close yourself away because it is easier.

Integrating Divinity

Integrating divinity can be a challenge. Sometimes people who are not ready to experience their divinity set their intentions to experience it not fully understanding the ramifications. Many don't realize that to experience divinity or oneness they may have to let go of their separate identity and their idea of what divinity is.

The full reckoning, when an individual's belief does not align with what is so, can result in all their closely-held religious constructs crashing down. If someone has one idea of what God is and they experience something completely different it can put them in a tailspin. I have seen many, many, individuals come out of a medicine experience with a completely new perspective that comes at the cost of the old.

Before even setting the intention to experience God, Divinity, or the Truth of the Universe ask, "Am I ready for that?" Future forecast what would happen if your intention was met? What would change? Are you really ready to face your own Divinity in whatever form it may be revealed to you? Are you prepared to let go of the old? If so, and you have an experience that rocks your world, congratulations! Integration is now your highest priority and you want to put everything into quarantine where you allow your body, mind and spirit adapt. The more you feel, contemplate, explore, and be with your revelations the more they will integrate.

Integration is a Way of Life

Once you know how to integrate you can take this process into your everyday life. You can have an argument with your partner and afterwards ask, "What did that altercation say about me or my behavior?" You put it into quarantine, ask questions: When did that behavior start? How did it serve me?

Who did I get from it? Do I still need this today?

And then when you're complete with it, you can move on.

You're terminating old new neuro pathways, creating new circuits, and processing information each time you go into the medicine space. You evolve, expand, and integrate, evolve, expand, and integrate. It's beautiful.

Medicine work is a learned skill. It's about mastering a set of protocols that allow you to go into places and get information that you can't get any other way. The goal is to make measurable progress with each medicine journey.

Hopefully this chapter gave you an idea of things that may challenge you in the medicine space and ideas on how to handle them.

The next few chapters may resonate if you find yourself exploring spiritual questions. We will explore one map of many on what healing may look like, the purpose of pain and suffering, and how to track your progress. We will end with a deep dive into divine integration.

PART 3

EMBODIMENT AND INTEGRATION

CHAPTER 9

THE PHASES OF HEALING

In this chapter I will share with you the different phases I have experienced on my own healing journey as well as what others have reported. Working with so many people going into and coming out of various medicine experiences has given me a unique perspective on how these medicines are working with us.

As you read through this chapter you will notice that you may be experiencing things in several phases at the same time. This is very normal as healing is not a linear process and it is different for every human.

The Revelation Integration Method's Map of Healing

What follows is, what I have come to treat as, a sacred map that identifies and outlines The Phases of Healing based upon my experience and the experiences of other individuals over five years of case studies and medicine work. This is not linear. It is common for individuals to jump from one phase to another.

1. Letting Go

This phase is marked by the feeling that you are constantly letting go. You slowly get more and more comfortable with the letting go process.

- You let go of negative thought patterns, such as "I am unworthy."
- You let go of limiting belief structures, such as "I am not safe to love."
- You let go of emotional imprints from your past, such as grief, fear, or anger.
- You let go of false identities and ego activity slowly recedes.
- You let go of trauma and any guilt, shame, or identification with it.

2. Healing

All phases contribute to healing and our ability to acclimate to being healed, whole, and complete. Healing often unfolds when we let go of a belief of unworthiness and experience ourselves as worthy. Healing can happen when we release all the pent-up grief, sorrow, sadness, and pain. It happens when we receive an insight that our parents did the best they could, that what we inherited in the form of behaviors, addictions, and beliefs weren't ever ours to begin with. We heal when we begin to work with the mind and explore who we are beyond thoughts. Healing is what happens when our hearts open and compassion flowers for ourselves and our fellow man and all the trauma we have collectively experienced. Healing takes place when we are cleansed physically, mentally, emotionally, and spiritually little by little by little. Healing also happens when we transform our relationship with food to the point when we no longer use food to feed, soothe or avoid our emotions, but to nourish the body.

3. Identity Crisis

This can happen when you have let go of so much you feel empty, or what was revealed to you about you was more intense than you thought you could handle. Identity crisis happens when the ego freaks out or you as the aware presence has a new perspective. This phase can feel like a collapse of all that you thought you were. You may go back and forth between "Am I a human in physical form? Am I this God nugget, or am I both?" And what the heck is this thing called aware presence? You realize you are not in Kansas anymore and other dimensions that you can sense and perceive become more real. Feelings of being lost, yet found, certain and uncertain, knowing, yet completely in the dark are normal. This is a commonly reported phase in which True Self is experienced in degrees.

4. Spiritual Significance

This phase usually happens when a person has an intense psychedelic experience in which they experience themselves in a way that is beyond words. It may be interpreted as "I am God, Source, Universe, Spirit, Consciousness, etc." and the experience is just so wonderful and powerful and intense the ego can't help but grab a hold of it and want to claim it for itself. This is when feelings of being spiritually advanced or superior creep in. "I need to save the world, I am more advanced than you, or I have this huge responsibility" are steeped in spiritual significance.

This is where a good integration guide can pull you down by your ankles and remind you that, "Yes, you are extraordinary, and so is everyone else. Tough love is sometimes needed to guide you away from both the feelings of unworthiness and the I am better than you complex. Remember, many people are encountering themselves in this way, yet each experience is unique, not special.

5. Tests of Virtue

It is almost guaranteed at some point you will experience uncertainty. You may doubt yourself. Opportunities for you to lie, cheat, steal, or not live up to your own moral and ethical code may arise. You may be tempted to give up and give in to apathy or resignation, or to avoid facing something that needs to be faced. You may use food, alcohol, or substances to manage your emotions instead of facing them and learning from them. You may be addicted to drama, sex, pain, or dysfunction. How you face these challenges, these "tests" tells you much about your character and the work that lies before you.

You may experience delusion; you will certainly experience fear. In many ways we could say integration is a path of growing up and learning who we are based upon how we respond to one situation, then another, then another, and each of those responses teach us about who we are and where we are with ourselves.

When a situation or experience occurs repeatedly, you know it has not been integrated. It is there to show you that the pattern or behavior has still not been resolved. Integration is the rewiring that prevents collapsing back into habit.

Tests of virtue help you train your mind and can teach you

how to operate the physical body and its impulses, cravings, patterns, and habits. Self-mastery is tested and it is normal to experience what feels like transfiguration, reconciliation, and crucifixion all at the same time. Or at least it feels that way.

Through all of these experiences and phases of healing, challenges arise. It is sticky here and it's easy to get sucked into the drama, the glamour, and the materialism that have prevailed for so long. Every experience we encounter as humans gives us the opportunity to fail, fall on our face, and feel unlovable. There are also experiences when we can overcome and be the hero of our own story. The road to healing is a long one and even in our moments of what we call "enlightenment" we may still doubt ourselves.

Some call this the path of initiation.

What we call it doesn't really matter. What does matter is how we pick ourselves up after each fall. What matters is how we respond to the world, the people we meet, the people we love, and whether we are in or out of integrity with ourselves.

A Note on Pain and Suffering: Tests of virtue often involve pain and suffering. The purpose of pain and suffering has been debated for millennia. One thing is for sure: pain and suffering give us resilience.

Let's use our imagination and propose there is a place souls visit to learn and grow. A soul school where we put on our virtual reality helmet, forget who we are, and see how we act or perform in certain situations that enable us to be tested. How we face challenges, deal with those challenges, how we overcome challenges that are designed within this game help us be better humans. To evolve our soul.

Therefore, perhaps we are here to struggle and grow. Perhaps when we die we wake up from the game and retrieve the wisdom we have received through challenges. Wisdom that can only be receive through being challenged.

Life here resembles the hero's journey.

We explored this in my first book, *The Extraordinary Ordinary You: A Manual for Self Discovery*.

Yet, there are some tests I would not wish on anyone.

When it comes to the horrific experiences one can only guess why that has to happen. It's a topic that philosophers have bantered about for ages: why if there is a loving God is there so much suffering?

Well, who created pain and suffering? Has God has ever interfered with our choices, no matter how horrible they were? That's what's called free will. We are so free we can destroy ourselves and each other. And boy, have we come close. Maybe it's time to take responsibility for our own creations and the things we've done to each other? Victims and perpetrators alike are suffering greatly. It's time we come together as a collective and wrap our arms around both so healing can take place.

This is a complex subject and it's important to acknowledge the difference between individual choice and collective inheritance. Regardless of the scale and complexity, pain and suffering seem to be the price of admission for some people to incarnate on this planet.

REFLECTIVE MOMENT: Without pain and suffering, what would push us forward? Do you think we can be challenged without pain and suffering?

Regardless, pain and suffering can bear gifts in the form of who we become. How we stand up to failure and duress can mark our progress in life.

For example, for most of us, our sufferings and experiences are the things we end up being most grateful for because they have enabled us to mature, grow wiser, and cultivate the spiritual qualities of compassion, wisdom, honesty, love, and joy.

6. Integrating the Mystery

This phase is inclusive of all the other phases but becomes more pronounced when the individual experiences moments of clarity, presence, and beingness. A moment of awareness can be a moment of enlightenment. These moments, over time, happen more frequently and begin to string themselves together until the individual gains more and more stability in their ability to hold awareness and presence.

Physical Adaptation: As one gains stability in presence and beingness the physical body begins to adapt and integrate higher and higher vibrational frequencies and levels of consciousness. Just as the physical body responds to your thoughts, both positive and negative, the physical body responds to consciousness. This includes adaptation of the cellular structures, what some experience as activations of dormant DNA, and balancing and harmonizing of your electromagnetic field. Your nervous system has to adapt to the higher frequencies of the divine without overloading your circuitry. This requires the individual interested in embodiment to continuously ground, balance, heal, harmonize, and reorient themselves. It's a divine balancing act.

Grounding: Many individuals go into the medicine space to experience the Mystery, especially if they are reaching for MDMA or 5-MeO-DMT. When not enough time is given between sessions these intense experiences can challenge the nervous system and overwhelm the body systems. It is very important that we set aside time to integrate these experiences. Too many people want to leave their body when they have these experiences and they don't want to come back.

278

This leads to an addiction and dependency on medicine for these high, ecstatic, dissociated states, instead of adapting and integrating that ecstatic state here in the body.

Integration is the process by which the mystical experience becomes lived reality. The Revelation Integration Method recommends always taking time to ground and embody your mystical revelations and establishing your new set point before continuing with more medicine. I can't emphasize the importance of this enough. Integration is also when an intense mystical state becomes how you live coherently afterwards without collapsing, retreating, fragmenting or inflating the ego. It is a peaceful way of living and being. While integration can be intense, most often it's the slow, ordinary and unglamorous process of letting your system reorganize.

Don't Depend on the Medicine: Divine integration encourages you to learn how to use your own chemistry to have these ecstatic experiences. Refer back to the exercise that teaches you how to journey without medicine in Chapter 5 for more information on this. Your body is a wonderful pharmacy. Just have an orgasm and you will know you can reach these high states without medicine.

Go Slow: When an individual goes too fast and doesn't allow for an integration period, they may experience joint pain and discomfort similar to arthritis, ringing in the ears, flu-like symptoms, brain fog, and confusion. Headaches, dizziness, and loss of equilibrium are indicators you may be going too fast and need to slow down and allow the body to adapt and settle into a new set point.

Stay Here: It's easy to want to dive out of this reality; it's tough here. But there's one reality you are living in right now and it's right here, and there's more to it than you think. As we continue to receive and work with these mystical experiences and the physical body adapts to expanding perceptive abilities, we may become more aware of synchronicities and see the patterns in others with clarity because our own patterns are being transmuted. We can communicate more easily and the body integrates a new way of being in the world beyond what we have known. Who knows what we will be able to do and what potentials lie ahead of us. That's all part of the mystery!

Make the most of the ecstatic divine experiences, not by leaving the body but by rooting, grounding, and balancing those experiences here in the body so we can live more fulfilling lives here. If you allow yourself to stay in the body while you have the ecstatic experience, the body will adapt. Use the Earth as an anchor point and it will help you. Go slowly and at a pace that enables you to deepen your rooting as you expand consciousness incrementally. You can build the circuitry to embody what you are experiencing. It does not matter if the frequency is from breathwork, meditation, or medicine. Ground, balance, and harmonize these frequencies. The body can heal as a result and you may stand firm in your knowing of yourself as a wonderful, conscious being with your own unique frequency right here, right now.

Track New Gifts: As you integrate, your sensitivity may increase. The clear intuitive senses—clairvoyance (clear seeing), clairaudience (clear hearing), clairsentience (clear feeling), and claircognizance (clear knowing), for instance—can be tracked as you progress. We are creating a new template, a new blueprint. As the body adapts to higher states of consciousness, it restructures the physical body in such a way that it can handle higher vibrational states.

Ground Some More: I will reiterate again, in order to tap into these new gifts, we must ground, we must center ourselves, we must orient ourselves to ever expanding and evolving perceptions over and over and over again, otherwise we may succumb to delusion and ego, and we may not be able to make the next evolutionary leap mankind has in potential.

We have to ground in order to expand. The depths of our roots determine how high our branches can grow. Today people go to high places, but they're not functioning well in the world. If people don't build the circuitry to embody these experiences, we as a collective won't be able to adapt. Glean everything you can from your experiences. Bring it down into the body as much as possible. Land it in the body, and remember, the deeper your roots the higher your branches can grow.

Balance, Heal, and Harmonize: Integrating the mystery can happen when you work with kundalini energy and the chakra centers of the body intentionally. When this energy and these centers balance and harmonize, you heal. The electromagnetic body animates and you have a higher realm version of who you are. You may even touch the mystery. Grounding, balancing, and harmonizing the energies will help you integrate what you are experiencing.

Orient to True Self: Integrating the ecstatic mystical moment isn't just about experiencing intense sensations; it can be higher states of consciousness being allowed to descend into the body to integrate as you.

At some point no more plant medicine is needed. You've cultivated awareness and you realize there is nothing to do but just be in the world. Interdependence become clear and you realize there is one God, one life, one heartbeat that is a mystery unfolding.

This is just one map of healing based on my experience and the experiences of others. It is not complete by any means nor is it linear. There are many other things people experience on the spiritual path, but I like to keep things simple. Having a map can remind us that we are not alone. It helps to know others are experiencing what we experience and enables us to identify where we are on our healing path.

Here is a quick recap of the RIM Map of Healing

1. Letting Go
2. Healing
3. Identity Crisis
4. Spiritual Significance
5. Tests of Virtue
6. Integrating the Mystery
7. The Healing Does End

There is a point where the healing can end if you allow it, and integration of being "healed and whole" can take place. This is not a process of perpetual healing but slow and steady progress that ebbs and flows and may require tune ups now and then to release the stickiness of being here. We do know how to heal. Many of us are doing it and chances are you are, too.

The Revelation Integration Method's Map of Healing empowers clients and practitioners alike to walk the integration path knowing what may lie ahead and how to move through difficulties into wholeness.

As we walk the path of healing, we grow up. We put aside our petty jealousies and comparisons and choose love and kindness instead. We alchemize fear over and over again, choosing to love instead of hurting each other. One thing I see in the medicine space all the time are realizations that love is the only reason we are here. This is experienced in a variety of ways.

- One person may see the universe as a computer simulation and all of humanity moving from chaos to entropy. When I ask what entropy is like they say unconditional love, balance, harmony, and peace.

- Another person may use the words density and light. They see that our whole reason for being here is to transform the density with light. When I ask how this is done, they say with love.

Yet another person may see the world in which we live from the perspective of good versus evil. They say it is a war we are fighting. When I ask how that war is fought they say with love.

The foundation of all religions is built on love.

Integrating the mystery is different for everyone. There is no one path, but there are commonalities, and love is the main one. So is the ability to put aside our differences, master our mind and remain un-triggerable no matter what shit hits the fan.

These perspectives are clues as to how to move from one phase of healing to another. If it is your desire to "awaken," "self-realize," or "become enlightened," love is certainly a good starting point. But consider for a moment what you would experience if you didn't need to go anywhere or achieve anything?

I meet with clients who have had the God experience often. And frequently this will bring tears. Unconditional, indescribable love are the words used to describe it over and over again. When people touch the mystery it is one of the most beautiful things to witness.

But don't take my word for it. Explore the mystery yourself and let me know what you discover.

Now let's talk more about the path every human is walking together and what to expect.

CHAPTER 10

WHAT TO EXPECT

Expect to let go of all expectations.

In this chapter we will dive even deeper into what you can anticipate as you move through the phases of healing and integrate divinity with the assistance of psychedelics. From fear of obliteration to the bliss of reconciliation. You will receive many ways to track your progress so you can be reassured that you are not walking this path alone. It has been walked. It is being walked by many humans at this time often with the aid of psychedelic medicines. It is important to emphasize that your path is yours alone and there is no way for you to expect what is around the corner for you.

Yet, as more people walk the path of healing, we are being given a loose map filled with symbolism, metaphors, and ideas—pointers to help us on our way. In reality, as mentioned, expectations lead to disappointment and even boredom or betrayal. This chapter represents signposts you may see on your healing journey, but don't hold on to them tightly. Be willing to change perceptions and ideas of the way things 'should be' again and again.

Destruction: In general, if you have an experience of knowing who you are as that which has no words, you may go through the unwinding of what you are not. The unwinding of the life that you created as a limited human. Realization often destroys previous creations and previous perceptions so something other can come through. It's uncomfortable. Yes. But that's what these medicines are good at; destroying old constructs and showing us new ones. This includes relationships that will evolve with you or be released.

Motivations: Executives, leaders, and entrepreneurs are often afraid they will lose their drive and end up on a mountain meditating and never get anything done. There is no need to fear this. From my experience they don't lose that aspect of themself that gets things done; they still chop wood and carry water. Drive and motivation become a pair shoes they can put on because they know they will be running. Then there are times when they can put on their slippers. They don't lose their edge; they can always put those shoes on. In addition, the action that one takes often shifts from ego driven action to inspired action. This increases the quality of the creation dramatically.

Loss of Identity: If you are working with identity it can be intense. It is common for people to understand that they are not the roles they play, the work they do, the car they drive or the money in the bank. But when the medicine strips you of all that it can shake your world. So be cautious and intentional and go slow when working with identity. It can be shocking and freeing depending on many factors to have identity striped away. Fear of obliteration is real, and while I can reassure you that you could never cease to exist, this is one fear you must work through on your own. Take it to the medicine and be so bold as to explore your existence. Knowing that most fear is protective but without foundation may help. I recommend you approach the medicine carefully and ask it to be gentle when working with identity.

Free Will Choice: At some point you may clearly know you are a divine articulation that chooses freely what to do with any thought, situation, or experience that arises within your field of awareness. Then you may forget again. Then you may remember. You may slowly begin to engage more and more with whatever arises or comes into your world from a place of choice. You stop reacting...most of the time and know that whatever comes into your field of awareness may be a reflection of the level of consciousness you hold. You may even come to realize the universe as a reflective mirror, whether you are ready to look at that mirroring is up to you.

Responsibility: Using medicine can help you realize you are no longer a victim. Whatever happened to you happened to you in the past and is no longer in your now-moment. You can't change the past, but you can take responsibility for how you respond to it now. If you were a perpetrator, whatever happened was done in the past and is no longer in your now-moment. You can't change the past but you can take responsibility for how you acted. You can take responsibility for your choices anytime you are ready to. You can forgive and choose to move on.

Reconciliation: You can expect to go through an acclimation or reconciliation phase where you get used to being that which cannot be described AND a human on Earth. It may not be what you thought it would be. Over time you may slowly get used to the mystery of knowing that which can never be known and wonder where your halo is. You may be slightly disappointed because you still chop wood and carry water.

Testing: As mentioned earlier you may be tested. When you say you are going to do something, do you do it? Are you paying lip service to your health? Or are you putting some energy and momentum behind your intentions to care for your body? Are you exercising your sovereign free will choice or are you being at the mercy of the world around you? How are you responding to these tests?

Please be compassionate with yourself. You really aren't being tested. Tested is a metaphor and there is no final grade. It's normal to fail one 'test' and then another. For instance, I have worked with my relationship with alcohol for most of my life. Time and time again I said I would not have more than one glass of wine and wine kicked my butt and I caved. Similar to that donut, I had to ask myself again and again, who is stronger? Alcohol or me? I'll be honest, most of the time it was alcohol. Now, one part of this 'test' with alcohol was not judging wine, or myself for caving, but acknowledging what I am after is the freedom of choice to be able to enjoy a glass of wine from time to time without needing it as a substance. Can you feel the difference? Freedom of choice is self-mastery.

Peace: You may transition to being even more present, in peace, and in the beautiful now-moment. You may reside more and more in a place of no thought. You may be able to leave time and space and in many ways feel empty yet full. The medicine may show you that the mind is a tool, a faculty that can be used for logistics to be able to function in time and space to communicate and share. You may get the cosmic joke

287

and laugh more frequently at your mind and the crazy things it comes up with.

Clarity: You may slowly become aware that everything is creation, including you. Your ability to clearly see other people's creations and your own grows. You may see other people's stories, drama, and emotional hairballs clearly. At first you may want to interrupt them and may do so until you realize it doesn't do any good most of the time. So, you let people have their creations as you work with your own creations.

Joy: It may be helpful to note that many people associate being holier than thou, strict, or pious with awakening or enlightenment. Not so. Others think life will be boring, bereft of any fun, emotions, or other traits. I certainly did. Rest assured, the divine does have a sense of humor and life without distortions is never dull.

Freedom: As you come into alignment, distortions can drop away. You may no longer feel you have to save the world or do things because you feel they make you a good person. You may realize your value is in your being and your only job is to just be you. The choices you make can then be implemented because you choose to, not because you should. You may stop driving other people's car and start driving your own.

Trust: It is common for people to marvel at the mystery that bridges the gap between the divine and the physical. In general, I see people learning how to trust that all is well, all unfolds. Some may trust so much that they give up sovereignty to that which is greater than they and allow themselves to be led.

Paradox Reconciliation: Knowing that which can never be known is an example of a paradox. As people heal it is common for paradoxes that were previously misunderstood to become clear.

Knowing: Intuition can get stronger and may nudge you to go to a coffee shop, take a walk, cook some dinner, say hello to a stranger. You may find yourself in a drug store not needing anything, wondering why you are there, then meeting someone to offer a smile or a message.

You Receive: Some people report periods where they feel like they are in a constant state of receiving. I have experienced this. It feels like resistance ends and flow begins. And your life and what you receive delights and surprises you...most of the time. You start to understand why all ascended masters laugh so much. You will still receive challenges that nudge you forward, but you see them for what they are and don't resist the lessons they hold...as much.

Oneness: Psychedelic medicines are famous for giving us the experience of Oneness. Yet, in all my years I have never heard it described the same way. If you stay on this journey long enough, at some point you may discover, in your own way, that we live as unique individuals with personal stories, while simultaneously recognizing ourselves as expressions of one shared Consciousness, God, Source, Spirit, Universe. At least this is as close as I can come to pointing you towards it. This unity experience is different for everyone. Your connection with God, Source, Spirit, Universe, Consciousness, and your fellow man and our beloved planet is yours alone to experience.

Acceptance: You may slowly realize that there is nothing you have to do, need to do, or should do. The phrases, "There is no such thing as worthiness. No good/bad, right/wrong, or judgment of any kind" may start to make sense. You may notice others functioning at different levels of awareness. You still chop wood and carry water and there may be what feels like a period of rest, integration, and reorganization as you transition from "shoulds" to "I choose."

Your Gifts May Be Realized: For many, purpose emerges. Gifts are pondered and seem to arise on their own spontaneously. Without seeking, without drive, without any outside forces. They can simply emerge and become clear when you allow yourself to be still. Opportunities for you to move into service may arise. Not because you have to be a good person, but because you can't help it.

These, of course, are just signposts that lead the way based upon my own experience and the experiences of others. Many more experiences are in between and beyond that are subtle and experiential, and it is not unusual to experience many at once. In general, as you heal, the level of chaos and compulsion die down to be replaced with simplicity, beingness, lightheartedness, and ease.

Certain thoughts that trigger experiences, such as judgment, fear, anxiety, worry, guilt, and shame, can arise, and fall throughout all healing and integration experiences. Again, this is not a linear process. As spiritual teacher Ram Dass said once, "If you think you're enlightened, go spend a week with your family," then you will know where your work lies. There's nothing like a good humbling among family. What we may call 'enlightenment' isn't perfection. It's the end of separation.

Ways to Track Your Progress

Tracking Your Thought Patterns: At first, you may catch a negative thought after it snagged you and you disappeared within it. Then as you continue to cultivate awareness, you may catch yourself in the middle of the thought. Then, you may witness the thought without getting snagged by it at all. You just witness it rise and fall within your awareness. This is one way you can measure your progress.

Tracking Emotional Reactivity: Patterns that used to

manifest as emotional triggers will get less intense and less frequent, fading into the background and becoming more and more subtle, requiring more and more awareness to dissolve them.

Tracking Identity: The degree to which you release false identity may fluctuate because you may not maintain consciousness. You may be conditioned to respond to certain things in certain ways based on old patterns, paradigms, social constructs, and old belief systems. It may take time to unknow these things. The ego will usually come out kicking and screaming once you decide to heal and wake up because it thinks it will be the death of it. The more you work with the ego by thanking it, loving it, and saying, "No," the quicker it will integrate. Know that if you are a writer, you may continue to write. If you are a business owner, you can continue on. But you may do these activities from a higher level of consciousness that brings more quality and joy to the experience or creation. You don't have to change your career or your life's work unless you are called to do so. Whatever you choose to do may give you a sense of knowing that your work is right for who you are and your gifts.

Tracking Integration: Integration is the process of experience becoming lived reality. There is no end to integration. No final moment when you declare, "I'm done! I made it!" Integration is what happens when an individual is willing to look at all the bits and pieces of themselves and let their system reorganize again and again.

Tracking the Need to Control: You may gradually trade control for trust. Instead of micromanaging everything you can choose to let go and trust that Source has you. You may still take action, but the action you take tends to be inspired action, which is taking action that feels like it's compelled by your soul—and the results of your action often produce higher quality results. Integrating inherent divinity requires courage and a leap of faith. The certainty of the known is left behind to realize that which is beyond the known. This means leaving the comfortable self you have created behind—the one who likes this, disagrees with those people, judges this and is ashamed of those things.

Tracking Love: As you integrate, little by little, you may experience more and more moments of love. Your idea of what love is may give way to what love really is. Here are a few signposts to guide the way:

- Conditional love may give way to unconditional love. Unconditional love has no conditions: "I will love you if you love me back." Nope. Not love. "If you take out the garbage I will love you." No. That's not love. That's manipulation.
- Unconditional love has no meaning. It doesn't mean anything if I love you. It doesn't mean you are good enough or I am good enough if you love me. No. It just is. The meaning you put on love may loosen over time.
- Unconditional love has no reason. "I love you because you have hair and bring home the bacon." No. That's not love either. Reasons to love decrease over time and you may find yourself loving just because it feels good.
- Unconditional love is not attached to outcomes. "I will love you, but only if you promise never to leave me." Nope. Attachments to love can also loosen over time.
- Unconditional love cannot be described in totality. It is beyond words.
- Unconditional love has no expectations. "I expect you to be with me forever." That's not love, that's bondage.

What would it feel like to leave all expectations behind?

Can you allow yourself to experience love without the conditions? Can you love without restraint? Can you open your heart and let it in? It's much better than expectations I can guarantee you that.

Many people say to me, "If I let go of expectations and open my heart, I may get rejected." To which I reply, "What if there is no such thing as rejection? Only preference and experience that you and others get to choose?" What if it didn't mean anything about you if this person chooses not to see you again? What if it doesn't mean anything about them if you decide not to see them? Preference takes the fear and judgment away. And if you decide to continue the engagement you can create mutual agreements.

As you grow, the way you love may evolve and expand. Your capacity for it may grow and the degree to which you honor and love the world can also grow.

Tracking Readiness: In the beginning you may not be ready to let go of everything you think you are to experience what you truly are. For me, I had to let go a little at a time.

Tracking Mastery: Self-mastery is what can empower you to fulfill your intentions and make the changes you desire. It is a combination of presence, intention, will and action that can turn insight into a way of life. It is a safeguard that can keep you from getting lost in illusion, distractions, or spiritual bypassing. It is a key that can prevent relapse. It can be the momentum that keeps you moving forward. Tracking your level of mastery is a great way to track integration. Over and over again people tell me that one psychedelic experience was like ten years of therapy. Yet it is integration and mastery that can prevent us from picking back up what was laid down in ceremony.

Tracking You: There is only one you. The you that

witnesses everything that arises within your filed of awareness and anything you witness cannot be you. That includes the ego. The degree in which you dissociate from ego and acclimate to who and what you are beyond identity can also be tracked.

These are just a few ways you can track your progress. As you move through the phases of healing, you may start to perceive what exists beyond your preconceived notions of what life is all about. Your understanding of what divinity is will definitely be challenged. The only insight I can give you is that it won't be what you expect!

In the next chapter we will dive even deeper into divinity. So, grab a cup of tea. Take a nice deep breath. Ground a bit more and continue on. You are ready for it.

CHAPTER 11

DIVINE INTEGRATION

Many people have had meaningful experiences that include psychedelic, spiritual, therapeutic, or existential experiences that touched something very real inside of them, but left them unsure how to carry it forward. The problem is not lack of insight. It is what happens after insight: confusion, oscillation, identity inflation, disorientation, loss of grounding, or a quiet sense that something important was touched but not integrated. This chapter addresses what divine integration may look like from many different perspectives.

Perspective is important because what we experience as "divine," "absolute," or "unity" are states of perception and embodiment. While these states can be intense, they are often misinterpreted as identities, missions, or roles to perform instead of states of being. Therefore, the more perspectives we explore, the more open we can remain in translating what words and language cannot convey.

The language of awakening is woefully inadequate, and often we must speak in metaphors. Some people may walk what they call the initiatic path. Others want to become enlightened. Others want to self-realize. Some religions say the only way is through Jesus; others insist their way is through prayer, others through meditation. Some scientists and mathematicians claim there is nothing left after we leave this world—that the path to God returns us back to the nothingness from whence we came. Others believe consciousness is the fundamental reality beneath all of existence. While there are similarities, no two paths are the same. There are as many paths to what we call God, Source, Spirit, Universe, Consciousness as there are people.

I will try to be as clear and concise as possible, while being vague enough not to set expectations. There really are no words for divine integration. We all experience the mystery differently, and my journey is not the same as your journey. We may use different language to describe the same thing and while there may be similarities along the way, it is wise not to get caught up in language or definitions, dogma or doctrine when it comes to divine integration, and instead, enjoy the signposts and metaphors along the way.

A Quantum Physics Perspective

From a quantum viewpoint, reality is not made of solid objects but of fields of potential—waves of possibility that become "real" when observed or interacted with.

Integration: Divine integration, from this lens, is the practice of recognizing that both you and your world are fluid, energetic, and influenced by attention. Where you focus your awareness shapes how potential becomes experience. Spend a day focusing only on play to see how your focus results in experience.

A Consciousness Perspective

From a consciousness-based view, pure consciousness is the ground of being—the unified field beneath all energy and matter. Waves and particles are simply consciousness expressing itself in different forms. Awareness, or observation, is what turns potential into actuality, allowing the unseen field of consciousness to manifest as the experiences, matter, and energy we perceive.

In simple terms: pure consciousness is the silent ocean; waves are its possibilities; particles are the moments it chooses to take form.

Integration: Honoring this perspective means living as the ocean while honoring the waves. It includes participating fully in form, while remaining rooted in the formless awareness that gives rise to it all.

The key distinction between these two is that the quantum physics perspective treats consciousness as an observer influencing an underlying physical field of potential, while the consciousness perspective sees consciousness itself as the fundamental field from which all matter, energy, and observation arise. You can explore both of these perspectives when you cultivate awareness to see what rings true for you.

A Vibrational Perspective

One thing we know for sure is that you and I exist within a universe made of atoms, subatomic particles, and fields of energy. When we look closely at matter, we find molecules, atoms, and then subatomic particles. At the deepest measurable levels, these particles behave both like particles and like waves, depending on how they are observed. While the exact nature of this wave–particle behavior is still not fully understood, science shows that matter is largely empty space and dynamic energy patterns that vibrate rather than solid substance.

In addition, the world you and I exist within is dynamic and in constant motion. This ever-changing field (sometimes called a matrix) exists in, through, and around us. How we interact with ourselves, others, and our environment shapes our experiences.

Thoughts, while not physical objects, are energetic processes in the brain and body that influence how we feel and act. You can't see a thought, but you can feel its effects. Simply think or say the word hate and notice the shift in your body. Then say love. The difference is immediate, experiential, and vibrational.

In addition, each person, and the planet itself, has a unique vibrational pattern and frequency. People truly do vibrate differently. You already know this and you actually read vibe quite well. When you walk into a room and see someone, you can very quickly intuit whether you want to spend time with them or not.

That's you reading someone else's vibe.

Everyone's personal vibrational set point is based on their habitual ways of thinking, feeling, and acting in the world. Your choices are reflected in your vibration.

Integration: Rub your hands together for 10 seconds then stop. Friction creates warmth; you are making yourself aware of the vibrational being that you are. When something vibrates, it's moving—creating waves or frequencies. Those vibrations carry energy and affect how matter behaves and how we feel or experience the world. It's your vibrational frequency that makes you, you.

Let's continue to explore the vibrational perspective.

Emotions: As I said before, David Hawkins conducted research on emotions as energy and devised a system that rates emotions on a scale from 1 to 1000. There are low vibrational frequency emotions that give you a certain experience, such as hatred, anger, fear, anxiety, depression, and self-doubt and you have high frequency emotions that give you experiences of contentment, gratitude, joy, and love. And a wide variety of vibrational experiences in between.

You can increase your frequency or decrease your frequency by consciously choosing thoughts and setting intentions that bring about certain feelings or emotional responses. You get to choose. This is self-mastery.

"If you want to find the secrets of the universe, think in terms of energy, frequency and vibration." ~Nikola Tesla

The Principle of Vibration: From a vibrational or metaphysical perspective, the principle of vibration states that like attracts like. Vibrational frequencies attract similar frequencies because they are resonant. Since everything in the totality of existence is energy in motion, the same goes for our thoughts and emotions. They just vibrate at a higher frequency and, like oxygen, we are unable to see them. For example, if you think one negative thought, that thought is a match for another negative thought, which then attracts another negative thought and the next thing you know you are headfirst into a pint of ice cream.

When we transmit lower vibrational frequencies in the form of negative thoughts out into the field they are returned to us in the form of our outer experience. Same goes for emotions. If you are happy inside your outer experience will reflect it. It's actually a really cool system once you understand how it works.

You are a part of a vibrating field of oneness. And you are always in relationship with it whether you are conscious of it or not.

As you explore this perspective you become aware of all the different emotions that are available to you, you can leapfrog your way up the vibrational ladder until you reach a point where you access what I call the God vibration. To describe the God vibration is extremely limiting. Think of the best orgasm you have ever had times 1000! It's pure ecstasy!

To experience this, practice the Journeying Without Medicine exercise mentioned in Chapter 5 and combine joy, love, and freedom altogether to experience bliss. Then magnify your awareness of bliss. Hang out there for a while! It makes the genital orgasm a puny thing compared to the bliss and ecstasy of a cosmic orgasm!

Some say the orgasmic state is the closest we can come to experiencing who we are beyond form.

Integration: From a vibrational viewpoint, divine integration is the process of attuning your physical, mental, emotional, and energetic systems to higher, more coherent frequencies and being able to balance and ground them. It involves becoming aware of the vibrations you create—your thoughts, emotions, actions—and choosing those that align with the qualities of the divine. As your inner frequency rises, and you are able to ground and balance it, all parts of your being begin to resonate in harmony, allowing you to interact with life from a more coherent state.

Note: As you cultivate awareness and achieve high states of consciousness be careful. If you approach your creator abilities with any kind of neediness, they will bring about experiences that reflect your state of being needy. In other words, if you think, "I need more money," you are going to reinforce that. Such is the creative power of "I am."

Let's continue to explore divine integration from another perspective.

A Light Perspective

In one of my self-mastery workshops a man said to me, "I was told the other day that we are all going to light." What does this mean? To answer his question I had to again delve a bit more into quantum mechanics.

This is what I said:

When we examine the building blocks of reality — molecules, atoms, and subatomic particles — the solid world we take for granted begins to collapse into frequency.

Visible light occupies a narrow band of frequencies, ranging roughly from 430 trillion hertz (red) to 750 trillion hertz (violet). Vibration and light are fundamental features of who and what we are.

He liked this response.

Note: I used to be enamored of the idea that as we evolve our physical body becomes a light body. Now knowing we all inhabit light bodies takes all of the ego out of it and all we have to do is become aware that we are inhabiting a body of light and voilà! There you are inhabiting a body of light.

Exploring these models, we see how physics, consciousness, and vibration are interconnected and may be what allows you as consciousness to inhabit a form that vibrates. And your physical form reflects your vibration and level of consciousness. Think of it like this:

- On one end of the spectrum beyond space and time you could say that a beam of pure consciousness inhabits a form that is the complete opposite of dense. It is as close to pure consciousness as possible while still maintaining form. This being has a very light, airy form, a high level of consciousness, and a very high frequency.

- On the other end of the spectrum is another beam of pure consciousness within space time that inhabits a very dense physical body or a biological form that is low in consciousness and vibrates at a low frequency, aka you. No offense intended. We are all inhabiting bodies of light. Some are just less dense, more conscious and more coherent than others.

Integration: Divine Integration, from a light perspective, is bringing unconscious patterns to the light of awareness, softening inner shadows, and letting the body, emotions, and mind reorganize around a clearer sense of self. Practically, this happens when you pause in moments of discomfort and breathe gently into the experience instead of resisting it. Slow, deep breathing supports this "inner light" indirectly by improving oxygen flow, calming the nervous system, and enhancing mitochondrial function. (Mitochondria naturally emit ultra-weak light biophotons as they produce energy.)

Other simple ways associated with increasing or supporting "light" in the body:

- Cultivate awareness to increase consciousness.
- Don't hold on to things, lighten your load. Stop being so dense. (Pun intended.)
- Spend time in natural sunlight to regulate circadian rhythms and cellular energy.
- Eat fresh, whole foods (especially plants), which support efficient cellular metabolism.
- Prioritize deep rest and sleep, when cellular repair and

energy balance occur.

- Reduce chronic stress through meditation, nature, or gentle movement, which lowers metabolic chaos and supports coherent cellular function.

Together, these practices create conditions where the body operates more efficiently and coherently, allowing more light to move through you.

A Color Perspective

Think of God, Source, Spirit, Universe, Consciousness as white light that passes through a prism. As the light passes through the prism, it slows and bends and it separates into distinct colors of the rainbow. This symbolizes the multiplicity of existence and all the different universes, beings, and expressions. Each one is unique, yet all are still light. The rainbow is not separate from the white light; it's simply the same light expressed in many colors.

In other words, God, Source, Spirit, Universe, Consciousness is the white light. Life is the rainbow of colors, the diversity and individuality that are expressions of one Source.

There is a common human fear: that union with God, Source, Spirit, Universe, Consciousness means losing our individuation, erasing our uniqueness, giving up our unique color. But in reality, even when reunited in white light, all colors still exist. White light is not the absence of color but the inclusion of all colors together in harmony. The brilliant hue that is you represents your choices and the path you have taken.

Perhaps, like I did, you fear that in order to return to white light, you must lose your hue, your individuality, yet all that is lost is the false sense of self. Again, white is not the loss of color; it is the embrace of all colors. Your uniqueness is never dissolved in the divine; it is cherished, woven into the wholeness, shimmering eternally as part of white light itself.

From a color perspective we are the many colors in the rainbow of existence. In fact, some people can read the colors or your aura, just like others read vibe through intuition. People see colors in the medicine space all the time.

Integration: Throughout time many have used color as a map for integrating divinity. Think of the chakra system and all it represents. Integrating divinity from this perspective means balancing these colors/qualities so they form a coherent, unified field often symbolized as a column of white light. White light contains all colors; likewise, your divine nature includes all these qualities in harmony.

- Red: may bring forth the qualities of vitality, grounding, and life force.
- Orange: may bring forth the qualities of creativity, desire, and joy.
- Yellow: may bring forth the qualities of clarity, willpower, and purpose.
- Green: may bring forth the qualities of love, balance, and compassion.
- Blue: may bring forth the qualities of expression and communication.
- Indigo: may bring forth the qualities of intuition and inner vision.
- Violet: may bring forth the qualities of unity, spirit, and transcendence.

There are various interpretations as to what the colors represent but I think you get my gist. To integrate divinity from a color perspective is to master and balance each chakra. It has been said that we are made in the image of our creator.

If this is true, then we are all white light, expressing uniquely. We may have just gotten out of balance on our journeys throughout creation. For example, you could over identify with one color, always living in green/heart energy while avoiding red/grounding, resulting in a love bug who can't hold a job or focus.

We could correlate this with what some might call the initiatic path where one must release an excessive focus on orange (sexuality) so that it is balanced and without distortion. Maybe an individual needs more yellow when they lack clarity or power and need to tone down the blue of communication to integrate the green of love more. There are many ways we can integrate using colors.

There is no other being like me in the entire universe. My human is awesomely me. And your human is awesomely you. It is based on all your choices, experiences, how you express, and how you create. You are your own creation. Isn't that beautiful? And if you don't like what you created you can re-create and rearrange the pattern of you anytime.

A Sound Perspective

Let's bring another metaphor into the conversation for further clarity. Let's explore divine integration from a sound perspective. Let's designate each human as one single musical note. On its own, it has beauty, tone, and presence. One note gives us a taste of music, but not the fullness of an entire chord: the harmony of all notes sounding together. The chord contains infinite depth and richness that no single note can carry alone. The full resonance of the chord only exists because of all the notes vibrating in relationship.

Yes, I said in relationship. As humans, we are unique notes within the divine chord. Our individuality is real and valuable, but our meaning, fullness, and beauty expand when we are heard as part of the whole. In the chord, our single note is not lost; it is fulfilled.

From this perspective, you are note within the chord of God. There is nothing wrong with you. Your sound matters because without you, the chord would be incomplete.

Sure, you've had a few rough lives; sure, you've picked up some distortions like fear, judgment, or shame along the way and experienced some pain. You may be off key a bit. That's where these psychedelic medicines can help. Set the intentions to let go of the past, forget about the future, and listen. The rest of the song can't be sung without you and we need your note!

Integration: Divine integration is the process of singing your one note until you find yourself in accord with All That Is. It is the end of separation. Allowing your reunion with the choir enhances your ability to realize you are a part of everything.

Here are some fun ways to use sound to integrate:

Divine Integration Through Sound & Toning

Toning: Begin by toning a single note (like "AH") and feel its vibration in your body. Then, invite others (or yourself in layers if recorded) to add notes, creating a harmony. The experience becomes a living metaphor: your individuality (one note) merges into the fullness of God/Source (the chord/symphony).

Divine integration from the perspective of sound is remembering that your unique sound is both distinct and part of the greater harmony of existence.

Chakra Toning: This bridges sound, color, and vibration. We are getting crazy now!

Each chakra or energy center can be activated through

sound. Two common methods are:

- Vowel Sounds: Pure tones that resonate naturally in the body.
- Syllables from ancient traditions, said to carry vibrational codes.

Color	Vowel	Syllable
Root (Red)	"UH" (cup)	LAM
Sacral (Orange)	"OO" (you)	VAM
Solar Plexus (Yellow)	"OH" (go)	RAM
Heart (Green)	"AH" (father)	YAM
Throat (Blue)	"EYE" (eye)	HAM
Third Eye (Indigo)	"AYE" (say)	OM
Crown (Violet/White)	"EEE" (see)	Silence or OM

Whether you use vowels, syllables, or mantras, the practice is the same. Sounding each tone to clear, balance, and unite the energy centers, allowing the full rainbow of your being to merge into white light. By toning through these sounds sequentially, you "tune" your body like an instrument, as the colors unify into white light, the tones unify into a resonant hum of wholeness.

Chanting OM: The chanting of OM (sometimes written AUM) originates in the Vedic and yogic traditions of India as the primordial sound of creation. Chanting OM is a way of remembering that beneath all forms, thoughts, and experiences, you are vibration itself, eternal, unified, and whole. OM is described as the primordial sound, the vibration out of which the universe itself arises. Chanting OM is traditionally used as both a mantra for meditation and a sacred invocation. It helps attune the body and mind to the vibrational field of existence, bringing the individual into resonance with the universal. In yogic practice, OM is often chanted at the beginning or end of meditation, yoga classes, or rituals to signify alignment with divine consciousness.

Are you noticing that many of these perspectives speak in metaphors? Sometimes in order to heal the illusion of separation we need to use illusion.

These are the perspectives I understand and resonate with the most. They are not complete by any means and do keep in mind they are told from my perspective, which is constantly shifting, evolving, regressing, and expanding! Lol!

Let's look at another perspective.

A Coherent Perspective

From a coherence perspective, divine integration is the process by which all aspects of a human being—mind, body, emotions, identity, and awareness—come into alignment and function together without internal contradiction. When a system is coherent, its parts are not fighting one another. Thoughts, feelings, actions, and values begin to point in the same direction. Life feels simpler, not because challenges disappear, but because inner fragmentation decreases. Coherence is felt as steadiness, clarity, and an increasing sense of "nothing being out of place," even in the midst of uncertainty.

As coherence increases, the nervous system stabilizes and the constant push–pull between desire, fear, and identity softens. The individual no longer swings as wildly between highs and lows or between spiritual insight and everyday reactivity. Instead of chasing peak experiences or avoiding discomfort, a person becomes more present and responsive.

Choices arise more naturally, without the need for excessive effort or self-correction. In this way, divine integration is not about becoming extraordinary, but about becoming whole.

Integration: From this lens, divine integration is not an escape from humanity but a deep inhabiting of it. Awareness does not hover above life; it moves through ordinary moments. The sacred is no longer something accessed only in altered states or special experiences. It is expressed through consistency, integrity, and the ability to remain present with what is. Coherence shows itself when insight translates into behavior and when compassion is embodied rather than conceptual.

Ultimately, coherence is a lived unity. The sense of separation between "spiritual life" and "human life" dissolves, not through belief, but through alignment. What one knows, feels, says, and does begin to match. This alignment is dynamic, not fixed; coherence ebbs and flows as life unfolds. Divine integration, from this perspective, is simply the ongoing return to internal harmony again and again until being oneself no longer feels divided.

A Mathematical Perspective

From a mathematical perspective divine integration can be seen as the process of aligning one's internal frequencies with a coherent, higher-order pattern, similar to tuning an instrument to a universal scale.

Mathematically, this involves bringing chaotic or fragmented waveforms (thoughts, emotions, and actions) into harmonic resonance. Imagine each part of you, your mind, body, and spirit as a waveform.

A waveform is a shape that shows how something changes over time. In math, it's usually drawn as a graph with time on one axis and the wave's value (like height or intensity) on the other.

In mathematics, waveforms describe how energy moves through space and time. These can be sound waves, light waves, or even probability waves in quantum physics.

When these waveforms are out of sync, they create interference, peaks and troughs that cancel each other out or amplify unpredictably.

There are four key parts of a waveform

- Amplitude: How tall the wave is. It shows the strength or intensity of the wave.
- Wavelength: The distance between two peaks (or two troughs).
- Frequency: How many waves pass a point in one second. Measured in Hertz.
- Phase: Where the wave starts. Two waves can have the same shape but be shifted left or right.

The simplest waveform is a sine wave, described by:

$y(t)=A \cdot \sin(2\pi ft+\phi)$

Where:

A = amplitude

f = frequency

t = time

ϕ = phase shift

Waveforms are used to model:

- Sound (audio waves)
- Light (electromagnetic waves)
- Heartbeats (ECG)
- Brain activity (EEG)
- Quantum particles (probability waves)

If you had a hard time following that don't worry. It took me a while to translate how math and a thought could be connected. Let's go back to imagining each part of you, your mind, body, and spirit as a waveform.

Bridging human thought and mathematics requires a shift in perspective where:

- Thoughts are mental waveforms, patterns of electrical and chemical activity in the brain.
- Emotions are energetic waveforms, vibrations in the nervous system and body.
- Actions are physical waveforms, expressions of internal states in the external world.

All of these waveforms can be represented by a mathematical graph. When these waveforms are fragmented, for example thinking one thing, feeling another, and doing something else, they create chaos, internal conflict, confusion, and fatigue. From this perspective, thoughts and emotions can be seen as waveforms or patterns that rise and fall, interfere, and resonate.

Integration: Integration occurs when these waveforms lock into a stable, coherent pattern in such a way that their peaks and troughs match. This creates coherence, a state where energy flows smoothly, without resistance. This alignment is not static; it's a dynamic equilibrium that is constantly adjusting to maintain coherence as new inputs in the form of experiences or insights arrive.

In you, this may feel like:

- Clarity of mind
- Emotional stability
- Aligned actions
- A sense of flow or presence

Practically, divine integration looks like living in a state of inner and outer coherence. It means your thoughts, words, and actions align with your highest values and intentions.

This manifests as clarity in decision-making, emotional stability, and a sense of purpose. You become less reactive and more responsive. Relationships improve because you're no longer projecting unresolved patterns onto others. You feel more connected to life and less driven by fear or ego. Integration doesn't mean perfection; it means you're aware of your patterns and actively harmonizing them.

Think of yourself as an orchestra: Each instrument (thought, emotion, action) is a waveform.

- Chaos is when the violins play jazz, the drums play metal, and the conductor is on a coffee break.
- Integration is when everyone plays the same song. You don't control the music, but you learn to groove with it.

Let's explore briefly some other perspectives of divine integration.

More Perspectives of Divine Integration

- **From a religious perspective:** It is the process of drawing closer to the divine and transcending worldly attachments and embodying higher virtues like love, compassion, and humility. No matter what religion you study, love is always the foundation.
- **The embodiment perspective** emphasizes that ascension is not an escape from the body but the anchoring of divinity within it, transforming the body into a radiant vessel of presence and vitality. There has been so much attention on enlightenment and ascension, but it is the embodiment piece many of us came here for. Yes, we can recognize our true essence AND we can live that here. This makes chopping wood any carrying water a whole new experience!
- **The collective perspective** sees awakening as

something that naturally shifts focus from the "me" to the "we," moving us all toward healing where we all contribute to humanity's evolution. If the individual continues to become aware of the greater "we," they become more and more aware of the planetary, solar, and universal collective. Universal awareness takes place.

- **The mystical perspective** speaks of union with the Beloved, a dissolving of the separate self into the infinite embrace of divine love.
- **The planetary perspective** views integration as part of Earth's own ascension, inviting humanity to rise with her by living in harmony with nature and honoring her rhythms.
- **The psychological perspective:** Psychologically, divine integration is often understood as the healing and unification of fragmented aspects of the self, bringing the conscious and unconscious mind into harmony. Rooted in Jungian ideas of individuation, it involves reconciling inner opposites, integrating shadow elements, and aligning personal identity with a deeper sense of meaning or self-transcendence. In this process, the psyche becomes a more balanced, coherent, and receptive vessel through which experiences of the sacred or transpersonal can naturally emerge.
- **The creative perspective** sees integration as the flowering of divine energy into art, expression, and innovation, allowing Spirit to move uniquely through each person.
- **Ascended masters' perspective:** This path is walked by those who have crucified their lower nature completely. Ascended masters (also known as

Mahatmas) are spiritually enlightened beings who, after numerous lifetimes as a human, have achieved a state of enlightenment and mastery.

A Healing Perspective

From this perspective, as one masters the mind, releases limiting beliefs, stops acting out emotional reactivity, and conquers the physical impulses of the body; as one quiets the mind and works with ego, lets go of fear, guilt, shame, and trauma, healing happens. The stuff of the past starts to feel like distant memories and feelings of being empty may arise.

Then you have to adapt to being empty of all that you held so that room can be created for something other to emerge; new ways of perceiving and being in the world. Identity crisis can happen. Confusion may arise, especially when the individual finds themself as an expression of one shared, infinite and unchanging Consciousness, God, Source, Spirit, Universe with a unique vibrational signature. An individuation and embodiment; a God nugget that perceives very differently the architecture of oneself and the universe. The being may then slowly start to remember and put together all the pieces that were lost, forgotten, given away, or taken away.

This has been my path. It has never been what I expected!

From my perspective you are an expression of the one. You are one with all of creation and you are individuated. A paradox reconciled. And your only purpose is to be you. You are not better than or less than. You are extraordinary and ordinary. You are you. Your body reflects your level of consciousness and choices, and other people's body reflects their level of consciousness and choices, and we all learn and gain wisdom as a result of our choices together.

I believe your unique individual vibrational signature

or body of light will continue to be a reflection of all your experiences, ideas, expressions, and choices that only you can make throughout all incarnations and eternity.

It's quite beautiful.

We still chop wood and carry water, which really disappointed me in the beginning. I really wanted that halo.

But as recommended in this book, I am willing to change and evolve my perspective over and over again. Who knows, maybe one day as I continue to integrate that halo will appear. For now, I am content just to know myself as healed and whole as I continue to integrate and explore the mystery and truth of my being.

Different traditions and teachers use different language to describe divine integration or ascension. There is no single "right" way to describe divine integration. Each path is valid, and each person must find the way that resonates with them.

REFLECTIVE MOMENT: Maybe existence is the convergence of all perspectives? Maybe quantum, consciousness, vibration, light, color, sound, and other perspectives are aspects of one being? Pointers or metaphors for that which cannot be described?

Yet, every perspective is both a doorway and a possible limitation. If held rigidly, even the most beautiful teaching can become a boundary or a detour that takes us off the path. Ultimately, divine integration is not found in clinging to belief or a process, but in living the direct experience of unity, where individuality shines as a unique color, and together, all colors return us to the wholeness of white light.

While the words may vary, the heart of the process is the same: Divine integration is the end of the belief in separation.

The Revelation Integration Method is but one map of healing. It is the Rhythm of Integration you engage with when you set the intention, take the journey and realize a new layer of all-of-you. You put the pieces of yourself back together. The root meaning of integration comes from the Latin integratio, meaning "to make whole, restore, or renew." At its root, integration means bringing parts together into a unified, whole state rather than keeping them separate.

You, my dear, are a divine puzzle!

CHAPTER 12

IN CLOSING

The books I have written contain all the tools I have used and found to be helpful on my spiritual journey.

- Within the pages of my first book *Good Decisions...Most of the Time Because life is too short not to eat chocolate,* I explored nutrition, created recipes, and dabbled in the psychology of food. That was the beginning of my journey back to myself as I explored intuitive eating and honoring the body.

- The second book was a fun project that I co-wrote with a good friend when I was single. She called me up one day and asked what I was doing. I told her I was creating a *Mandala for Manifesting My Man.* She laughed and said, "Oh my goodness we need to write that book!" And we did.

- *The Extraordinary Ordinary You: A Manual for Self-*

Discovery, contains all the tools and processes I went through as I learned how to release negative thought patterns, beliefs of unworthiness, and how I processed emotional imprints and worked with ego. It was dealing these things that enabled me to experience who I truly am beneath those constructs.

- Then with the help of sacred medicines, the power of intentions and consistent integration this book was born to help myself and others integrate broader perspectives of our beingness.

You will find all the tools I used in these books.

Eventually though, you may let go of all tools, all metaphors, all ideas, all constructs, all perspectives and experience your own unique divine nature. When you do, don't try to put it in a box or try to understand it. Instead, just be with it. Explore it. Integrate it in your own way.

Tools give the impression there is someplace to go. They can help us, but when you realize there is no place to go, you may release the tools. They are designed to help you return to what was always there.

When you need clarity, take it to the medicine. When you get stuck, take it to the medicine. When you need healing, take it to the medicine. Be intentional and remember everything I have taught you about setting intentions, navigating the medicine space and integrating your revelations.

I am saying one last time: DO NOT Overuse Medicine.

When medicines are overused or used recreationally they are no longer medicine. Drug culture is not medicine. Using medicine as a crutch is not medicine. Using medicine to avoid pain instead of heal pain does not move you forward.

You will intuitively know when to take a break, when you need it, and when your path with the medicine has ended, if you listen.

Eventually you may realize you can bliss out using your own chemistry and that your body has everything you need within it to heal and transcend.

The medicine can point the way, but it is up to you to integrate. I have seen those who are unwilling to do the work return to the medicine over and over, and in those cases, medicine becomes a drug, another addiction, another substance to numb the pain, avoid the past or check out. Please, don't do this.

Use the medicine wisely. Use it to heal. Use it to remember. And look within. Everything you need is there.

Your Path Is Uniquely Yours

The way you meet God, Source, Spirit, Universe, Consciousness is yours and yours alone. The way you integrate that experience is yours and yours alone. There is no one right way or wrong way.

There is no other being like you in the entire cosmos. I like to think of the "light body" as something that is created by the light a person has manifested throughout all incarnations. I mean, wow! Look at you and what you have created!

I like this idea because it reflects the choices we have made, the experiences we have had, and our level of consciousness. It's not good or bad, it just is...us. There is no hierarchy. No one is more spiritually advanced than another. Some are just still asleep.

We Know How to Heal

As you witness negative thought patterns and watch

319

them vanish, as you unravel beliefs about yourself that have no foundation, as you face the ego and process emotions and trauma from the past, as you master the impulses and cravings of the physical body, the personality self goes through something akin to a spiritual car wash.

You heal.

Yes. We know how to heal. You strip away everything that you are not so you can experience all that you are. Then, what you are needs integrating. It's not linear and it's not easy. If it was easy everyone would be doing it.

At some point you may be able to see that everything is creation, including you, and you may experience what exists beyond creation.

You might even get a glimpse of what I call undistorted creation.

Undistorted Creation

Undistorted creation is creation that occurs in full awareness.

Humanity is coming into full awareness. Little by little we are increasing consciousness and dropping the distortions and coming into balance and harmony. Yes, old systems are falling down so that the new can come through. While this looks like destruction, and it is, it is simply creating space for free expression and undistorted creation.

Creation without fear, anxiety, or depression. Creation without self-doubt, guilt, or shame. Creation without judgment or comparison.

Can you imagine it?

Creation just for the sake of creating, not because you have to but because you choose to. Creation that vibrates in resonance with wisdom, unconditional love, and acceptance.

Creation that celebrates individual expression, knowing full well we are all One. Because we are.

Creation that is not distorted by the belief in separation or the fear that arises from it.

I wonder if we will still chop wood and carry water? I think we will. I think it will be a time when we have all realized our special gifts and work together to create this beautiful new Earth everyone keeps talking about.

In the meantime, here are some final tips I have found useful.

You could call them the last of my tools before I leave them all behind.

★ TIPS

- Stop chasing.
- Stop needing to know.
- Let experiences be what they are—experiences.
- Find right ways of thinking and being in the world.
- Surround yourself in beauty.
- Cultivate an attitude that allows you to enjoy the human experience.
- Stay aware of True Self.
- Live beyond all stories, notions, and constructs. See things as they are.
- Stop taking things so seriously. Play, dance, and have fun!

Oh, and cultivate awareness. Definitely.

As you move forward on your healing journey, you will move through many phases, many initiations. You will be tested and you will be challenged. How you respond to these challenges is what will help you move forward or keep you stuck. Don't worry though if you decide to stay stuck. Eventually something will come along to nudge you out of your stuckness. But don't wait that long. That's what medicine is for.

Only you know when you are ready to know yourself in truth, and I am happy to hold your hand along the way. It's what I do. As someone once said, we are all walking each other home. And watching a fellow human wake up to who and what they are is my favorite thing on this planet. I will stay as long as I get to witness this.

The important thing to remember is that your journey is your journey. Please do not compare it to anyone else. From my perspective, I know who you are and what you are beyond any stories you have created about yourself or any stories that others have created about you. You are wonderful. You are brilliant. You are beautiful. You are you.

And I'm so grateful you've taken this time to journey with me.

XxxOoo...

Love,

Dani

www.ingramcontent.com/pod-product-compliance
Lightning Source LLC
Chambersburg PA
CBHW060409130626
46555CB00005B/2011